"R2P is now a globally accepted norm, but universally effective atrocity prevention in practice remains a battle barely half-won. This is the guide to the task ahead the world has been waiting for. The richness and precision of Luck's and Bellamy's analysis should satisfy the most demanding academics, while the sharp practicality of their prescriptions – supported by a wealth of real-world lessons-learned examples – will be of enormous help to policymakers. This is not just one for the bookshelves: it demands to be read."

Gareth Evans, Co-Chair of International Commission on Intervention and State Sovereignty; former Australian Foreign Minister; President Emeritus of International Crisis Group; author of *The Responsibility to Protect: Ending Mass Atrocity Crimes Once and For All.*

The Responsibility to Protect

In Memoriam

Richard H. Stanley (1932–2017)

The Responsibility to Protect: From Promise to Practice

ALEX J. BELLAMY AND EDWARD C. LUCK

polity

First published in 2018 by Polity Press

Polity Press
65 Bridge Street
Cambridge CB2 1UR, UK

Polity Press
101 Station Landing
Suite 300
Medford, MA 02155, USA

ISBN-13: 978-1-5095-1243-0
ISBN-13: 978-1-5095-1244-7(pb)

A catalogue record for this book is available from the British Library.

Library of Congress Cataloging-in-Publication Data

Names: Bellamy, Alex J., 1975- author. | Luck, Edward C., author.
Title: The responsibility to protect : from promise to practice / Alex J. Bellamy, Edward C. Luck.
Description: Cambridge, UK; Medford, MA, USA : Polity, 2018. | Includes bibliographical references and index.
Identifiers: LCCN 2018004117 (print) | LCCN 2018018806 (ebook) | ISBN 9781509512478 (Epub) | ISBN 9781509512430 | ISBN 9781509512447 (pb)
Subjects: LCSH: Responsibility to protect (International law)
Classification: LCC KZ4082 (ebook) | LCC KZ4082 .B45 2018 (print) | DDC 341.4/8–dc23
LC record available at https://lccn.loc.gov/2018004117

Typeset in 9.5 on 12 pt Swift Light
by Toppan Best-set Premedia Limited
Printed and bound in Great Britain by CPI Group (UK) Ltd, Croydon

For further information on Polity, visit our website:
politybooks.com

Contents

Acknowledgments

We have accumulated more than two decades of experience working with and on the Responsibility to Protect (R2P). Along the way, we have acquired many debts of gratitude, both personal and professional. Chief amongst them are the debts owed to our long-suffering but endlessly patient and supportive families. They have endured our frequent absences and anxieties with grace and have listened far more than is healthy to our ramblings about the fortunes of atrocity prevention and machinations of the UN system. We would also like to thank all at Polity Press, and the anonymous reviewers, for their deep engagement with this project. Any errors of fact or interpretation are, of course, our own.

Introduction

Following more than a decade of decline, the incidence of atrocity crimes is again rising.[1] The tide of forcibly displaced populations is at its highest level since the end of World War II. We need to do far better at preventing such horrific crimes and at protecting vulnerable populations. That is the purpose of the responsibility to protect (R2P), a set of rules and principles that has advanced far more rapidly in debating halls than in national and international policies and actions.[2] This book is about how to turn the promise of R2P into practice.

The outpouring of books, articles, and reports about R2P has been nothing short of breathtaking. They have enriched our understanding of the etiology of mass murder, of its persistence throughout human history, and of the political hurdles to the successful implementation of R2P. As scholars and practitioners, however, we felt that something was missing, that the literature has been incomplete in four respects.

First, while the scholarly and analytical work on R2P as a normative innovation and political enterprise has been truly impressive, there has been far less attention to what R2P looks like in practice. The study of R2P has attracted throngs of acute observers and commentators, but, to date, only a handful of those engaged in the practice of prevention and protection have reflected publicly on their experiences. Practitioners, whether in governments, international organizations, or civil society, have been largely learning by doing, with little opportunity to reflect on what has and has not worked and why. There is a need, in our view, for a more systematic assessment of the strategies, doctrines, policies, procedures, mechanisms, and tools for preventing atrocities and protecting populations. So this book takes R2P out of the international meeting halls and academic debates that have defined its formative years and into the prevention and protection trenches.

Second, much of the existing literature lacks context. The evolution of R2P, either as principle or practice, has not occurred in a vacuum. It is one of many political priorities competing for space, resources, and attention. This becomes abundantly clear at the implementation stage. How R2P interacts with other conflict resolution, peacekeeping, peacebuilding, development, humanitarian, and human rights agendas – not to mention other security and counterterrorism imperatives – helps determine R2P's trajectory within the United Nations (UN) system, just as cost-risk-benefit calculations will continue to shape national responses. R2P has emerged and developed within an international system that is dynamic and at a historical moment in which that system is under stress, as geopolitics, non-state actors, and domestic political forces impose new strains on international institutions, principles, and commitments. R2P does not have the luxury of coming of age in propitious times.

Third, following a decade of normative development and maturation, R2P principles have now been tested in practice for a decade as well. The principles have reached a settled state, but their practice is still far down the learning curve. We believe, nevertheless, that there is now enough of a track record to begin to offer some rough assessments of what is or is not working. Some of our initial observations may seem counterintuitive – and quite debatable – but we believe that it is time to shift the conversation from theory to practice, from what sounds good to what might make a difference on the ground when lives are at stake.

Fourth, as scholars and practitioners, we have each spent some quality time on the practice side of the equation. Between us, we have amassed more than a quarter of a century working on, and with, R2P. From 2008 to 2012, as the United Nations' first Special Adviser on the Responsibility to Protect, Edward Luck was responsible for its conceptual, political, institutional, and operational development. He was the architect and drafter of the UN's three-pillar strategy for implementing R2P, crafted all of Secretary-General Ban Ki-moon's speeches and reports on R2P over those years, and advised the Secretary-General and member states on the application of R2P principles to numerous crisis situations. Alex Bellamy has directed the Asia Pacific Centre for the Responsibility to Protect for much of the last decade and served as Secretary to the High Level Advisory Panel on R2P in Southeast Asia, a group chaired by former Association of Southeast Nations (ASEAN) Secretary-General Surin Pitsuwan. More recently, he has served as a consultant to the UN Office on Genocide Prevention and R2P, supporting the work of Luck's successors in the Special Adviser role, Jennifer Welsh and Ivan Simonovic. In that capacity, he contributed to Ban Ki-moon's 2013 and 2016 reports on R2P, and was responsible for drafting Antonio Guterres's first two reports on the subject.

Timing matters. The conceptual and normative struggle to design and advocate R2P is now largely behind us. Most of the operational challenges, however, remain before us. Unless these are overcome, the promise of R2P will turn to cynicism and despair. So this book calls for fresh thinking and a more comprehensive approach to the practice of R2P – one that moves beyond states and the UN to include the full range of actors that could play a role in inhibiting atrocity crimes and protecting vulnerable populations. It calls for situating efforts to implement R2P within the broader context of world politics, emphasizing the role played by regional arrangements, individual states, non-state groups and individuals, as well as the UN. It seeks to reorient the way we think about and study R2P away from the normative and conceptual (important as these are) and toward the practices of atrocity prevention and human protection necessary to make the principle a living reality for the world's most vulnerable populations.

Three key ideas run through the book. First is the notion of individual responsibility.[3] Collective responsibility ultimately rests on individuals, whether on the ground or in state and international institutions. Prevention and protection depend on the choices people make. Yet initial articulations of R2P were too state centric, underplaying the role of individuals and groups. Second is the contention that the normative arguments about R2P have largely prevailed and that the priorities now are political and practical in nature. These political and practical tasks are made more difficult by the emergence of new challenges, such as violent extremist non-state armed groups, that were not foreseen by R2P's architects. Third is that R2P relates to different aspects of sovereignty in different ways. In practice, varying degrees of progress have been achieved vis-à-vis the different types of sovereignty. In particular, "decision-making sovereignty" – each state's right to determine its own course of action – has proven more central than some anticipated, whereas territorial sovereignty – long thought to be the principal obstacle to collective action against atrocities – has proven somewhat less critical to the implementation of R2P than expected.[4]

This book includes seven chapters and a conclusion. The first three chapters consider the origins and evolution of R2P against the backdrop of larger political and historical forces. Chapter 1 traces the conceptual and doctrinal development of R2P, beginning with its roots in the human security paradigm and the focus on vulnerable populations in the 1990s, seminal conceptual breakthroughs in the African experience, and the searing atrocities in Rwanda and Srebrenica. It compares the three iterations of R2P in 2001, 2005, and 2009 and addresses why the doctrinal expression of R2P needed to be adjusted along the path from promise to practice. Chapter 2 places R2P in a larger historical and political context, recognizing that the evolution and development of R2P have not occurred in a vacuum. Given the demanding dynamics of contemporary national and international politics, it emphasizes that R2P poses, at the very least, a responsibility to try. Chapter 3 looks at a series of challenges and opportunities that had not been anticipated at the inception of R2P in 2001. On the one hand, the rise of violent extremism and the increasing commission of atrocity crimes by non-state armed groups have required R2P to move beyond its initial state-centric formulation. On the other hand, there has been a growing recognition that regional, sub-regional, and national actors, including those from civil society and the private sector, can play critical roles in the implementation of R2P.

Chapters 4 through 6 address three critical operational challenges: building an international community of commitment and practice; getting states to live up to their primary responsibilities for preventing atrocity crimes and for protecting populations; and making the emphasis on prevention into a "lived reality." Chapter 4 both details the efforts well underway at the United

Nations to operationalize R2P and comments on the uneven, but often encouraging, initiatives at the regional and sub-regional levels. Chapter 5, in considering the essential, but often overlooked, work being pursued within countries to help them fulfill their primary responsibility for prevention and protection, finds some evidence that R2P is beginning to move well beyond international debating halls. In asserting the imperative of prevention, chapter 6 considers not only the place of prevention within the larger R2P project but also how actors ranging from peacekeepers to the International Criminal Court (ICC) can contribute to prevention objectives.

In chapter 7 and the Conclusion, the authors reflect on the lessons from R2P's first decade of implementation experience. Chapter 7 looks at eight cases, four that were relative failures (including two that predated R2P) and four that were relatively successful, in order to highlight some factors that appear to be associated with more negative or positive outcomes, respectively. Many of the findings, though decidedly tentative, are strikingly counterintuitive. They point the way for further, more rigorous, study. The Conclusion draws eight lessons from what it terms the third stage of R2P metamorphosis as it moves, ever so slowly, from aspirational principles to more consistent practice. Though this remains the challenge of our times, it finds that experience demonstrates that the key to making a difference is trying to make a difference.

CHAPTER ONE

R2P as Principle and Policy

The responsibility to protect (R2P) is a normative response to a particular set of challenges to public policy. It did not emerge from nowhere, as its roots can be traced to decades of failure to anticipate, prevent, and curb atrocity crimes. These failures had consequences not only for the tens of millions of people who had lost their lives, their dignity, or their loved ones to such crimes, but also for the viability and character of their societies and for the legitimacy of international law and institutions. These episodes of mass killing, forced displacement, and sexual and gender-based violence had left deep and lasting scars on the human condition. The repeated inability or unwillingness to develop principles, strategies, policies, instruments, and practices for effective prevention and protection had raised troubling doubts about public policy priorities and about the efficacy of institutions on many levels. So this book begins with a brief look at the seminal events and conceptual innovations of the 1990s that both shaped the etiology and evolution of R2P and laid the political foundation for its development as a core principle of and standard for public policy.

The first four sections of this chapter address critical elements of the 1990s' experience that led to the birth of R2P: (1) the human security paradigm; (2) the focus on vulnerable populations; (3) normative, institutional, and operational developments in Africa; and (4) lessons from the searing atrocities in Rwanda and Srebrenica. These developments both propelled and shaped the effort to develop more effective responses to the challenges to public policy presented by atrocity crimes. The final three sections of the chapter assess the main elements of the three successive conceptions of R2P that emerged in 2001, 2005, and 2009 respectively, as the principle moved closer to implementation. The fifth section considers the mandate, assumptions, and conclusions of the pathbreaking 2001 report of the International Commission on Intervention and State Sovereignty (ICISS) that coined the term "responsibility to protect." In the sixth section, the three paragraphs of the Outcome Document of the 2005 World Summit that were devoted to R2P are compared and contrasted to the initial conception of R2P presented by the ICISS report four years earlier. The seventh and final section explains how the 2009 implementation report by United Nations Secretary-General Ban Ki-moon strove to translate the agreed language of the 2005 Outcome Document into a comprehensive and sustainable strategy for moving from promise to practice.

In relating the 2001, 2005, and 2009 versions of R2P, the chapter addresses how and why the following five fundamental questions were handled somewhat differently at each juncture:

- What is the problem that R2P is meant to address?
- Who is responsible for addressing it?
- What tools could be both effective and appropriate for addressing it?
- Who should be authorized to wield those tools in various circumstances?
- How should the articulation and application of the R2P principle be conditioned by other widely accepted norms and principles?

Understandings about what R2P is and is meant to accomplish changed in substantial ways over those eight years. On the operational side, R2P was refined through a combination of political exigencies and practical experience. On the normative side, R2P's metamorphosis from a concept to a principle to an emerging norm proceeded with unusual alacrity. As explained in chapter 2, there are compelling reasons to conclude that R2P has developed since 2009 into a norm (or standard of behavior), as the term is defined in the social sciences.[1] By focusing on how rapid and far-reaching the evolution of R2P was over those years, chapter 1 also sheds light on why the concept so often has been subject to manipulation or misunderstanding despite (or sometimes because of) all of the attention it has garnered in scholarly and intergovernmental debate. This chapter also concludes, more hopefully, that R2P has reached a stage of conceptual and normative maturity, so that its implementation in policy and practice – the focus of this volume – can proceed as conditions permit.

The Promise of the 1990s: Human Security

The decade of the 1990s opened with high expectations. The conclusion of the four-decades-long Cold War appeared to offer unprecedented opportunities for forging international consensus, including in the UN Security Council, for easing tensions and identifying common ground for resolving a number of long-running conflicts and for strengthening international law and institutions. In September 1991, UN Secretary-General Javier Pérez de Cuéllar welcomed the "renaissance of the Organization," as "the extinction of the bipolarity associated with the cold war has no doubt removed the factor that virtually immobilized international relations over four decades."[2] When the Soviet representative – the USSR had not yet imploded – voted for Security Council Resolution 678 (1990) of November 29, 1990 to authorize the member states "to use all necessary means to uphold and implement" its earlier resolutions aimed at reversing the Iraqi invasion of Kuwait, it was the first time that the coercive use of force under Chapter VII of the Charter had been authorized in a vote that included all members of the Council.

Indeed, the number of vetoes cast in the Council dropped dramatically during the first half of the 1990s, while the number of enforcement resolutions passed under Chapter VII soared.[3] Meeting for the first time at the heads-of-state level in January 1992, the Council asked the new Secretary-General, Boutros Boutros-Ghali of Egypt, to prepare a report on a range of peace and security challenges.[4] Though stemming mass atrocity crimes was not among the issues to be considered, the Secretary-General's subsequent report, *An Agenda for Peace: Preventive Diplomacy, Peacemaking, and Peacekeeping*, did flag the importance of humanitarian assistance for preventing conflicts.[5] More consequently, he acknowledged that "the time of absolute and exclusive sovereignty...has passed; its theory was never matched by reality."[6]

The end of the Cold War permitted capitals and international institutions to shift some attention from more globally existential issues, such as nuclear annihilation, to more immediate threats to individuals, communities, and societies. A range of scholars, experts, and commentators called for raising the political profile of human security concerns alongside more traditional concerns about the security of states and borders. At the United Nations, the concept of human security was introduced in the 1994 *Human Development Report*. As it commented, "The concept of security has for too long been interpreted narrowly: as security of territory from external aggression, or as protection of national interests in foreign policy or as global security from the threat of nuclear holocaust. It has been related more to nation-states than to people."[7] The following year, the independent Commission on Global Governance took this notion a bit further, linking it more specifically to sovereignty and atrocity crimes committed by governments:

> In many countries the security of people has been violated on a horrendous scale without any external aggression or external threat to territorial integrity or state sovereignty. To confine the concept of security exclusively to the protection of states is to ignore the interests of people who form the citizens of a state and in whose name sovereignty is exercised. It can produce situations in which regimes in power feel they have the unfettered freedom to abuse the right to security of their people.[8]

The Commission urged that the Security Council be granted the authority to defend people within borders and asserted that "all people, no less than all states, have a right to a secure existence, and all states have an obligation to protect those rights."[9] In 1999, the Canadian Foreign Minister, Lloyd Axworthy, told the Security Council that "the promotion of human security is the bedrock upon which all other objectives of the United Nations Charter must rest."[10]

During the early 1990s, there was a growing awareness across the international community that the apparent growth in the number and complexity of intra-state conflicts was presenting a particularly difficult set of peace and security challenges. As the 1994 *Human Development Report* put it, "with the dark shadows of the cold war receding, one can now see that many conflicts are within nations rather than between nations."[11] As that report noted, "Of the 82 armed conflicts between 1989 and 1992, only three were between states."[12] According to a 1996 report to the General Assembly, prepared by Graça Machel, on the impact of armed conflict on children, all 30 major conflicts in 1995 "took place within States, between factions split along ethnic, religious or cultural lines."[13] Over time, a number of commentators came to recognize that even civil conflicts could have significant international dimensions.[14] Often they entailed the trans-border movement of weapons, armed groups, and funding for one side or another, the political involvement of diaspora, the forced displacement of large numbers of people across borders, and/or adverse regional or sub-regional economic effects. With the emergence of the so-called "CNN effect," the humanitarian tragedies that often resulted from such transnational conflicts were becoming increasingly difficult to ignore, even in distant capitals. Secretary-General Boutros-Ghali expressed ambivalence about this development, for while the increased media coverage could encourage support for humanitarian efforts, it "also may create an emotional environment in which effective decision-making can be far more difficult."[15]

At the United Nations, it became widely accepted that, in these intrastate or transnational conflicts, non-combatants were increasingly becoming the primary targets of violence, not just the incidental casualties of more traditional wars. Long-accepted international humanitarian standards, it was believed, were under siege by armed groups with narrow political, economic, ideological or sectarian agendas.[16] Both institutional and normative initiatives would be needed to meet the growing humanitarian imperative. Growing concern "about the suffering of the victims of disasters and emergency situations, the loss in human lives, the flow of refugees, the mass displacement of people and the material destruction" led the General Assembly in December 1991 to adopt Resolution 46/182 on the coordination of UN emergency assistance.[17] Its Annex contained a set of Guiding Principles for humanitarian assistance that stressed state responsibility, urged increased efforts at early warning, and called for the appointment of an emergency relief coordinator, among other measures. The next year, the incoming Secretary-General, Boutros Boutros-Ghali, appointed Francis M. Deng to be his new – if unpaid and part-time – adviser on the growing problem of internally displaced persons. Seeking to bolster the world body's decidedly modest staff capacity for dealing with human rights, in December 1993 the General Assembly established the post of High Commissioner for Human Rights. In retrospect, it is remarkable that it took 45 years from the adoption of the Universal Declaration of Human Rights to gather sufficient political will to take this critical step toward implementation.

As international conflict-resolution efforts multiplied during the post-Cold War years, the question of how to deal with leaders of governments and non-state armed groups that had committed mass atrocity crimes became increasingly problematic. In a number of situations, the short-term exigencies of peace and justice seemed to push in different directions. Though the tribunals for Rwanda and the Former Yugoslavia offered an ad hoc response to the growing calls for ending impunity, their operations raised questions of selectivity, effectiveness, efficiency, and cost. So over the course of the decade, international discussions about establishing a more permanent and universal court to address individual culpability for the commission of serious international crimes gained momentum, culminating in the negotiation of the Rome Statute of the International Criminal Court in July 1998.

Vulnerable Populations

Though reliable statistics on civilian casualties in most of these situations did not exist, United Nations reports and statements began to repeat quite high (and varying) estimates that suggested that, in the 1990s, combatants overwhelmingly targeted civilians as their victims of choice. The *1994 Human Development Report*, for instance, asserted that "at the beginning of this century, around 90 percent of war casualties were military. Today, about 90 percent are civilian – a disastrous shift in the balance."[18] Two years later, the report by Graça Machel on the *Impact of Armed Conflict on Children* suggested that this shift had occurred in a much shorter period: "In recent decades, the proportion of war victims who are civilians has leaped dramatically from 5 percent to over 90 percent."[19] In his 1995 *Supplement to the Agenda for Peace*, Secretary-General Boutros-Ghali drew the attention of the member states to the trend toward increasing civilian casualties, a point that had been missing from the original report 30 months earlier.[20] Foreign Minister Axworthy told the Security Council that "the number of casualties from armed conflict has almost doubled since the 1980s to about 1 million a year, of those, 80 percent are civilians."[21]

There were growing qualitative concerns as well. It was not only that the numbers of civilian casualties appeared to be expanding, but the commission of violent acts against vulnerable populations – especially refugees and displaced persons, children, and women – gained increasing attention in the media, policy circles, and academia. The relative success of Operation Provide Comfort, a US-led coalition effort to protect and provide assistance to beleaguered Kurdish populations in Northern Iraq launched in 1991, appeared to open a new chapter in the employment of military force for humanitarian purposes. The operation drew international attention to the fact that forcibly displaced populations, whether or not they had crossed borders and achieved refugee status, were both growing and at increasing risk. Their plight was further compromised by the increasingly common attacks on unarmed humanitarian workers, whether they were affiliated with independent non-governmental organizations or with international agencies. In his first report to the United Nations Commission on Human Rights, in 1993, the Secretary-General's Representative, Francis Deng, noted that the surging number of internally displaced people had come to exceed the number of refugees (24 to 17 million).[22] His reporting in the 1990s was confined to the Commission on Human Rights in Geneva, from which his mandate originated, and did not officially reach the General Assembly and Security Council in New York. Nevertheless, after extended consultations over a number of years, he did develop a set of Guiding Principles on Internal Displacement in 1998 that was "welcomed" by the Commission, though never formally adopted by it.[23] In terms of the building blocks for R2P, Principle 25 was particularly relevant:

> 1. The primary duty and responsibility for providing humanitarian assistance to internally displaced persons lies with national authorities. 2. International humanitarian organizations and other appropriate actors have the right to offer their services in support of the internally displaced. Such an offer should not be regarded as an unfriendly act or as interference in a State's internal affairs and should be considered in good faith. Consent thereto should not be arbitrarily withheld, particularly when authorities concerned are unable or unwilling to provide required humanitarian assistance. 3. All authorities concerned should grant and facilitate the free passage of humanitarian assistance and grant persons engaged in the provision of such assistance rapid and unimpeded access to the internally displaced.

Though these principles have never achieved legal status, they have been widely accepted by international humanitarian agencies and used as a standard by a number of governments.

In terms of children, much of the impetus came from graphic press and NGO accounts of the plight of child soldiers and others abducted by armed groups, the parallel public campaigns to ban landmines and limit the flow of small arms and light weapons, and the General Assembly's adoption of the Convention on the Rights of the Child in late 1989.[24] Four years later, in December 1993, the Assembly adopted its first resolution devoted to the plight of children caught in the midst of armed conflict.[25] Expressing profound concern about "the grievous deterioration in the situation of children in many parts of the world as result of armed conflict," the resolution found that "children affected by armed conflict require the *special protection* of the international community [emphasis added]."[26] It went on to request that the Secretary-General engage an expert – he chose Graça Machel, then the former First Lady of Mozambique – to write a report on children and armed conflict for the Assembly's review.[27] Among other threats to children, her report addressed the forced recruitment of child soldiers, the substantial portion of refugees and internally displaced who were children, and their vulnerability to sexual exploitation and gender-based violence, as well as to landmines and unexploded ordnance. Estimating that "two million children have been killed in armed conflict" over the past decade, the report noted that "some fall victim to a general onslaught against civilians; others die as part of a calculated genocide. Still other children suffer the effects of sexual violence or the multiple deprivations of armed conflict that expose them to hunger or disease. Just as shocking, thousands of young people are cynically exploited as combatants."[28]

The vulnerabilities of children and women could not be separated. Not unlike the attention generated by the phenomenon of child soldiers, the systematic employment of rape and sexual violence in the war in the former Yugoslavia in the early 1990s shocked world opinion. Strategically, such gender-related violence became associated with campaigns to compel "ethnic cleansing," a notion that quickly gained international notoriety, if not formal legal standing. In May 1993, in the preambular language to Resolution 827 (1993), which authorized the establishment of the International Criminal Tribunal for the Former Yugoslavia (ICTY) as a subsidiary body of the UN Security Council, the Council included rape as an international crime for the first time. It noted "reports of mass killings, massive, organized and systematic detention and rape of women, and the practice of 'ethnic cleansing.'"[29] Less than eighteen months later, the Council established a second international tribunal "for the sole purpose of prosecuting persons responsible for genocide and other serious violations of international humanitarian law" in Rwanda.[30] As with the Yugoslav tribunal, the Statute of the International Criminal Tribunal for Rwanda (ICTR) included rape as a crime against humanity.[31] It would be another six years before the Security Council adopted its first resolution devoted to women, peace, and security. That landmark resolution, 1325 (2000), "[e]mphasizes the responsibility of all States to put an end to impunity and to prosecute those responsible for genocide, crimes against humanity, and war crimes including those relating to sexual and other violence against women and girls, and in this regard stresses the need to exclude these crimes, where feasible from amnesty provisions."[32]

As these initiatives on women and children suggest, by the turn of the century the Security Council had begun to grapple seriously for the first time with the perplexing question of how to protect civilians caught in the midst of armed conflict. Some Council members, of course, initially were quite cautious about the implications of this evolving agenda. At an early debate in the Council on the protection of civilians, Russian Permanent Representative Sergei Lavrov contended that the situation in Somalia demonstrated that "sometimes the decision to use force, if not fully thought through and calculated in terms of its consequences, may lead to a situation in which such unsuccessful humanitarian interference only exacerbates the conflict and, inter alia, aggravates the situation for the civilian population – the very population which we wanted to protect."[33] Cautioning against using force without Council authorization or stretching the scope of the Council's "primary responsibility for the maintenance of international peace and security" under Article 24 (1) of the UN Charter, Lavrov warned against putting Council members in the position of "opposing the need to implement international humanitarian law with the need to implement the Charter."[34] Calling "for the elimination of double standards in the humanitarian field," China"s representative, Qin Huasun, urged that "the question of the protection of civilians in armed conflict be placed on the agenda of the General Assembly and the Economic and Social Council for more thorough and comprehensive discussions."[35] Yet, for all these caveats, widely held perceptions about the changing nature of conflict and about public expectations continued to propel these concerns forward over the course of the decade. As Foreign Minister Axworthy, who convened and chaired that Council debate, put it, "There should be no mistake. Promoting the protection of civilians in armed conflict is no sideshow to the Council's mandate for ensuring international peace and security; it is central to it."[36]

On most of these thematic concerns, the General Assembly was usually in the vanguard and then the Security Council followed with the authorization of more specific measures. For instance, responding to a report by the Secretary-General, the Council adopted its first thematic resolution on the protection of civilians (POC) in September 1999, just weeks before the release of the UN's mea culpa reports on the fall of Srebrenica and the genocide in Rwanda. In the preambular language of the POC Resolution 1265 (1999), the Council emphasized "*its deep concern* at the erosion in respect for international humanitarian, human rights and refugee law and principles during armed conflict, in particular deliberate acts of violence against all those protected under such law."[37] In operative paragraph 6, the Council "*[e]mphasizes* the responsibility of States to end impunity and to prosecute those responsible for genocide, crimes against humanity and serious violations of international humanitarian law." The Council also called for "safe and unhindered access of humanitarian personnel to civilians in armed conflict" (paragraph 7) and expressed "its willingness to respond to situations of armed conflict where civilians are being targeted or humanitarian assistance to civilians is being deliberately obstructed" (paragraph 10).

The African Experience

Over these years, the normative and institutional foundations for the responsibility to protect were being laid at a regional level as much as at the United Nations. Though the signs of renewed interest in human protection were most pronounced in Africa, they were visible in most other regions as well. During the late 1980s and early 1990s, peacekeeping operations were undertaking a broader and more ambitious range of functions, including post-conflict peacebuilding, a notion that had been introduced by Secretary-General Boutros Boutros-Ghali in his 1992 *Agenda for Peace* report.[38] In Cambodia, Mozambique, Angola, Rwanda, and the Balkans, among other situations, these peacebuilding efforts were asked to put the pieces back together in societies that had been riven by the commission of notoriously horrific atrocity crimes. The geographical reach of peacekeeping and peacebuilding was also expanding, with major operations launched in Europe, Asia, and Latin America, as well as the more numerous ones in Africa and the Middle East. The operations in Central America and Haiti broke the centuries-old Monroe Doctrine limit on international military intervention in the Western Hemisphere. No longer could mass atrocity prevention be dismissed as only a concern for Africa.

As in other cases of successful normative development, it was the synergy between the global and regional efforts that shaped and propelled the birth of R2P. Politically, the readiness of the African regional group – the largest and among the most active in the world body – was critical to gaining broader acceptance of R2P (as addressed later in this chapter). Africa's experience with humanitarian intervention had certainly been varied, from the widely accepted unilateral Tanzanian incursion into Uganda to overthrow the government of Idi Amin in 1978–9, to the ill-fated effort by the United States and the United Nations to protect the delivery of humanitarian assistance in Somalia during 1991–5, to the utter failure of the international community to curb the 1994 genocide in Rwanda, despite the presence of an undermanned UN peacekeeping force. Among the reactions in African capitals to Somalia and Rwanda was a sense that Africans could not expect others to be willing or able to respond to humanitarian emergencies on the continent. In West Africa, subregional cooperation appeared to be an alternative, as ECOMOG (the Economic Community of West African States [ECOWAS] Monitoring Group) intervened forcefully with Nigerian leadership to bring the bloody civil war in Liberia during 1989–96 to an end. At times, the peacekeepers there appeared to be as much a part of the problem as the solution, but their persistence made a difference in the end. A subsequent ECOMOG intervention in Sierra Leone did not fare as well, though it laid a political foundation for subsequent interventions by forces from the United Kingdom and the United Nations.[39]

Over the course of the 1990s, a number of leading African scholars and practitioners began to grapple with the place of inadequate or irresponsible governance as one of the contributing factors to conflict in Africa, particularly of the intrastate variety. One stream of these reflections was captured in a book by Francis Deng and colleagues that developed the notion of "sovereignty as responsibility." They posited a relationship between sovereignty and legitimacy, because "to be legitimate, sovereignty must demonstrate responsibility, which means at the very least ensuring a certain level of protection for and providing the basic needs of the people."[40] Moreover:

No government that will allow hundreds of thousands, and maybe millions, of its citizens to starve to death when food can be made available to them, allow them to be exposed to deadly elements when they could be provided with shelter, or permit them to be indiscriminately tortured, brutalized, and murdered by contending forces can claim sovereignty. A government that allows its citizens to suffer in a vacuum of responsibility for moral leadership cannot claim sovereignty in an effort to keep the outside world from stepping in to offer protection and assistance.[41]

Conceptual advances such as this arose more from Africa's searing experience with atrocity crimes than from parallel deliberations in the conference halls of Addis Ababa, Geneva, and New York. That experience demanded new policy and normative responses, including the reconsideration of long-held norms against non-intervention. If Africans were to take the lead in addressing the challenges posed by human security and human protection on the continent, then the core principle of non-interference championed by the Organization of African Unity (OAU) for more than three decades would need to be revisited. The shift could be seen in the philosophy and the principles adopted by the member states to guide the OAU's successor organization, the African Union (AU), which was to embody a growing sense of unity and common purpose. The emphasis was now to be on "non-indifference" rather than on "non-interference."[42]

In important respects, the AU's Constitutive Act, agreed in 2000, a year before the ICISS report, foreshadowed the enunciation of R2P principles. Five of the principles enumerated in Article 4 of the Act ((f) through (j)) are especially relevant. Three of these principles sound quite consistent with those in Article 2 of the UN Charter: "(f) prohibition of the use of force or threat to use force among Member States of the Union"; "(g) non-interference by any Member State in the internal affairs of another"; and "(i) peaceful co-existence of Member States and their right to live in peace and security." These three points refer to the rules that should guide relationships among the member states of the African Union. The other two, which address relationships between the Union and individual member states, come closer to R2P formulations: "(h) the right of the Union to intervene in a Member State pursuant to a decision of the Assembly in respect of grave circumstances, namely: war crimes, genocide, and crimes against humanity" and "(j) the right of Member States to request intervention from the Union in order to restore peace and security."

Article 4 (h) has gained the most attention, given its identification of atrocity crimes, including three of the four included in the definition of R2P adopted at the World Summit five years later, as "grave circumstances" warranting the possibility of intervention by the Union. This principle, though a striking contrast to the emphasis on non-interference in the OAU charter, should be understood in the wider context of the other principles listed in Article 4. Clearly, the rights and responsibilities of the collective Union were to be much greater than those of individual member states. This provision, in large part, echoes the exception to the non-intervention clause granted to the United Nations Security Council under Article 2 (7) of the Charter.

Article 4 (j), on the other hand, has not received much attention from scholars or practitioners. However, it anticipates the kind of situation under Pillar Two of the UN Secretary-General's 2009 strategy in which a sovereign government could request international intervention to help deal with atrocities committed by armed groups or factions of the military that have escalated out of its control. That had been the case, for instance, in Sierra Leone when the Revolutionary United Front (RUF) occupied much of the country's territory and was committing horrific atrocity crimes. As discussed later in this volume, there have been several recent situations when the implementation of R2P entailed such consent-based international intervention or engagement.

Lessons from Rwanda and Srebrenica

In March 1999, Secretary-General Kofi Annan informed the Security Council of his "intention to set up an independent inquiry into the actions which the United Nations took" before and during the genocide in Rwanda.[43] In its report that December, the Inquiry urged a series of unexceptional steps to improve early warning, peacekeeping and civilian protection capacity, coordination and cooperation, security of staff, the flow of information to the Security Council, and rules of engagement. It called on the United Nations to "acknowledge its part of the responsibility for not having done enough to prevent or stop the genocide in Rwanda."[44] From an R2P perspective, however, some of the findings and recommendations of the Independent Inquiry were quite striking. As part of its recommended "action plan to prevent genocide," "States must be prepared to identify situations as genocide...and to assume the concomitant responsibility to act."[45] In its third recommendation, the Inquiry underscored that "the United Nations – and in particular the Security Council and troop-contributing countries – must be prepared to act to prevent acts of genocide or gross violations of human rights wherever they may take place. The political will to act should not be subject to double standards."[46]

Given the way that so much of the R2P debate has revolved around questions of territorial sovereignty, it is remarkable how little such matters surfaced in the report of the Inquiry. Indeed, rather than suggesting ways to accommodate state sovereignty, the Inquiry recommended that the Security Council or General Assembly find a way of "suspending the participation of a representative of a member state on the Council in exceptional circumstances such as that related to Rwanda."[47] The unusual circumstance, of course, had been that the genocidal regime in Kigali happened to be serving a non-permanent term on the Council at the time of the mass killings. It provided false and misleading information to the Council deliberations.[48] Neither the Security Council nor key member states were inhibited about launching an intervention to stop the genocide because of concerns about sovereignty and non-interference norms.[49] Indeed, that would have been a moot point, given that the Council had already deployed a modest peacekeeping mission to help discourage further unraveling of the ceasefire there. As the Inquiry recognized, but did not explicitly say, the sovereignty issue at stake in this situation had actually been about the decision-making sovereignty in those capitals with the wherewithal to have intervened militarily at the time of the unfolding genocide.[50] They did not want to cede their freedom of choice to the Council or any other international body. Though never stated in such bald terms, it was their sovereignty that was at question in the deliberations of the Security Council, not that of Rwanda.

Released just weeks earlier, the General Assembly-mandated assessment of the failure to protect the safe area in Srebrenica reached similar conclusions – though in a very different context – about the place of sovereignty in explaining the failure to act. In Bosnia-Herzegovina, as in Rwanda, UN peacekeepers were already on the ground. They, too, had ambitious mandates – in this case under Chapter VII – and insufficient forces to carry them out. The Security Council had authorized them to employ force, if necessary, to ensure the delivery of humanitarian assistance, to enforce the no-fly zone, and to protect the safe areas. Yet in practice, as in Rwanda a year earlier, there was a hesitancy to use coercive military force until after the worst atrocities had already been committed. Again, the barrier to effective action to protect populations and curb atrocity crimes was decision-making sovereignty, not territorial sovereignty. There is every reason to believe that doubts about the legality or appropriateness of circumventing international norms of non-intervention were not high on the list of inhibitors to a decision by major capitals to employ force to protect the safe areas. National decision makers undoubtedly found plenty of other reasons, such as risk, cost, domestic politics, and geopolitical consequences, which weighed against more timely and decisive action.

The soul-searching report on Srebrenica by Secretary-General Kofi Annan reached some candid and sweeping conclusions, especially about misperceptions and misjudgments by top UN officials. But it did not enumerate specific policy and institutional recommendations as the Rwanda Inquiry had. Of particular relevance to efforts to prevent or end atrocities, he underscored "the failure to fully comprehend the extent of the Serb war aims" and "an inability to recognize the scope of the evil confronting us."[51] In his view, "the men who have been charged with this crime against humanity reminded the world and, in particular, the United Nations, that evil exists in the world. They taught us also that the United Nations global commitment to ending conflict does not preclude moral judgements, but makes them necessary."[52] There had been a failure to comprehend that the Serbian policy of "ethnic cleansing" contemplated "employing savage terror, primarily mass killings, rapes and brutalization of civilians, to expel populations."[53] As a result, the international community had conducted negotiations that "amounted to appeasement," resisted the use of force, and applied "a philosophy of impartiality and non-violence wholly unsuited to the conflict in Bosnia."[54]

The UN's cardinal failing in Srebrenica, as confirmed by the Secretary-General's assessment, did not stem from barriers imposed by sensitivities over territorial sovereignty. Indeed, the notion of establishing safe areas had been pushed by smaller developing countries serving on the Security Council as non-permanent members.[55] The shortcomings lay, instead, in the institutional culture of the world body and in the lack of will in major capitals. The Secretary-General criticized "the pervasive ambivalence within the United

Nations regarding the role of force in the pursuit of peace; an institutional ideology of impartiality even when confronted with attempted genocide."[56] In his words:

> the cardinal lesson of Srebrenica is that a deliberate and systematic attempt to terrorize, expel or murder an entire people must be met decisively with all necessary means, and with the political will to carry the policy through to its logical conclusion....Otherwise, it is surely better not to raise hopes and expectations in the first place, and not to impede whatever capability they may be able to muster in their own defence.[57]

This was a remarkably clear acknowledgement of the moral hazard inherent in promising far more in the way of protection than one is prepared to deliver.

The Rwanda and Srebrenica reports were released at the time of an animated debate inside and outside of the world body over sovereignty, humanitarian intervention, and atrocity prevention that had been spurred by a series of eloquent addresses by Kofi Annan in 1998 and 1999.[58] The first of these, delivered at Ditchley Park in June 1998, offered "reflections on intervention." "State frontiers," he contended, "should no longer be seen as a watertight protection for war criminals or mass murderers. The fact that a conflict is 'internal' does not give the parties any right to disregard the most basic rules of human conduct."[59] Echoing, but not quoting, Francis Deng, he noted that "sovereignty implies responsibility, not just power."[60] Moreover, "since genocide is almost always committed with the connivance, if not the direct participation, of the State authorities, it is hard to see how the United Nations could prevent it without intervening in a State's internal affairs."[61] The Secretary-General also referred to what he called the "duty to interfere" (*le devoir d'ingérence*), as proposed by Bernard Kouchner before he entered the French government, under which "non-governmental organizations had a duty to cross national boundaries, with or without the consent of governments, in order to reach the victims of natural disasters and other emergencies."[62] Though Kofi Annan did not specifically endorse the parallel notion of a right or duty to intervene by military means in extreme circumstances, many critics, especially from the developing world, thought that they could see the writing on the wall.

The Secretary-General's most direct appeal to the member states to give more reflection to these dilemmas came in his annual address to the General Assembly in September 1999.[63] In it, he contrasted the notion of state sovereignty, which "is being redefined by the forces of globalization and international cooperation," and individual sovereignty, which encompasses "the human rights and fundamental freedoms of each and every individual as enshrined in our Charter." He regretted that, in the case of Kosovo, the international community had not been able to resolve the dilemma of "humanitarian intervention: on one side, the question of the legitimacy of an action taken by a regional organization without a United Nations mandate; on the other, the universally recognized imperative of effectively halting gross and systematic violations of human rights with grave humanitarian consequences." At the same time, he applauded the unity in the Security Council when it came to intervention in East Timor and Sierra Leone. In the former case, Indonesia gave consent under considerable pressure from members of the Council and in the latter case, as noted above, consent was readily provided by a government beset by armed groups that were committing atrocity crimes. Predictably, most member states wanted neither to engage in a profound philosophical debate nor to be put in a position of choosing between two contrasting conceptions of sovereignty. The reaction to Annan's call to reconsider the bounds of territorial sovereignty, especially from the global South, was decidedly unenthusiastic.

The Secretary-General's next foray into this controversial territory was a brief section of his Millennium Report for the 2000 World Summit on "the dilemma of intervention."[64] In it, he commented that, though his Assembly speech had "emphasized that intervention embraced a wide continuum of responses, from diplomacy to armed action, it was the latter option that generated most controversy in the debate that followed." He acknowledged the critics' concerns that "the concept of 'humanitarian intervention' could become a cover for gratuitous interference in the internal affairs of sovereign states," that "secessionist movements" could deliberately provoke human rights violations "in order to trigger external interventions," that interventions would not be undertaken consistently, and that "weak states are far more likely to be subjected to it than strong ones." Humanitarian intervention, he concluded, poses "a real dilemma. Few would disagree that both the defence of humanity and the defence of sovereignty are principles that must be supported. Alas, that does not tell us which principle should prevail when they are in conflict." So, as the twentieth century came to a close, the Secretary-General seemed to be reconciled to the political reality that, as pointed as his questions about humanitarian intervention had been, it would have to be for others to provide more persuasive and viable answers.

2001: The International Commission on Intervention and State Sovereignty (ICISS)

It was at the Millennium Summit in September 2000 that Canadian Prime Minister Jean Chrétien announced his government's intention to support the establishment of an independent International Commission on Intervention and State Sovereignty (ICISS). As the name selected for the new Commission made abundantly clear, its mandate would be to find new approaches to resolve the sovereignty/intervention dilemma identified by the Secretary-General in a manner that could receive broader, and hopefully consensus, support among the member states. Before turning to the substance of the Commission's findings and conclusions, it is worth reflecting on why the Commission's task was framed the way that it was, rather than asking it to address the lessons learned from the tragic failures in Rwanda and Srebrenica. The disconnect between the findings of the Rwanda and Srebrenica reports of the previous year and the ICISS mandate was nothing short of remarkable.

Clearly, the architects of this initiative expected the Commission to emphasize issues of territorial sovereignty, not decision-making sovereignty. This may have been due, in part, to the prominence of the divisive debate – including in Canada – over the use of force in the Kosovo conflict in 1999. Many characterized the use of force by the North Atlantic Treaty Organization (NATO) in Kosovo and Serbia as legitimate, but not legal, given that it lacked authorization by a divided Security Council. As Ramesh Thakur, an active and influential member of the Commission, recently put it, "in Kosovo in 1999 western leaders for the first time challenged the non-intervention norm itself. NATO claims of an emerging new norm of 'humanitarian intervention' were emphatically rejected by a majority of the world's countries. The ensuing controversy highlighted a lacuna in the existing legal regime governing the international use of force."[65]

Undoubtedly, the leaders behind the establishment of the Commission had the most immediate crisis – Kosovo – more in mind than the larger failures to prevent or curb the atrocity crimes in Rwanda and Srebrenica. The framing choice may also have reflected the fact that the General Assembly was the venue for the Secretary-General's most pointed address on the subject of intervention, one that gave the subsequent debate a distinctly North–South flavor. It may also be that some of those favoring the launch of the Commission realized that the conversation on adjusting traditional notions of territorial sovereignty was already quite advanced – including through contributions by three successive Secretaries-General – and might be ripe for further reflection, despite the widespread opposition to the notion of humanitarian intervention in its baldest form. The question of decision-making sovereignty, in contrast, was potentially even more controversial, not least because it touched on the prerogatives of the most powerful military powers, including the five permanent members of the Security Council, to decide when, where, and how their military capacities would be used.

In retrospect, all of this seems quite sensible politically, but it should not be forgotten that the framing of the ICISS mandate did not reflect the core conclusions of the two contemporary reports on the lessons learned from the international community's failure to act in a timely and decisive manner in Rwanda and Srebrenica. The decision to focus on the issue that was most contentious politically – military intervention – is also eminently understandable, but it is not equivalent to concentrating international attention on the more fundamental question of how best to prevent atrocity crimes and protect populations. In some ways, the focus on the former may even have distorted the debate and detracted attention from the latter, making it harder to sustain a productive international conversation on atrocity prevention. The latter is now taking place in the policy as well as academic realms, but that seminal conversation was distorted and delayed by years of debate about territorial sovereignty and military intervention instead.

The Commission, ably co-chaired by Gareth Evans of Australia and Mohamed Sahnoun of Algeria, was not given the luxury of a leisurely pace of work. It was asked to complete its work, including an extensive round of international consultations, in a year (apparently so that Canada would have results to announce at the Assembly's next general debate). By all accounts, the question of how to reconcile humanitarian imperatives and non-intervention norms provoked lively exchanges within the Commission, as they had outside its confines. Reaching a consensus among its members proved neither simple nor quick. The fact that they managed to agree on so much in such a relatively brief period, therefore, is quite remarkable.

The mandate of the Commission, moreover, was cast quite broadly, leaving much leeway to the commissioners. According to their report, "our mandate was generally to build a broader understanding of the problem of reconciling intervention for human protection purposes and sovereignty; more specifi- cally, it was to try to develop a global political consensus on how to move from polemics – and often paralysis – towards action within the international system, particularly the United Nations."[66] This was not to be an academic exercise, as the Commission's work was to serve an explicit political purpose. The Commission underscored that "the objective from the outset has been for our report to have a practical and concrete political impact, rather than simply provide additional stimulation to scholars and other commentators – though we hope to have done that as well."[67] It was to find reasons for action, not excuses for inaction. The mandate appeared to be based on several implicit assumptions. One was that "action" was a good thing, and that there had been too little of it when lives were at stake. Second, international decision making had been too slow and uncertain when decisive and timely leadership was most needed. Third, intervention, including military intervention, could save lives under the right conditions. Fourth, it would be unwise to try to ignore or deny the concerns that had been voiced about violating sovereignty and non-intervention norms. Those concerns had to be addressed, co-opted, finessed, or circumvented. And lastly, though the task was not to contribute to the "polemics" surrounding these matters, the Commission was to recast or reframe the debate because that was deemed to be a necessary step toward permitting an effective and timely response to pending atrocities.

The mandate left much unsaid. The Commission was not asked to find a better way to prevent atrocity crimes or to curb them once they were underway. As noted below, to their credit, the commissioners did devote considerable attention to atrocity prevention, at least in the text of their report, if not in its recommendations. But their mandate was about intervention, not prevention. The mandate failed either to refer to atrocity crimes as the reason for such interventions or to provide a generally accepted definition of what constitutes humanitarian intervention. Was it, for instance, limited to coercive action or did it include other forms of international engagement, such as preventive diplomacy? Definition aside, were the commissioners to find a more persuasive rationale for humanitarian intervention, a firmer legal footing for it, or a successor notion that would prove acceptable to a wider swath of the member states? Were they, in other words, to identify ways of making humanitarian intervention work or of circumventing it altogether? Were their proposals to fit entirely within existing norms and institutions, or could they recommend innovations in international structures and decision-making processes? Most critically, what circumstances would trigger or justify such an intervention, who would decide to take such measures, and who would be responsible for carrying them out and then for dealing with the consequences?

Given the diversity of its members, time pressures, and the breadth of its mandate, it is not surprising that there appears to have been some unresolved ambivalence in the Commission's approach toward humanitarian intervention. As Ramesh Thakur aptly notes, "the key innovation in 2001 was the reconceptualization of 'humanitarian intervention' as R2P; everything else in the discourse flows from that distinction."[68] In his view, "R2P was the ICISS answer to reconciling the neuralgic rejection of humanitarian intervention by the global South with the determination by the North to end atrocities."[69] Tom Weiss, who had served as the research director for the Commission, put it even more bluntly: "ICISS sought to drive a stake through the heart of the term 'humanitarian intervention.'"[70] Fair enough, but in its opening words the Commission underscores that "this report is about the so-called 'right of humanitarian intervention': the question of when, if ever, it is appropriate for states to take coercive – and in particular military – action against another state for the purpose of protecting people at risk in that other state."[71] As the report readily acknowledged, "external military intervention for human protection purposes has been controversial both when it has happened – as in Somalia, Bosnia and Kosovo – and when it has failed to happen, as in Rwanda."[72] According to the report:

> The kind of intervention with which we are concerned in this report is action taken against a state or its leaders, without its or their consent, for purposes which are claimed to be humanitarian or protective. By far the most controversial form of such intervention is military, and a great part of our report necessarily focuses on that. But we are also very much concerned with alternatives to military action, including all forms of preventive measures, and coercive intervention measures – sanctions and criminal prosecutions – falling short of military intervention.[73]

The commissioners decided "not to adopt" the terminology of "humanitarian intervention," which they reportedly found to be both controversial and prejudicial.[74] But they also determined that "if intervention for human protection purposes is to be accepted, including the possibility of military action, it remains imperative that the international community develop consistent, credible and enforceable standards to guide state and intergovernmental practice."[75]

The centerpiece of the ICISS report, of course, was its introduction of the notion of a "responsibility to protect" as an alternative to assertions about a right or duty of humanitarian intervention. This conceptual shift was, more than the Commission's specific recommendations, the seminal contribution of its report. Sustainable ideas for implementation came later, but the critical conceptual breakthrough came in this 2001 report. As it put it, "The Commission is of the view that the debate about intervention for human protection purposes should focus not on 'the right to intervene' but on 'the responsibility to protect'":

> First, the responsibility to protect implies an evaluation of the issues from the point of view of those seeking or needing support, rather than those who may be considering intervention....
>
> Secondly, the responsibility to protect acknowledges that the primary responsibility in this regard rests with the state concerned, and that it is only if the state is unable or unwilling to fulfill this responsibility or is itself the perpetrator, that it becomes the responsibility of the international community to act in its place....
>
> Thirdly, the responsibility to protect means not just the "responsibility to react," but the "responsibility to prevent" and the "responsibility to rebuild" as well. It directs our attention to the costs and results of action versus no action, and provides conceptual, normative and operational linkages between assistance, intervention and reconstruction.[76]

Though the Commission made a real effort to situate this new principle in existing international law and practice, it struggled a bit between the need to demonstrate continuity and the desire to appear innovative. It cited a number of reasons to assert that "there is an emerging principle in favour of military intervention for human protection purposes."[77] Though "there is not yet a sufficiently strong basis to claim the emergence of a new principle of customary international law, growing state and regional organization practice as well as Security Council precedent suggest an emerging guiding principle – which in the Commission's view could properly be termed 'the responsibility to protect.'"[78] In terms of sovereignty, the report called for a "re-characterization" from "*sovereignty as control* to *sovereignty as responsibility* in both internal functions and external duties...in a way that is being increasingly recognized in state practice."[79]

The Commission did not devote much attention to defining who should be protected. At various points, the report speaks of "populations at risk" and "people in mortal danger," of the way states treat "their own people" or their "citizens," and of the need to protect "civilians."[80] This imprecision did not detract from the thrust of the report, though the choice of terms here is not insignificant. References to "citizens" or a state's "own people" have proven contentious in places, like Côte d'Ivoire, where nativism has been part of the problem and some groups have charged that others do not belong and are not real citizens. The term "civilians" has a specific meaning in international humanitarian law, where it is employed in situations of armed conflict, while atrocity crimes do not always occur in wartime circumstances. As addressed in the next section, the 2005 World Summit Outcome Document only used the term "populations" to avoid these distinctions.

Perhaps because of time constraints or differences among its members, the Commission never settled on concise parameters regarding what kind or severity of events would trigger the R2P principles. Again, this was addressed at the 2005 Summit instead. The apparent definitional confusion may have stemmed partly from the Commission's careful attention to the human security roots of the responsibility to protect and partly from the lack of a reference to atrocity crimes in its mandate. According to the Commission, "Secretary-General Kofi Annan himself put the issue of human security at the centre of the current debate, when in his statement to the 54th session of the General Assembly he made clear his intention to 'address the prospects for human security and intervention in the next century.'"[81] R2P, they noted, "focuses attention where it should be most concentrated, on the human needs of those seeking protection or assistance" and "the security of *people* against threats to life, health, livelihood, personal safety and human dignity." [82] The Commission then criticized countries that "fail to protect their citizens from chronic insecurities of hunger, disease, inadequate shelter, crime, unemployment, social conflict and environmental hazard" and concepts of security that fail to take into account cases "when rape is used as an instrument of war and ethnic cleansing, when thousands are killed by floods resulting from a ravaged countryside and when citizens are killed by their own security forces."[83]

The Commission never clarified which of these situations might qualify as the kind of "conscience-shocking" event referred to at several points in the report as possible triggers for R2P-based intervention.[84] At two points, the report suggests that genocide, massacre, and ethnic cleansing would be acts that would be conscience shocking.[85] Another passage refers to "conscience-shocking situations of great humanitarian need crying out for that {international R2P} action."[86] "Starvation" is included along with "slaughter" and "ethnic cleansing" at one juncture and with "mass murder and rape" at another.[87] The looseness of the terminology is understandable, as the Commission was an independent group charged with making a conceptual contribution for political purposes, not with negotiating a precise legal document. Nevertheless, some critics, especially from skeptical UN member state delegations, have been quick to point to these ambiguities as evidence that R2P is an open-ended concept that could readily be misappropriated for other purposes.

In presenting its recommendations, the Commission was more rigorous in describing potential triggers to R2P action. Under the heading "Basic Principles," the report notes that "where a population is suffering serious harm, as a result of internal war, insurgency, repression or state failure, and the state in question is unwilling or unable to halt or avert it, the principle of non-intervention yields to the international responsibility to protect."[88] How that international responsibility would be exercised, however, would depend on the circumstances of each case. Under its discussion of "the just cause threshold," for instance, the Commission underscored that:

> Military intervention for human protection purposes is an exceptional and extraordinary measure. To be warranted, there must be serious and irreparable harm occurring to human beings, or imminently likely to occur, of the following kind:
>
> A. large scale loss of life, actual or apprehended, with genocidal intent or not, which is the product either of deliberate state action, or state neglect or inability to act, or a failed state situation; or
>
> B. large scale "ethnic cleansing", actual or apprehended, whether carried out by killing, forced expulsion, acts of terror or rape.[89]

As the text notes, "for political, economic and judicial measures the barrier can be set lower, but for military intervention it must be set high: for military action ever to be defensible the circumstances must be grave indeed."[90] Adapting "just war" criteria, the Commission also enunciated four "precautionary principles" for the use of force: right intention; last resort; proportional means; and reasonable prospects.[91] The group also emphasized the need for "right authority," namely authorization by the UN Security Council, for military intervention. Should the Council fail to act, then the General Assembly's "Uniting for Peace" procedure could be invoked or regional arrangements might act under Chapter VIII of the Charter. The Commission warned that if the Security Council failed "to discharge its responsibility to protect in conscience-shocking situations crying out for action, concerned states may not rule out other means to meet the gravity and urgency of that situation."[92]

Given its origins and mandate, it was not surprising that the Commission devoted most of its report and recommendations to the question of military intervention. As Kofi Annan had lamented in his Millennium Report, as noted above, the same had been the case in terms of the General Assembly's response to his 1999 address. The disproportional emphasis on coercive military action, however, has had a distorting effect on both academic discussion and intergovernmental deliberations on R2P ever since the 2001 release of the Commission's report. Subsequent chapters of this volume address the consequences that this bias has had for efforts to put R2P into practice, as well as for the continuing dialogue on R2P among the member states. As noted above, the ICISS report outlined a "responsibility to prevent" and a "responsibility to rebuild," as well as a "responsibility to react."

The ICISS report contained a detailed and nuanced discussion of possible measures, both structural and operational (or what the Commission called "root cause prevention efforts" and "direct prevention efforts"), to prevent "deadly conflict and other forms of man-made catastrophe."[93] It asserted that prevention was "first and foremost the responsibility of sovereign states," but that "strong support from the international community is often needed, and in many cases may be indispensable."[94] The Commission echoed the Brahimi Report's call for improvements in the United Nations' institutional capacities for gathering and analyzing early warning signs of impending conflict, including from non-governmental sources.[95] The commissioners understood, as many observers have not, that "some states are becoming reluctant to accept any internationally endorsed preventive measures at all – even of the softest and most supportive kind," fearing the "internationalization" of their domestic problems and the granting of "legitimacy" to political opponents.[96] Sovereignty issues did not begin or end with military intervention, they seemed to say. According to the report, moreover, "direct prevention" tools could take a range of forms, including "straightforward assistance, positive inducements or, in the more difficult cases, the negative form of threatened 'punishments.'"[97] The latter could include prosecution by the newly formed International Criminal Court.[98]

Though broad ranging, the ICISS's treatment of prevention could have been more compelling. The Synopsis section of the report does assert that "prevention is the single most important dimension of the responsibility to protect: prevention options should always be exhausted before intervention is contemplated."[99] This bold declaration, however, is undermined by the lack of any recommendations for preventive measures and by the much greater space and precision devoted to rules and procedures for the use of force. This imbalance has provided ample material for critics who wrongly claim that R2P is really about finding more acceptable ways of justifying armed humanitarian intervention. Also, the section of the report on prevention focuses solely on preventing deadly conflict, not atrocity crimes. As discussed in subsequent chapters, preventing armed conflict and preventing atrocity crimes may require distinct policy and tactical approaches in dealing with specific situations, despite the statistical fact that atrocities occur most often in cases of armed conflict. This is somewhat better understood at the time of this writing than it was in 2001, when little sustained policy attention had been devoted to the difficult question of how to prevent atrocity crimes in particular crises. One of the more valuable and durable legacies of the Commission's work has, in fact, been to stimulate much more focused analytical and policy work on atrocity prevention.

As noted above, the third element of the deceptively simple three-part architecture given by ICISS for R2P, following a responsibility to prevent and a responsibility to react, was a responsibility to rebuild after any international intervention undertaken under the response basket. As the report puts it, "if military intervention action is taken…there should be a genuine commitment to helping to build a durable peace, and promoting good governance and sustainable development."[100] This third component drew from the substantial efforts to develop the conceptual, operational, and institutional dimensions of peacebuilding following Boutros Boutros-Ghali's introduction of this term in his 1992 *Agenda for Peace* report. The Commission, in that regard, quoted extensively from Kofi Annan's 1998 report on conflict in Africa.[101] Neither of these reports from the Secretaries-General, however, addressed the question of how societies could best recover from atrocity crimes, as distinct from other forms of armed conflict.

The ICISS discussion of the third – peacebuilding – function embodied some of the same strengths and weaknesses as did its treatment of the first one on prevention. As the report acknowledged, peacebuilding could well encounter similar sovereignty concerns as would intrusive preventive measures by the international community. In both cases, obtaining and maintaining a sustainable balance between local ownership and global engagement could be a demanding and delicate task. In a post-conflict situation, the Commission advised, international actors should strive "to do themselves out of a job."[102] It might well be even more difficult to achieve this balance in countries that had been engulfed in horrific communal violence, as had been the case in the Balkans, but this point was not explored by the report. The third basket, like the first, received thoughtful attention in the text of the report, but was not included among the recommendations. Once again, it was accorded secondary or tertiary coverage compared to the centerpiece question of military intervention. In fact, the report had suggested that peacebuilding would be particularly needed where military intervention had occurred. Also, as discussed in the next two sections of this chapter, the chronological sequencing of the three baskets was widely questioned in the debates that followed the release of the report. In real-life crises, there was not always such a clear differentiation between prevention, reaction, and rebuilding, nor did events or policy choices uniformly follow such an orderly sequencing and progression.

2005: The World Summit

The 2001 ICISS report, whose release was delayed by the horrific events of 9/11, was greeted with a polarized mix of praise and scorn. Among its biggest champions, naturally, were the Canadian government and UN Secretary-General Kofi Annan. To its supporters, the introduction of R2P principles represented the long-awaited conceptual breakthrough that could offer a politically viable bridge between humanitarian and sovereignty norms. But the report had its share of skeptics as well, and these questioning voices came from developed as well as developing countries. It is important to understand their concerns, particularly those coming from constructive critics rather than complete rejectionists, because the nature of those reservations largely explains why the conception of R2P was altered in several key respects before it could be adopted by the World Summit in 2005. First, however, it would be useful to see how R2P's most prominent proponents, including Kofi Annan and Gareth Evans, worked to frame the issues at stake during the four years from the completion of the ICISS report in September 2001 to the World Summit in September 2005.

The Secretary-General assembled a High-level Panel on Threats, Challenges and Change to spur fresh thinking among both member states and independent policy analysts in advance of the Summit. The Panel's December 2004 consensus report, *A More Secure World: Our Shared Responsibility*, presented incisive analysis and policy recommendations on a wide range of issues, including a sub-section on "Chapter VII of the Charter of the United Nations, internal threats and the responsibility to protect."[103] This discussion was embedded in a larger section of the report on "Collective Security and the Use of Force." Clearly, the two dimensions of the ICISS report on prevention and rebuilding were once again de-emphasized in favor of the core themes related to intervention by military means. With Gareth Evans as one of its more energetic members, the High-level Panel endorsed "the emerging norm that there is a collective international responsibility to protect, exercisable by the Security Council authorizing military intervention as a last resort."[104] The group failed, however, to clarify what circumstances might trigger an R2P response, giving five different formulations in the course of five paragraphs:

- saving lives in countries in situations of mass atrocity (para. 199);
- the principle of non-intervention in internal affairs cannot be used to protect genocidal acts or other atrocities, such as large-scale violations of international humanitarian law or large-scale ethnic cleansing (para. 200);
- there is a growing recognition that the issue is not the "right to intervene" of any state, but the "responsibility to protect" of *every* state when it comes to people suffering from avoidable catastrophe – mass murder and rape, ethnic cleansing by forcible expulsion and terror, and deliberate starvation and exposure to disease (para. 201, emphasis in the original);
- when sovereign governments "are unable or unwilling" to exercise their "primary responsibility to protect their own citizens from such catastrophes," then "that responsibility should be taken up by the wider international community – with it spanning a continuum involving prevention, response to violence, if necessary, and rebuilding shattered societies" (para. 201); and
- the "emerging norm" is exercisable "in the event of genocide and other large-scale killing, ethnic cleansing or serious violations of international humanitarian law which sovereign Governments have proved powerless or unwilling to prevent" (para. 203).

Some of this language was retained by the Summit, but references to "citizens," to a chronological "continuum," and to whether a state was "unable or unwilling" and/or "powerless or unwilling" were deleted by the assembled heads of state and government less than a year later.

Four months after the publication of the High-level Panel's report, Secretary-General Kofi Annan presented his own wide-ranging report to help frame the agenda for the Summit. *In Larger Freedom: Towards Development, Security and Human Rights for All* counseled that "we must embrace the responsibility to protect, and, when necessary, we must act on it."[105] At points, this report also referred to the need to protect "citizens," but it also spoke of "civilian populations," a formulation closer to that adopted by the Summit.[106] The report introduced the term "national authorities," which was employed by the Summit, but again repeated the "unable or unwilling" phrase that was not.[107] It spoke of a range of possible responses, including "diplomatic, humanitarian and other methods" to help protect civilian populations, in words close to those employed by the Summit.[108] Most importantly, though the text included various terms – "genocide and comparable crimes," "genocide, ethnic cleansing and other such crimes against humanity," "genocide, crimes against humanity and mass human suffering," and "victims of atrocity crimes" – it was much more centered than previous reports on atrocity crimes as the trigger for R2P responses.[109] In retrospect, that step toward a more focused understanding of the scope of R2P helped to open the door to finding common ground on these matters at the Summit a few months later.

Sovereignty concerns were abundant in the intergovernmental debates leading up to the Summit. On the one hand, many developing countries expressed caution about the possibility that R2P principles could be misused by the powerful as a pretext for circumventing long-held norms of non-interference in domestic affairs.[110] Notions of territorial sovereignty, in short, could be at risk. Loose and flexible interpretations of the scope of possible R2P triggers had only served to heighten these worries. On the other hand, a number of developed countries with substantial military capabilities had their own sovereignty concerns about the implications of R2P. China, Russia, and the United States, the three largest permanent members of the UN Security Council, had doubts about R2P from the outset.[111] They were cautious about embracing international principles that could be read as imposing obligations on them to employ their military capacity in ways and situations beyond their national interests and for which there was insufficient domestic political support to be sustainable. They did not want to compromise their decision-making sovereignty.[112] In the weeks before the Summit, these concerns were expressed particularly sharply by John Bolton, the US Permanent Representative to the United Nations. From the perspective of decision-making sovereignty, as of territorial sovereignty, a loose conception of R2P triggers would also have been problematic.

Sometimes practical and constructive solutions come from unlikely sources. Though R2P advocates had tended to cast him as an R2P skeptic, Munir Akram, the UN Permanent Representative of Pakistan, is credited with proposing that the key to gaining broader support among the member states lay in linking the invocation of R2P principles to a discrete set of atrocity crimes.[113] This suggestion was well received for several reasons. One, it echoed the language of Article 4 (h) of the Constitutive Act of the African Union, as noted earlier. Two, it could tie R2P to existing and generally accepted international legal standards. And three, it would confirm the direction in which the Secretary-General's *In Larger Freedom* report was already pointing.

Despite these positive signs, when the heads of state and government began to assemble in New York in September 2005, there were still deep doubts about the possibility of finding common ground on R2P. These doubts were compounded by the Summit's inability to agree on such core security issues as disarmament and non-proliferation, which were deleted from the Outcome Document because of lack of agreement. In the end, the Outcome Document – subsequently adopted unanimously by the General Assembly as Resolution 60/1 – included the following three paragraphs of agreed language in its R2P section:

138. Each individual State has the responsibility to protect its populations from genocide, war crimes, ethnic cleansing and crimes against humanity. This responsibility entails the prevention of such crimes, including their incitement, through appropriate and necessary means. We accept that responsibility and will act in accordance with it. The international community should, as appropriate, encourage and help States to exercise this responsibility and support the United Nations in establishing an early warning capability.

139. The international community, through the United Nations, also has the responsibility to use appropriate diplomatic, humanitarian and other peaceful means, in accordance with Chapters VI and VIII of the Charter, to help to protect populations from genocide, war crimes, ethnic cleansing and crimes against humanity. In this context, we are prepared to take collective action, in a timely and decisive manner, through the Security Council, in accordance with the Charter, including Chapter VII, on a case-by-case basis and in cooperation with relevant regional organizations as appropriate, should peaceful means be inadequate and national authorities are manifestly failing to protect their populations from genocide, war crimes, ethnic cleansing and crimes against humanity. We stress the need for the General Assembly to continue consideration of the responsibility to protect populations from genocide, war crimes, ethnic cleansing and crimes against humanity and its implications, bearing in mind the principles of the Charter and international law. We also intend to commit ourselves, as necessary and appropriate, to helping States build capacity to protect their populations from genocide, war crimes, ethnic cleansing and crimes against humanity and to assisting those which are under stress before crises and conflicts break out.

140. We fully support the mission of the Special Adviser of the Secretary-General on the Prevention of Genocide.

These three paragraphs, adopted without dissent by one of the largest gatherings of heads of state and government ever assembled and then approved by the General Assembly, became the official articulation of R2P. They superseded the original formulation of R2P as proposed by the independent ICISS commission in 2001.

The Summit text on R2P began, logically, with the responsibility of "each individual State," rather than with the responsibilities of the international community. The state was to be responsible for protecting "its populations," a term used consistently and frequently – five times – in paragraphs 138 and 139. There is no talk of "citizens" or "civilians." Populations were to be protected from the three crimes mentioned in the AU Constitutive Act – genocide, war crimes, and crimes against humanity – plus ethnic cleansing, a mass atrocity associated more with Europe than Africa at that point. Ethnic cleansing was not explicitly categorized as a crime in international law but had been frequently referred to in the various reports and commentaries leading up to the Summit. Such acts, moreover, clearly constitute one of the other more established and better defined crimes. In an interesting twist, the state was to offer protection by preventing the four crimes, including their incitement. This both established a close linkage between acts of prevention and protection and raised the profile of incitement as a potentially serious crime in itself. As discussed later in this volume, the integrated manner in which the Summit brought these elements together would later prove very useful for efforts to actually implement R2P principles in specific situations.

Paragraph 138 includes the kind of personal pledge – "we accept that responsibility and will act in accordance with it" – that had not been anticipated, as the 2001 version of R2P did not contemplate its adoption by heads of state and government at a World Summit. In that sense, the state-centric image of R2P projected in the recommendations of the ICISS report seemed a bit more nuanced in the Summit language. That would certainly be so if the "international community" referred to in paragraph 139 in connection with Chapters VI and VIII of the Charter encompassed civil society and the private sector, as would seem to have been the intention. The "will act" phrasing of the prevention pledge in paragraph 138 certainly sounded like a much firmer commitment than the more conditional language of paragraph 139: "also has the responsibility to use appropriate diplomatic, humanitarian and other peaceful means, in accordance with Chapters VI and VIII" of the Charter; "we are prepared to take collective action" under various caveats; and "we also intend to commit ourselves" to assistance and capacity building.

Several of the preventive measures contained in the Outcome Document had appeared, in one form or another, in the text of the ICISS report, though not in the latter's conclusions and recommendations. One was the endorsement in paragraph 138 of a United Nations early warning capability. On the surface, that might have appeared to have been an obvious recommendation, but, given the long history of member-state resistance to giving the UN

Secretariat such a capacity, this was a significant step forward, at least in declaratory policy. Also, the ICISS text had paid much more attention to measures under Chapters VI and VIII than had its recommendations. The Summit put considerable emphasis on helping or assisting states – notably including those "under stress" – as a preventive measure, not a rebuilding one. Here, the treatment of collective military measures as just one of many options made the need for rebuilding afterward a much lower priority in the overall conception of R2P in 2005.

Not surprisingly, the most striking difference between the ICISS report and the Summit's rendition of R2P came in the terms and conditions for the use of force. Gone was the detailed presentation of "precautionary principles" or "principles for military intervention." The members of the Security Council had never accepted guidelines for their decision making beyond the provisions, purposes, and principles of the Charter, with those open to plenty of interpretation by various members at various points. Even if some nonpermanent members had found elements of the "just war" approach favored by ICISS to be of interest, there was little likelihood that the five permanent members would accept rules that might shed doubt on the legitimacy of their use of the veto in some contentious situations.

In four other respects, the presentation of R2P evolved substantially from 2001 to 2005, as follows:

1 The Member States at the World Summit abandoned the three-step chronology proposed in the ICISS report. No continuum or sequencing of policy choices was foreseen in the redefinition and refinement of R2P adopted at the Summit. Perhaps the difference in perspective reflected both the authors and their perceived mandates. The independent commission included experienced policy makers, but their assignment was to produce a coherent conception, not precise policy guidance. The government representatives who drafted and negotiated the Summit Outcome Document sought to retain flexibility, given the unpredictability and variance among crisis situations. Neither prevention nor capacity building, for instance, had clear beginning and ending points. The integration of prevention and protection noted above had a similar implication, as sequencing and continuums tend to break down in practice.
2 The Summit eschewed terms like "unable or unwilling," substituting the simpler term "manifestly failing." The key point was whether there was a need to protect populations, whatever the motives or intentions of the government in question. In practice, this formulation provided a much more straightforward test of whether R2P measures were needed, while avoiding indeterminate and contentious debates in the Security Council about the intentions of the government in question.
3 Though R2P advocates sometimes ignore paragraph 140, its inclusion under the R2P section of the Outcome Document underscored the conceptual,

institutional, and operational ties between R2P and genocide prevention. In an ironic historical twist, Kofi Annan had appointed the first Special Adviser for the Prevention of Genocide just a year before the Summit as part of his effort to commemorate the tenth anniversary of the Rwandan genocide. Otherwise, it should have been possible to integrate these two mandates more fully from the outset.

4 The Summit's call for the General Assembly to "continue consideration" of R2P had not been anticipated either in the 2001 ICISS report or in subsequent ones. Yet, as addressed below, this somewhat obscure provision became a central pathway for the normative development of R2P.

Clearly, the filter of intergovernmental negotiations produced a conception of R2P that differed from that first envisioned by the International Commission in 2001 in important respects. Gone was the heavy focus on the use of coercive force as the centerpiece of R2P, though the Summit's acceptance of the phrase "timely and decisive" as the criterion for collective action was a promising step toward greater international responsibility. In many other respects, as noted above, the Summit produced a much broader and more actionable agenda for preventing atrocity crimes and protecting populations. Though the words of the Outcome Document left some ambiguities and open spaces, these three paragraphs offered a relatively coherent framework on which to build a workable and sustainable implementation strategy. Most importantly, they imparted an invaluable sense of urgency and legitimacy to the continuing project of developing R2P normatively, institutionally, and operationally. With the Summit Outcome, the reframing of R2P from a new way of expressing humanitarian intervention to a platform for developing better ways to prevent atrocities and save lives was well underway.

2009: The Three-Pillar Implementation Strategy

The inclusion of a substantive section of the Outcome Document on the responsibility to protect was a remarkable achievement, but it did not offer much assurance about the depth, breadth, or sustainability of the political support for the concept among member states, particularly in their capitals. One of the reasons that Luck encouraged Ban Ki-moon in 2006, when he was a candidate for the post of Secretary-General, to become engaged with moving R2P forward was concern about signs of significant backsliding among the member states, including in Africa. The United Nations had often been rightly criticized for being much better at words than deeds and for not following up on historic normative advances. As noted earlier, this had sometimes been the case with human rights standards and international humanitarian law (IHL), where critical institutional and implementation steps had sometimes lagged by decades. When it came to R2P, as one of the Secretary-General's policy advisers commented in 2007, there was a palpable sense of "buyer's remorse" among some member-state representatives. Without leadership by the new Secretary-General and visible implementation efforts, there was a real danger that all of the forward momentum for R2P achieved at the Summit could be lost, perhaps irretrievably.

In February 2008, Luck was appointed the first Special Adviser to the UN Secretary-General for the Responsibility to Protect, with a three-part mandate to develop R2P conceptually, politically, and institutionally/operationally. The task was challenging not only because of the lack of staff support or compensation, but also because of the need to work all three aspects of the mandate in tandem and simultaneously. It would have made no sense to design an impressive conceptual architecture for R2P that would not be sustainable politically or achievable operationally. Gaining the confidence and support of cautious and/or skeptical member states would not be possible without an implementation strategy that met their legitimate political concerns and that looked feasible in terms of making a difference on the ground. Institutional and operational progress, moreover, could not be achieved without conceptual innovation, sustained political support, and strategic coherence. In other words, the three elements of the mandate were interdependent and needed to be pursued together.

These tasks required, first and foremost, extensive consultations with member states, the broader UN secretariat, and civil society about where they saw both the potential and the limits of R2P. With the member states, greater clarity was needed on just what they thought they had agreed to on some issues. It was readily apparent that the language of the Outcome Document represented both a framework and a starting point for the further development of R2P: it had to be rigorously respected, but it also left significant gaps in interpretation and content that would need to be filled. At points, the ambiguities and vagueness of the language offered both an opportunity and a risk. From the Special Adviser's perspective, among the openings for further conceptual progress offered by the Outcome Document were the following:

- The term "populations" should be understood as including all persons within the borders of a state, whether citizens, legal or illegal immigrants, refugees, or internally displaced people. If people were within a state's territory, the state had a responsibility to protect them from the four specified crimes and their incitement.
- When non-state armed groups control territory, they should be held to the same R2P standards as governments. There had been many situations in which governments had not been able to exercise effective sovereignty over portions of their territory and armed groups had committed atrocity crimes. The purposes of R2P, in such situations, included assisting the state to exercise its sovereign responsibilities, including protecting populations from the four crimes and their incitement.
- States, therefore, should be treated, whenever possible, as part of the solution, not just of the problem. The 2001 version of R2P appeared to view the state primarily as a perpetrator, while the 2005 edition put greater emphasis

on the state's primary role as a protector of populations, with the international community assisting as possible and when needed.[114] As the Secretary-General put it, R2P "seeks to help States succeed, not just to react when they fail."[115]

- The inclusion in 2005 of "incitement" for the first time as an integral part of a state's responsibility was quite significant from an operational perspective, particularly when trying to prevent or de-escalate such crimes. Practice has shown that incitement is often the most visible and least ambiguous sign of impending atrocity crimes. The crisis in Kenya in late 2007 and early 2008, for instance, illustrated how helpful a focus on incitement could be for both regional and global efforts at preventing an escalation of violence.
- Though it did not employ this phrasing, the Outcome Document presented a vision of R2P that was narrow and deep – narrow in scope by restricting R2P's application to the four crimes and their incitement, deep in terms of utilizing any of the expansive array of tools envisioned by Chapters VI, VII, and VIII of the Charter. The 2005 version, moreover, did not stress the value of some tools over others, tacitly recognizing that each crisis situation presents a unique set of opportunities and limitations.

These openings offered real promise in terms of recasting R2P in a way that might encourage some of the skeptics, especially from the global South, to rethink their instinctive opposition based on non-interference norms. The further development of R2P had the potential of offering a fresh perspective and perhaps new tools for addressing real problems that they or their neighbors had experienced.

Since the member states had not taken to ICISS's prevent-react-rebuild paradigm, a new conceptual architecture was badly needed and the Outcome Document had not provided one. Paragraph 138 was largely about prevention and 139 more about response, but both paragraphs also contained scattered references to helping or assisting states, including in 139 those "under stress." So the Secretary-General proposed a three-pillar implementation strategy as follows:

- Pillar One: the protection responsibilities of the state, as affirmed in paragraph 138 and derived from well-developed legal principles;
- Pillar Two: a concomitant responsibility of the international community (broadly conceived) to provide assistance and capacity building to support the efforts of states to meet their R2P-related protection and prevention responsibilities; and
- Pillar Three: an international commitment to a timely and decisive response, employing the full range of tools under Chapters VI, VII, and VIII, as appropriate and under the Charter, to protect populations from the four specified crimes and their incitement.

The three pillars were first articulated publicly by Ban in Berlin in mid-2008.[116] In subsequent reports by the Secretary-General and presentations by Luck as his Special Adviser, it was repeatedly stressed that the three pillars should be thought of as of equal length and strength and should not be approached sequentially or chronologically. Recognizing that no two crises were alike, their strategy called for an "early and flexible response tailored to the specific circumstances of each case." The approach placed a premium on "early engagement" rather than on "early intervention."

This new architecture – R2P's third makeover in eight years – was captured in greater detail in the Secretary-General's January 2009 report on implementing the responsibility to protect.[117] As in 2001 and 2005, the report's treatment of the use of force was controversial. In 2001, critics thought that the Commission had overemphasized rules for the use of force compared to preventive and non-coercive measures, particularly in its recommendations. In 2005, critics questioned whether the Summit had not gone too far in de-emphasizing the importance of military measures. In 2009, Ban accepted several conceptual innovations concerning the use of military assets proposed by his Special Adviser. Two of these new elements came under the assistance pillar (Pillar Two). One was to draw attention to preventive deployments of peacekeepers, as had been undertaken in the Former Yugoslav Republic of Macedonia and in Burundi, as a step to help "stabilize a country facing ethnically defined tensions both internally and externally."[118] It was also pointed out, again under a Pillar Two umbrella, that in several situations the international community, with the consent of the government concerned, had employed coercive military force to protect populations and even to restore effective sovereignty.[119] This option could prove increasingly relevant in places where non-state armed groups, including those employing terrorism, were challenging state authority and controlling portions of their territory.

Also, under Pillar Three, the new strategy rejected the notion that the use of force should always be the last measure to be considered, when all others had failed. Rather than declaring that the use of force would be a "last resort," as the ICISS report had, the Secretary-General's report termed it "a measure of last resort."[120] Invoking the "timely and decisive" phrasing of the Summit, the report cautioned against "following arbitrary, sequential or graduated policy ladders that prize procedure over substance and process over results."[121]

The 2005 Summit wording offered two other avenues for moving R2P forward that were taken up by the Secretary-General. One was subtle, the other not. The less obvious opening came from the references to "the international community" at several points in paragraphs 138 and 139, particularly in reference to assisting states and to "diplomatic, humanitarian and other peaceful means" under Chapters VI and VIII. These are tasks frequently undertaken with the collaboration of civil society and the private sector. Recognizing the critical role played by individual decision makers at every level, including within vulnerable populations and groups of potential perpetrators, as well as within governments and international institutions, the Secretary-General underscored that "one of the keys to preventing small crimes from becoming large ones, as well as to ending such affronts to human dignity altogether, is to foster individual responsibility."[122] This was the inaugural reference in a UN document to the notion of an "individual responsibility to protect," a theme that runs through this volume.[123]

The second, more obvious, opening was the call in paragraph 139 for the General Assembly "to continue consideration" of R2P, "bearing in mind the principles of the Charter and international law." Though many R2P advocates were concerned about R2P getting bogged down and watered down in the Assembly, Luck championed the initiation of an annual cycle of reports from the Secretary-General and subsequent dialogues with the membership. He saw this as a means both of giving the member states some sense of owner-ship in R2P's development and of spurring a continual process of reevaluation and sharpening of R2P methods by the Secretariat. After multiple rounds of reports and informal interactive dialogues, this ongoing process appears to be facilitating the normative development and political acceptance of R2P principles and practice. That continuing process of norm building, against the backdrop of the dynamics of international politics, is one of the central concerns of chapter 2 below.

CHAPTER TWO

R2P in World Politics

Like all international norms, R2P does not exist in a vacuum and neither does it sit above the fray of world politics. It is, instead, both a product of those politics and part of them. As such, the meanings attached to R2P, its capacity to influence practical action, and its effects on the ground are all shaped by world politics. This chapter attempts to lay out precisely what that means in terms of how we understand what R2P is, the world it operates within, and the expectations that we ought to have for it. Indeed, we argue that one of the principal contributions made by a norm like R2P is to help establish shared international expectations about appropriate behavior vis-à-vis atrocity crimes – how do we, as an international community, expect states to behave toward their own populations and what should the international community at large do to support the prevention of atrocity crimes and protection of vulnerable populations? It is through the setting of shared expectations that gaps between what we would like and what we have are exposed, galvanizing action to remedy those gaps. In the pages that follow, we will argue that R2P should be understood as a norm that challenges the international community to do better than it has in the past to protect people from atrocity crimes. We will also suggest that because practical action, and its effects, are shaped by a wide variety of considerations and forces, R2P should be understood primarily as a "responsibility to try," the exercise of which is evidenced in the intentions, actions, and outcomes achieved by relevant actors.

To make these arguments, we proceed in three steps. First, we posit that R2P should be understood as an international norm or, more accurately, a composite of different rules and principles relating to the domestic behavior of states and the responsibilities of the international community. We then examine how norms influence, but do not determine, political practice. Second, we turn more directly to practical politics and examine both the practical limitations of external action for atrocity prevention and protection and the impact of sovereignty and political will on decision making. R2P is necessarily part of the international political equation and we need to understand those dynamics in order to make sense of its operationalization. Finally, we consider how R2P might be evaluated and suggest an approach built upon the notion that R2P is, first and foremost, a "responsibility to try" to do what can be reasonably done to prevent and end atrocities, bearing in mind the practical and political limitations.

R2P as International Norm

It seems fair to suggest that the responsibility to protect (R2P) has become an international norm inasmuch as it sets widely shared expectations about how states *ought* to respond to the problem of atrocity crimes, even though – as with most international norms, including sovereignty itself – state practice commonly falls well short of the mark. In its first decade, R2P has moved from being a controversial and indeterminate concept seldom utilized by the international community to a norm invoked almost habitually by international institutions charged with responsibility for international peace and security. This is an assessment that stands in contrast to the widespread view that R2P is facing "growing controversy," but the sense of crisis confronting the field is in part a consequence of the principle's normative success: because R2P has succeeded in setting the standard of expected behavior, the pronounced gap between the shared norm and collective practice is now all too obvious. Strong agreement on the meaning and scope of the principle has emerged in the annual informal interactive dialogues on R2P held by the General Assembly; the principle has been unanimously reaffirmed in its entirety no fewer than four times by the UN Security Council and has informed more than 65 other Security Council resolutions; and R2P is now being utilized by the wider community of UN member states. With only a few exceptions, states accept that they have committed to R2P and agree on the principle's core elements. As a result, the international community can no longer hide – as it once did – behind questions of sovereign rights and the proper allocation of international responsibility. It has enunciated and accepted a clear standard of behavior (the very essence of a "norm" in international politics) and is increasingly being judged against that standard.

Evidence abounds that, after the somewhat rocky start charted in the previous chapter, R2P has become an international standard setter – a "norm" in the language of international relations theory. As UN Secretary-General Ban Ki-moon observed in 2012, international debate about R2P has moved from a focus on the merits of the principle itself to matters of implementation.[1] Organizations and regions once considered hostile to R2P have themselves begun to utilize the norm. At the General Assembly's September 2014 Informal Interactive Dialogue on the Responsibility to Protect, China went so far as to describe R2P as a "prudential norm," arguing that "states should establish relevant policies and mechanisms" for implementing it and noting that it was appropriate for the international community to adopt measures to support R2P, including the use of force "as a last resort"; India noted that R2P "was agreed by all" as early as 2005; Indonesia offered emphatic support, saying it "fully subscribes to the finest purposes and objectives of the concept of R2P"; Nigeria declared that "R2P is apt, based on humanitarian and human rights law, representing a global conceptual and policy shift in the notion of sovereignty and security";

Iran noted that "we cannot agree more with the Secretary-General" and his approach to R2P; the Philippines observed that "we subscribe to our shared responsibility" in relation to R2P; and Argentina declared that "since the beginning, Argentina supports the concept of R2P." These statements – all from the global South and including governments once considered quite hostile to the very idea of R2P – provide strong support for the idea that R2P, once considered deeply controversial, is now an established international norm.

Two issues complicate the question of evaluating whether R2P is a norm and what sort of norm it is. First, governments and international relations experts mean different things when they use the word "norm." Governments tend to view norms as binding legal principles: China, for example, questioned whether R2P is a norm on the grounds that it is not legally binding.[2] International relations scholars, however, understand norms as broader social phenomena: shared expectations of appropriate behavior for actors with a given identity.[3] From this perspective, norms need not be legally binding or viewed as synonymous with law. It is this wider social understanding of norms that we use here, not least because we share the view that R2P is a political rather than a legal principle, and one that does not even strive to become a legal principle. In essence, R2P is a political commitment to implement existing international law, not a legal principle itself.

The second complicating factor is that R2P refers not to a single norm but to two quite distinct sets of norms: those relating to how states treat their own populations and those relating to a state's responsibilities to contribute to the protection of populations in other countries. It is now commonly understood that the first cluster (Pillar One of R2P) relates to well-established principles of international law.[4] No state has demurred from this view in the General Assembly. Focusing on the second cluster of responsibilities, those associated with the protection of populations in other countries, this section will argue that R2P, which was described as an "emerging norm" by the International Commission on Intervention and State Sovereignty (ICISS) in 2001, has now become an established international norm.[5] That is because there are now "shared international expectations" (1) that governments and international organizations should exercise this responsibility; (2) that they recognize both a limited duty and a right to do so; and (3) that failure to fulfill this duty should attract criticism and/or punishment or remedial action. Taken together, the combination of practice (in which measures have been adopted in the hope of fulfilling R2P), and the ongoing consideration of the norm (in the General Assembly and Security Council), have been central to its emergence. Both have helped establish precedents and shared expectations that limit the decisions that can be legitimately taken in response to genocide and atrocity crimes, making it more difficult (but by no means impossible) for those institutions charged with protection responsibilities, most notably the Security Council, to avoid acting upon them altogether.[6]

To understand changes in behavior associated with the emergence of R2P, we first need to understand earlier practice. We showed in the previous chapter that R2P did not emerge as a fully formed norm from the 2005 World Summit. Indeed, most of the permanent members of the Security Council were initially deeply cautious about R2P, reflecting more generalized attitudes among sections of the UN membership that were concerned that R2P might constitute a potential challenge to territorial and decision-making sovereignty and provide a license for external intervention. Within that context, the inclusion of R2P language and considerations in substantive Security Council resolutions initially proved difficult and controversial. A reference to R2P in the draft preamble of Resolution 1769 (2007) on the situation in Sudan had to be removed before the resolution was adopted; and the Security Council decided not to refer to R2P in Resolution 1814 (2008) on Somalia despite its inclusion in a report by the Secretary-General's Special Representative.[7] After these unpromising early debates, it was some years before the Council referred once again to R2P in relation to another country situation. The apparent success of preventive diplomacy in Kenya (2008), which explicitly utilized an "R2P lens," was set against a number of other crises where states were more reticent about accepting and acting upon their protection responsibilities. During this time, there were major protection crises in Darfur, the Democratic Republic of Congo (DRC), Guinea, Kyrgyzstan, Somalia, Sri Lanka, and Sudan/South Sudan. The 2009 protection crisis in Sri Lanka, which saw up to 40,000 Tamil civilians killed, was not even placed on the formal Council agenda. As Ekkehard Strauss observed, "the lack of unity in the Council or, in fact, the opposition of some Member States prevented the Council so far from applying the responsibility to protect on a specific country situation."[8]

Since early 2011, however, and the adoption of a series of landmark Security Council resolutions on Libya (Resolutions 1970 [2011] and 1973 [2011]) and Côte d'Ivoire (Resolution 1975 [2011]), the situation has changed in at least two important ways. First, protection crises characterized by atrocity crimes have tended to generate international responses, usually marshaled through or supported by the Security Council, to a much greater extent than previously (see Table 2.1). As we observed earlier, the Security Council has referred to R2P in more than sixty-five resolutions and has employed the principle in different ways, including to remind governments of their protection responsibilities (e.g. Resolution 2014 [2011] on Yemen and Resolution 2165 [2014] on Syria), to demand that the parties to an armed conflict take active steps to protect civilians (e.g. Resolution 2139 [2014] on Syria), to task peacekeepers with assisting governments to protect their own populations (e.g. Resolution 1996 [2011] on South Sudan and Resolution 2085 [2012] on Mali), and to demand that perpetrators of mass violence be held legally accountable for their crimes (e.g. Resolution 2211 [2015] on DRC). The Council has also connected its work on R2P with its efforts focused on preventive diplomacy and conflict prevention more broadly, the control of small arms and light

Table 2.1 R2P and the response to new crises (2011–2015)

Crisis	UNSC Resolution?	R2P Referenced?	Tools
Syria	Yes	Yes	Diplomacy, inquiry, monitors, destruction of chemical weapons, humanitarian access
Libya	Yes	Yes	Diplomacy, use of force, no-fly zone, economic measures, inquiry
Yemen	Yes	Yes	Diplomacy, humanitarian
Iraq (Islamic State)	Yes	Yes	Humanitarian, military force, diplomacy, support for armed groups
Central African Republic	Yes	Yes	Peacekeeping, diplomacy, economic measures, accountability measures (International Criminal Court)
South Sudan	Yes	Yes	Peacekeeping, diplomacy, humanitarian, inquiry, accountability, statebuilding
Sudan (Darfur and Abyei)	Yes	Yes	Peacekeeping, diplomacy, humanitarian, inquiry, monitors, accountability measures (International Criminal Court)
Mali	Yes	Yes	Use of force, peacekeeping, diplomacy, statebuilding, humanitarian, inquiry, accountability
Gaza	Yes	No	Humanitarian, diplomacy, inquiry
DRC	Yes	Yes	Use of force, peacekeeping, diplomacy, statebuilding, humanitarian, inquiry, accountability
Somalia	Yes	Yes	Use of force, peacekeeping, diplomacy, statebuilding, humanitarian, inquiry
Cote d'Ivoire	Yes	Yes	Use of force, peacekeeping, diplomacy, economic measures, statebuilding, humanitarian, inquiry
Nigeria (Boko Haram)	No	No	Support for the Nigerian government
Myanmar (Rohingya)	No	No	Bilateral and multilateral support for political transition including capacity building
North Korea	No (but informal meetings held)	No (but UN Human Rights Council and General Assembly have)	Commission of inquiry, diplomacy, economic sanctions (weapons proliferation)

weapons, the prevention of genocide, counterterrorism, and international policing.

The Council has adopted measures in relation to relevant crises since 2011. The two principal outlying cases are the situation of Boko Haram in Nigeria, where the Nigerian government itself has pushed back against international activism, and the situation of the Rohingya in Myanmar, which has not made it onto the Council's formal agenda but which elicited informal responses through the Association of Southeast Asian Nations, the UN Secretary-General's Special Representative, and a range of bilateral initiatives. A further outlying case is North Korea, whose atrocity crimes predate R2P. Despite the difficult politics, R2P has been associated with some progressive change. In 2014, an independent panel of inquiry, commissioned by the UN Human Rights Council, reported that the government of North Korea was perpetrating systematic crimes against humanity against its own population and called on the government – and the international community – to fulfill their responsibility to protect the civilian population.[9] These recommendations were adopted by the UN General Assembly's Third Committee (Human Rights), which referred the matter to the Assembly's main session. The Assembly then resolved to refer the human rights situation to the UN Security Council, and the Council, in turn, held its first ever meetings on human rights in North Korea in late 2014 and then again a year after. Although the Council has not yet resolved to take action, the very fact that the decades-old human rights crisis in North Korea is now firmly on its agenda – over Chinese, and to a lesser extent Russian objections – is an important step forward. The fact that R2P played a catalytic role in that process is also significant.[10]

In many cases, the international community marshaled a multifaceted response comprising the deployment of significant international resources, including peacekeepers and/or military force, with the explicit intention of supporting the protection of populations. It is possible to see in all this an emerging pattern of response that is establishing precedents through practice and that is strongly suggestive of the emergence of shared expectations about the international community's responsibility to protect. Simply put, in assuming an almost habitual quality, collective international action to support the protection of populations from atrocity crimes has become "the norm." Not only has complete failure to act become rare, so too have entirely tokenistic responses. Of course, just how timely and decisive these responses have been – and whether the international community can be said to have actually fulfilled its responsibility to protect – is another matter entirely and is a question we will return to at length.

Behind this trend is a pronounced shift in the level of controversy associated with R2P. In sharp contrast to the controversy surrounding the inclusion of R2P in Resolution 1706 (2006) on Darfur, since early 2011 the inclusion of R2P language has become much easier to negotiate. Several UN officials and diplomats from member states intimately engaged in the Security Council have expressed this view privately, and public evidence also points in this direction. With the exception of Resolution 1973 (2011) on Libya, each of the resolutions mentioning R2P since early 2011 has been adopted unanimously. Further, even including the case of Resolution 1973 (2011), no Council member expressed concern about the inclusion of R2P in these resolutions in their formal statements to the Council. Nor is there evidence suggesting that the inclusion of R2P language in a draft resolution delayed its adoption.

There is therefore good reason to think that shared expectations have emerged that governments and international organizations, especially the United Nations, have a responsibility to protect populations from genocide and other atrocity crimes. Moreover, the general notion that the international community has a responsibility to adopt measures aimed at protecting populations from atrocity crimes is now largely uncontroversial among states – though, of course, the question of how that responsibility should be exercised in actual cases is often hotly contested, and deep sensitivities remain about the use of measures, coercive or not, without state consent – questions we will return to later.

This brings us to a related question: to what extent do states recognize a "right" or a "duty" to act? These matters go to the heart of the relationship between R2P and decision-making sovereignty – the heart of the problem as identified by the UN's reports on Rwanda and Srebrenica, but not seen as central to R2P in its initial articulation (see chapter 1). The question of "rights" is the more straightforward issue. In contrast to earlier times, when the Security Council's authority over "internal" matters was considered quite controversial, no state now disputes the right of the Council to adopt measures in respect of R2P or the right of individual states and regional organizations to provide encouragement and assistance to states on a consensual basis. These points have been clearly expressed by member states in the General Assembly's informal dialogues on R2P.[11] Even the more cautious Council members, such as China and Russia, do not now openly question the appropriateness of including R2P matters on the Council's agenda. When justifying their first Security Council vetoes on Syria in October 2011, Russia argued that it undertook "intensive, constructive efforts to develop an effective response on the part of the Council" (including an earlier Presidential Statement[12]) while China called for the Council to do more to encourage domestic reform and indicated its support for an alternative draft resolution focused on political dialogue.[13] Neither questioned whether it was legitimate for the Security Council to involve itself in Syria, despite the fact that the situation was then still a largely domestic affair.

Beyond the Security Council, important questions remain about the extent to which institutions such as the UN's human rights and peacebuilding architectures, regional and sub-regional arrangements, and international secretariats, as well as individual states, can take it upon themselves to advance protection efforts without the express consent of the states concerned. By and large, states hold the view that consent is a prerequisite for action not authorized by the Security Council under Chapter VII of the Charter, but there are indications that some other global institutions are beginning to identify their own roles in this area. Notably, in his 2017 report on R2P, the new UN Secretary-General, António Guterres, proposed that the Human Rights Council's Universal Periodic Review (UPR) process be utilized to support R2P goals. This suggestion has enjoyed some support from states. India, for example, has argued that "we need to activate an advance early warning system of potential dangers to civilian population by the UN Human Rights System when the country concerned is being reviewed by the UPR system."[14] A few years earlier, in December 2013, Ban Ki-moon unveiled a new "Human Rights up Front" action plan, which called on UN missions and country teams to prioritize human rights protection.[15] In late 2015, the UN in Geneva hosted an event to mark the tenth anniversary of R2P. Attended by more than a hundred member states, including China, India and Russia, not a single state questioned the applicability of R2P to the UN's human rights and humanitarian work based in Geneva.

The associated question of whether there exists a "duty" to protect other populations from genocide and atrocity crimes is altogether more difficult to untangle and speaks more directly to the thorny problem of decision-making sovereignty, the element of sovereignty most assiduously defended by the UN's most influential member states. It is also, of course, an issue that has animated moral philosophers with as yet no definitive resolution. While the 2005 agreement on R2P did not extend the international community's legal rights with respect to interference in the domestic affairs of states, it did acknowledge the special responsibilities of the Security Council, highlighting an expectation within the broader community of states that the Council would adopt the measures necessary to protect populations from atrocities, whatever they should be. Recall that in paragraph 139 of the World Summit Outcome Document, member states acknowledged an international responsibility to "use appropriate diplomatic, humanitarian and other peaceful means, in accordance with Chapters VI and VIII of the Charter of the United Nations, to help protect populations from genocide, war crimes, ethnic cleansing and crimes against humanity." This responsibility should be exercised "through the United Nations" and specifically through Chapters VI (peaceful measures), VII (enforcement measures), and VIII (regional arrangements) of the UN Charter, awarding a special role to the Security Council. These expectations have made it more difficult for the Council to justify complete inaction in the face of atrocity crimes.[16]

One of the principal critiques of the claim that R2P is an international norm rests on the observation that the Security Council has stopped short of recognizing or legislating the *international community*'s responsibility to protect. That is, that it has not formally recognized constraints on its decision making with respect to situations where atrocities are perpetrated or judged to be imminent. While it is true that the Council has not recognized a specific action or menu of steps necessary to fulfill the international responsibility to protect in its resolutions on individual country situations, no doubt owing to decision-making sovereignty-related concerns about the need to balance different sets of responsibilities (such as for peace and security and for human protection) and to avoid establishing precedents that could limit its future freedom of action, it is not the case that the Council has *never* affirmed the notion of an international responsibility to protect.[17] On several occasions the Council has expressly reaffirmed the *whole* R2P principle agreed to in 2005, including the special responsibilities that agreement bestows upon the Council itself.[18] Thus, while influential states jealously guard their decision-making sovereignty, they have started to recognize that R2P might impose constraints – however limited – upon it. Council members retain a right to abjure from taking timely and decisive action in response to atrocity crimes but they should not expect to avoid formal censure by the wider UN membership when they do – as indeed occurred in response to the situation in Syria.

Outside the Security Council, although the term "R2P" is used less often by other actors and institutions, similar trends are evident in terms of the patterns of engagement with atrocity crimes. For instance, although significant gaps remain, regional organizations are getting more, not less, engaged in their own peacekeeping operations and those operations are also becoming larger, more complex, and more focused on protection.[19] Given that both the AU missions in Somalia (AMISOM) and Central African Republic (MISCA) and the NATO and EU missions in the former Yugoslavia included protection advisers, it seems fair to suggest that the prioritization of protection practices applies to these organizations, as well as to the UN. Elsewhere, it is well recognized that an increasing proportion of violent conflicts and episodes of one-sided violence attract international mediation arising from both regional organizations and the UN, and sometimes (as in Kenya 2007–8 and Syria 2011–present) both simultaneously, as well as from more informal sources.[20] Meanwhile, international peacebuilding has expanded in breadth and depth largely as a response to the demands arising from mediated settlements; despite problems, international human rights machinery has expanded, as have regional processes in the global South, international criminal justice, transitional justice and truth commissions have proliferated; and widespread or systematic sexual and gender-based violence has come under the spotlight through regular UN reporting, targeted collective actions, a specifically targeted UK-led initiative to prevent sexual violence (PSVI), and a range of regional programs.[21] So, while member states may not yet formally recognize that R2P establishes a duty to act in a particular manner, and therefore imposes constraints on their decision-making sovereignty, there are signs that the normative expectations created by the principle are beginning to point in that direction.

This is best exemplified in our third test for a norm, which is the extent to which clear compliance failures attract criticism from peers. Clearly, states and non-state armed groups that perpetrate atrocity crimes are routinely condemned and ostracized. But what of failures to exercise the international responsibility to protect – is there evidence that the international community *expects* timely and decisive action by relevant actors? Because norms set expectations of appropriate behavior, it is somewhat easier to see them at work when they are violated than when they are complied with. Failures to comply with a norm should elicit criticism – because the actions fall short or transgress community expectations. Criticism is a clear indication that a society judges a course of action to be inappropriate because it does not comply with its norms. Conversely, if clear failures to comply with a norm do not elicit criticism from within the relevant society, this is an obvious sign that the shared expectations related to it are nonexistent, weak, or else easily trumped by competing norms.[22]

Since the upswing of normative commitment to R2P that coincided with the landmark 2009 report of the Secretary-General, the most obvious failure to comply with international expectations associated with R2P has been in Syria, where the Security Council has been too weak and divided to lead a timely and decisive response. The international community's response has left little doubt that the Council has failed to meet collective expectations. The General Assembly responded to the Council's ineffectualness by signaling its strong disapproval of the Council's actions and endorsing a more resolute approach. Large majorities in the Assembly voted to recommend many of the measures vetoed in the Security Council. On February 26, 2012, the Assembly voted by 137 to 12 (with 17 abstentions) to condemn "widespread and systematic human rights violations by the Syrian authorities"; to call on all armed groups to end the violence; and to support an Arab League peace initiative.[23] Among the supporters of that resolution were Brazil, India, Pakistan, and South Africa. In addition, the General Assembly expressly criticized the Security Council's handling of the crisis in Syria. On August 3, 2012, the Assembly voted 132 to 12 for a resolution that "deplored" the Council's failure to adopt effective measures to protect civilians.[24] Brazil and South Africa were among the countries that supported this resolution. More recently, the UN Human Rights Council's Commission of Inquiry on Syria, led by Paulo Pinheiro, argued that the Security Council "bears responsibility" for allowing the continuation of war crimes and crimes against humanity by all sides.[25] The willingness of the General Assembly and UN Secretariat to criticize the Council offers clear evidence of international expectations about the Security Council's responsibility to do what it can to protect populations from genocide and atrocity crimes.

Taking the three tests together (practice, recognition of rights and duties, criticism of clear violations), there are strong grounds for concluding that over the past few years R2P has emerged as an international norm. What that means is that there are shared expectations that states ought to protect their populations from atrocity crimes and that when they are manifestly failing to do so, the international community should adopt measures to protect vulnerable population. Precisely what the norm requires in specific cases, in terms of the exact configuration of measures, the resources that should be expended, and the degree of risk that should be borne by outsiders, is difficult to determine. This is partly because the best course of action is seldom clear and always determined by context and partly because states remain committed to their decision-making sovereignty which makes each response an ad hoc one to a certain extent. Judgments about what can be done and the political contexts that make actions possible or not are always necessarily conditional, relative (in terms of speaking of "better" or "worse" responses) and dependent on context. As such, Jennifer Welsh argues that R2P is primarily a responsibility to *consider* taking action to protect populations from atrocity crimes. We would go further and suggest that when atrocities are perpetrated or imminently apprehended, the international community has a "responsibility to try" to protect populations.[26]

The Practical and Political Limits of R2P

Having said that R2P establishes a clear set of expectations about the need to respond to atrocity crimes – a responsibility to try – it is important to be clear eyed about the limits of what norms can achieve. Indeed, it is precisely to address these limits and help R2P make a difference that we articulate a wider and more inclusive definition of actors, tools, and objectives. Some of these limits are inherent in norms themselves: they can influence behavior and shape social reactions to different types of behavior, but they cannot determine behavior. Some actors may be willing to pay the social costs of non-compliance. Moreover, R2P does not exist in a normative vacuum – it cohabits with other norms, interests and cherished values and sometimes these collide, forcing decision makers to choose between different sets of norms. Finally, there are some basic practical limitations to what outsiders can do to protect populations at a reasonable cost and risk.

We need to first recognize that there are important limits to what norms – all norms, including sovereignty (in all its different guises) – can do. Much like the law itself, norms cannot by themselves *compel* people or states to take particular actions or physically *prevent* them from doing so. Norms, like law, depend upon physical institutions, such as a police force, judiciary, and prisons system, to achieve these effects and neither norms nor law has ever been able to do so perfectly. Moreover, because it is a system of sovereign states rather than a single-world government, the international community has few of the institutions usually associated with law enforcement – the closest we have to such an institution is the UN Security Council. Instead, therefore, international laws and norms influence behavior indirectly by shaping governments' own judgments about appropriate and inappropriate behavior and influencing the way in which other governments will respond to that behavior. Behavior compliant with shared norms is likely to be welcomed and praised; non-compliance is likely to be met with criticism, punishment, and social exclusion. Just as some people can cope better with ostracism than others, so some states are more able than others to withstand these costs, at least in the short run, and might calculate that what they can secure by breaking the norms is more valuable to them than what they expect to lose. But there are limits to the costs that even the most powerful actors can withstand – as the terrible price the United States paid for its invasion of Iraq, widely seen as illegitimate, shows only too well.

A norm's capacity to shape behavior is also influenced by its specificity. In general, the more precisely a norm indicates the behavior it expects in a given situation, the stronger its "compliance-pull."[27] That is part of the reason why R2P's first pillar (states should protect their own populations) is a stronger norm than the third (the international community should respond to atrocities in a timely and decisive fashion): the first pillar is very clear about who is responsible for what and violations are relatively obvious; the third pillar is less clear on who has responsibility (though the Security Council clearly has a special responsibility) and more ambiguous still on what precisely is required in any given situation.

Finally, what counts as a breach of a norm, and the consequences that flow from that, are not decided objectively or in a mechanistic fashion. Judgments are contingent on their context and are highly political – usually influenced by the situation itself. There are at least four particularly relevant factors that shape judgments about norm compliance and violation: first, how a situation is perceived at the time is based on usually imperfect contemporaneous knowledge. Second is the nature of the relationships involved. *Who* is presenting an argument about norm compliance/violation may sometimes matter more than what is being argued. We are more likely to be persuaded by those we think are good and legitimate than those who we do not hold in such high esteem. Third, decision-making sovereignty remains important, so how the issue relates to the interests and priorities of relevant states matters. The importance attached to the issue or the norm relative to other concerns might dictate whether someone is prepared to turn a blind eye to norm violations or react more strongly to them. Fourth, another nod to decision-making sovereignty is the relative power of the various groups involved. The powerful are less likely to be punished or socially excluded because of the costs this imposes on those doing the punishing. What is more, the powerful are often able to use their political clout to protect their friends and allies.

Norms, then, are therefore understandings of appropriate behavior shared by members of a group. They influence behavior indirectly through social pressures that promote compliance and threats of punishment and exclusion.

As a result, they do not determine or compel behavior and their role in any given situation is influenced by a range of other contextual factors. It is not surprising, therefore, that the application and role of a norm such as R2P in actual crises is shaped by the political context at hand. It is the responsibility of those charged with implementing R2P to think creatively about how best to utilize these contextual factors to support implementation of the norm.

Even when the normative and political context allows for it, the effective protection of populations from atrocity crimes confronts significant practical challenges. It is important to be up-front about what these challenges are – since some advocates and many critics of R2P tend to underestimate the practical scale and immense difficulty of the task of preventing atrocities and protecting vulnerable populations. Preventing and ending atrocities is difficult and demanding. Even if there were abundant enthusiasm, consensus, and resources available for protection and atrocity prevention, it would likely still prove impossible to prevent every atrocity and protect every individual – absent some fundamental reforms to the human condition. To understand the operational practice of R2P, we need to appreciate the significant limitations imposed by the global context. We must draw an important distinction between failures that result from inadequacies in the international community's response from those that result from problems beyond the power of external actors. It also helps to sound a note of caution about what can be realistically expected and to contextualize the difficult politics of protecting populations.

The first point is to recognize that there are significant limits to what outsiders can do to prevent atrocity crimes. Many internal conflicts are not readily susceptible to outside mediation whether (as in the case of Rwanda or Iraq [Islamic State]) because one or more of the parties have embarked implacably on a course of action leading to atrocities or (as in the case of Syria and South Sudan) because a situation is so complex and fraught with danger as to defy easy resolution.[28] International efforts can facilitate protection and prevention either through massive and costly interventions or where there is local will and capacity, and the levels and types of resilience can be different in different parts of a country, producing different patterns of violence, but the so-called "structural" or "root" causes of atrocities are often not easily influenced by external actors. While outsiders can play important enabling and facilitative roles, foreign assistance cannot by itself achieve structural change except through massive intervention, and even then there are inherent limits and high risks. As Scott Straus observed, "[i]n the long-run…domestic actors are likely to be more effective than international ones at prevention."[29] Well-targeted programs and engagements can, however, support local sources of resilience to genocide and atrocity crimes and change the cost-benefit calculations of would-be perpetrators. But although concerted international action can sometimes protect populations or prevent atrocity crimes (e.g. as in Cote d'Ivoire, Guinea [Conakry], Kenya, Kyrgyzstan, and Libya), the primary determinants of violence or peace typically rest within the country itself and the disposition of its leaders.[30]

From the UN's perspective, this problem is compounded by the fact that it tends to be confronted by some of the world's most difficult cases. Situations usually reach the UN Security Council only when others have tried, and failed, to resolve them. As a rule of thumb, where conflicts have an easy remedy, solutions tend to be found at the local, national, or regional level and without the need for the UN. As the UN Charter specified, the Security Council was to assume the lead only on those crises for which others had found no solution. In such circumstances, a modest success rate might partly reflect the sheer difficulty of the cases presented to the UN system.

A second limiting fact of life is that R2P operates in a world of finite global capacity and competes with other cherished norms and values for resources. This problem of limited resources is compounded by the ongoing climate of financial austerity. Many major donors have cut national budgets and have imposed austerity measures on their own populations, putting pressure on their support for external activities. Unsurprisingly, the UN continues to cut its budget. The Secretary-General has asked the whole system to find savings, principally through cuts to personnel and reductions to the budget for Special Political Missions. Other research suggests that member states are close to their collective capacity to contribute peacekeepers and police for UN missions.[31] The harsh reality, therefore, is that in the near term the implementation of R2P will not be able to call upon significant new resources. What is more, although states often do manage to find resources to support new or expanded missions when necessary, concerns about resource limitations and overstretch do play a role in shaping decisions about the prevention of imminent atrocities in marginal cases. As such, major efforts to address atrocities will have to draw upon resources dedicated to other fields of work.

It is now something of a truism that, case for case, the prevention of atrocities is cheaper than responding to atrocities and rebuilding societies afterward, as the Carnegie Commission on Preventing Deadly Conflict found in relation to conflict prevention more generally.[32] But things are not so simple in practice. According to some critics, a fully comprehensive approach to atrocity prevention, comprising efforts to reduce the underlying structural and systemic sources of risk and to respond to imminent emergencies, could be judged to require determined action to raise living standards, improve governance institutions, and resolve disputes in every country thought to be harboring factors associated with risk, rather than only those countries where risks are imminent or violence present. Pursued holistically, they argue, the costs of implementing this agenda on a global scale could be both substantial and open-ended.[33] This, though, needs to be set against substantial evidence pointing to the massive costs associated with violent conflict. The mathematics are further complicated by the fact that – as the Secretary-General pointed out in 2012 – in most situations "preventive" and "responsive" actions are not easily distinguished from one another.[34] Most often, international engagement with specific crises includes elements of both prevention and response, sliding up and down a continuum of mindsets and measures, rather than being easily distinguishable as one or the other. This is one of the reasons that the pillars of the Secretary-General's 2009 implementation strategy are to be pursued simultaneously, not chronologically.

It is also important to recognize that the implementation of R2P is political, and sensitive, all the way down. The practice of R2P is both enabled and constrained by politics and can generate acute controversies and disputes by, for instance, requiring that some states be identified as being at risk of atrocities and demanding actions that some governments might object to. Often, even long-term preventive measures entail a significant degree of intrusion into the domestic affairs of states, which is not always welcome because it could, amongst other things, empower and legitimize a government's domestic opponents.[35] In this context, it is important to recognize that "in the nation-state era there will be limits to both the practicality and the wisdom of formally breaching the proper boundaries of sovereignty."[36] Typically, states jealously guard their sovereign prerogatives and are sensitive about perceived incursions on their rights or criticisms of their conduct or domestic conditions. As such, they rarely invite assistance or look kindly upon external efforts to prevent atrocities within their jurisdiction. As a result, it is false to assume that preventive action will always be less contentious than intervention once atrocities have erupted.[37] The general unwillingness of states to recognize atrocity risks at home and cooperate with international actors constitutes a significant barrier to effective early prevention, much of which must be done with the support and consent of the state. This, of course, can make prevention a politically sensitive and sometimes highly contentious undertaking. (As chapter 7 notes, experience suggests that the willingness of a government to work with the international community has sometimes been a key to successful prevention.)

When it comes to prevention, in particular – though it is also a powerful consideration in shaping responses since the precise consequences of an action or inaction are unknowable in advance – the field is plagued by the problem of uncertainty, what Colin Keating describes as the "prevention dilemma."[38] This dilemma stems from the fact that, despite significant advances in conflict forecasting, early warning models remain insufficiently accurate to provide a firm foundation for confident action and there is never any way of knowing – precisely – the overall effect of a course of action. This is a problem that exacerbates governments' predisposition to risk averseness arising from concerns about opportunity costs, their capacity to influence events on the ground at a reasonable price, and the political dangers associated with preventive action. As a result, although early action is imperative, there is seldom a sufficiently strong evidentiary basis on which to marshal international action in advance of the actual commission of atrocities. Moreover, since any type of action entails risks, the cards are stacked firmly in support of inaction: better to stand aside and minimize risk to oneself than to act and incur potential costs. Often, the best that can be achieved is an early response to atrocities that might prevent further escalation, as in Kenya 2007 and – through the Organization for Security and Cooperation in Europe (OSCE) – Kyrgyzstan in 2010.

The role of confidence in enabling preventive action was demonstrated when lessons learned from Kenya in 2008 spurred a genuinely preventive approach to that country's 2013 elections that made that exercise a largely peaceful affair, despite the presence of the same centrifugal forces that had caused violence five years earlier. It is that sort of precision about the triggers and timing of potential atrocities that is needed to give leaders sufficient confidence to act. Sometimes, circumstance and past experience provides such clarity, as with South Sudan's 2011 referendum, Gaddafi's imminent attack on Benghazi in 2011, and Kenya's 2013 election. In those situations, preventive action is more likely. In most cases, however, there is a much greater degree of uncertainty about whether, when, and where atrocity risks might be actualized and this is a significant obstacle to decisive preventive action.

R2P, Sovereignty and World Politics

In early debates and frameworks for R2P, it was widely, even generally, assumed that the biggest challenge, conceptually and politically, would be territorial sovereignty – the reluctance of states to involve themselves in the affairs of others *because* of their fidelity to non-interference and commitment to the sovereignty of the affected state. As we observed in the previous chapter, much of the early effort was focused on addressing the territorial sovereignty concerns of the global South, Russia, and China. While those concerns have not been entirely allayed, the international community has made far more progress on that front than had been anticipated by most observers. The more stubborn sovereignty issue has been the decision-making sovereignty of those states with the wherewithal to respond militarily. That resistance should have come as no surprise, but it points to the different aspects of sovereignty and what has and has not changed as a result of R2P. Among the unexpected successes would be the General Assembly debates and cycles of the Secretary-General's reports and the conceptual refinements and broader political ownership they produced.

The fact that the international community is comprised of sovereign states that pursue their own interests (however defined) and privilege domestic over foreign concerns also creates structural obstacles for atrocity prevention. The UN's activities are overseen by *political* (as opposed to judicial) organs comprised of sovereignty-wielding member states whose ideologies, interests, allegiances, and preferences influence their positions.[39] Most significantly, these states are often unwilling to commit more than very limited resources to the prevention of atrocities in foreign countries.

The central issues here are often labeled "political will," though that term can be used to obscure as much as to illuminate. At stake is the state's determination to cling on to its prerogative to decide for itself how to respond to atrocities, unconstrained by international norms and other considerations. One facet of the problem is that states sometimes judge that their own interests are best served by not preventing atrocity crimes. For example, the link between Russia's obstinate support for the al-Assad regime in Syria and its political, strategic, and economic interests in the region are well known. But the West has also sometimes put its own interests ahead of the prevention of atrocities. For example, in the 1980s and 1990s, the United Kingdom helped to fund, arm, and even train the Khmer Rouge, the United States supported a genocidal government in Guatemala, and France continued to aid the government in Kigali, even as the Rwandan genocide began to unfold.[40] The UN's position on Sri Lanka in 2008–9 was made particularly difficult by the collusion of the world's major powers in shielding the Sri Lankan government from blame. This collusion derived from a shared interest in the elimination of the Tamil Tigers (LTTE). Historically, the UN has struggled to assert its primacy in situations where the interests of powerful states, especially permanent members of the Security Council, are engaged (e.g. United States on Iraq; Russia on Chechnya).

Another facet of the problem relates to the fact that states are self-interested actors that prioritize their own interests or those of their governing elites. As such, they are generally reluctant to commit extensive resources to prevent atrocity crimes in other countries. The issue here is not whether governments support atrocity prevention as a goal, but the depth of their support relative to their other goals – including cherished domestic objectives such as healthcare and social welfare. Political and diplomatic capital is also a finite resource. Sometimes, states may judge that trade-offs have to be made to achieve the greatest good or least harm overall. For example, at the outset of the crisis in Darfur, several states decided not to press the government of Sudan too hard, fearing that this might jeopardize negotiations to end the government's war with the SPLM/A in the south.[41]

These different political considerations have a significant effect on the fortunes of atrocity prevention because not only do the UN's principal organs play a critical role in determining the mandates and policies, the effectiveness of the UN's resolutions and the work of its Secretariat, missions, and country-teams depend to a great extent on their capacity to *persuade* member states to implement their decisions.[42] Although the UN's Secretariat, agencies, funds, and programs can work preventively without specific mandates from the political organs, the UN has limited material resources at its direct disposal for atrocity prevention and therefore relies almost entirely on the goodwill of member states to provide the (sometimes extensive) resources required. As a result, even the implementation of Security Council decisions has been patchy at best.

Setting Expectations: A Responsibility to Try

How, then, should we evaluate R2P? One of the principal problems with the debate thus far is the use of different metrics to determine whether the principle is having an effect and whether or not that effect is beneficial. Keenly aware of the arduous diplomatic struggles that lay beneath international acceptance of R2P, advocates have sometimes rushed with undue haste to describe some actions, such as the NATO-led intervention in Libya, as "textbook examples" of R2P in practice.[43] Critics, meanwhile, have sometimes gone to equally great lengths to suggest that those same actions had little to do with the principle, despite clear references to it.[44] More often, though, they have pointed to signs of international inaction or ineffectual engagement in crises as indicative of R2P's "failure" or "irrelevance."[45] The problem with ascertaining R2P's influence, of course, is that pinning an actor's motive is a notoriously difficult business, especially when that actor is a state or an international organization. Meanwhile, the problem with focusing on outcomes is that it radically simplifies the interplay of decisions, factors, and forces that gives rise to them.

In trying to unravel this knot, perhaps the first thing that should be said is that R2P has helped to raise global expectations about prevention and protection. Norms, as we mentioned earlier, are all about establishing shared expectations. Notwithstanding the difficulties of the situation, the lamentations of the General Assembly and the popular media about the UN Security Council's failure to protect Syrians evinces a deep sense of shared expectation that the Council *ought* to protect Syrians from their own government. It was not always the case that the Security Council was thought to have this protection role, yet today its legitimacy – indeed that of the whole UN system – rests largely on judgments about its performance in the field of protection. This elevation of expectations makes it possible to see "failure" everywhere, for even with the best of intentions the international community will seldom have the wherewithal to prevent every atrocity. But while we should be careful to ensure that expectations are realistic, the goal should not be to tame R2P principles to such an extent that all states are comfortable with them all of the time or that advocates are able to claim perpetual success. Some norms do little more than codify existing patterns of behavior, while R2P, like other human rights and humanitarian norms, has an aspirational quality in that it challenges governments, groups, and individuals to do better and to aim higher. Without some level of discomfort and dissatisfaction with current practice, the international community would never get better at prevention and protection. We should not forget that R2P was created because the status quo was not acceptable: horrific crimes, with hundreds of thousands of casualties, had unfolded with no one taking responsibility or acting effectively to prevent or curb them. R2P was created to embody a new political dynamic for change, one that would affect attitudes, priorities, policies, and practices. This edge should not be dulled or lost since it is precisely through exposing the gap between expectations and lived reality that the political momentum needed to drive change arises. States, international organizations, and individuals are driven to act to support R2P in practice precisely because they are aware that existing practice does not meet shared expectations. Where, to the extent that it was a norm at all, "humanitarian intervention" was a permissive principle in that it permitted intervention without requiring it, R2P has codified a set of responsibilities that states and others ought to attempt to discharge in good faith.

And, although R2P is primarily a state-based initiative, its development has also sparked increasing expectations that non-state actors, including NGOs, private- sector actors, and individuals, ought to show initiative in taking steps to support the prevention of atrocity crimes.[46]

Wherever we set the expectations associated with R2P, clear international failures to protect, by which is commonly meant failures to forcibly intervene to halt atrocities as in, for example, Darfur and Syria, are commonly taken as evidence of limited commitment and the norm's fragility.[47] As Jennifer Welsh explains, however, whether or not armed intervention occurs is an inappropriate measure of R2P's effectiveness for at least two reasons. First, because the norm is indeterminate with respect to which courses of action the international community should adopt and there are often genuine disagreements over the most prudential courses of action. Second, as Justin Morris shows, in determining a course of action, states have to weigh multiple considerations, not only the potential effects on the crisis at hand.[48] For example, in the early stages of the Darfur crisis (which actually preceded international agreement on R2P, making this an unreliable test case), the international community had to weigh the protection demands that crisis created against the very real risk of Sudanese defection from ongoing peace talks with the south Sudanese aimed at resolving a civil war that had consumed far more lives than the conflict in Darfur.

What, though, does it mean to say an actor is fulfilling its R2P and how do we ascribe value to the norm's contribution? Common definitions of humanitarian intervention tended to emphasize the humanitarian *motivations* of the interveners. Wil Verwey famously defined humanitarian intervention as "the threat or use of force...*for the sole purpose* of preventing or putting a halt to a serious violation of human rights."[49] Writing in the early 1990s, Verwey argued that there had not yet been any genuine humanitarian interventions because in practice interventions had always been motivated by a mix of different concerns. For Verwey, humanitarian action must be singularly concerned with the welfare of humans regardless of who they are and where they are. Using this standard, as many of R2P's critics have, a particular policy or intervention can be ascribed the label "R2P" only if it is motivated exclusively by that norm. But there are at least three reasons to doubt this approach and think that a more differentiated account – comprising intent, practices, and outcomes – might be a better way of evaluating R2P.

First, organizations – be they states or non-state actors – always have mixed motives. States, for instance, are not black boxes guided by singular interests or motivations. They are composites of multiple bureaucracies guided by governments themselves comprised of multiple individuals. What is more, the issues states confront are never monocausal and neither does state action produce only singular effects. Atrocity crimes are complex, multicausal phenomena, and actions directed at stemming them have multiple effects not limited to atrocity crimes themselves. In practice, states have to weigh up competing practical considerations and make normative judgments about the relative weight of different ethically sound norms which may sometimes pull in different directions. For instance, should states risk the lives of their own citizens to potentially save populations in other countries? If so, how much risk should they expose their own to? Less dramatically, should states pursue policies aimed at preventing atrocities in third countries when those policies impose economic costs – for instance by diverting funds from national social policies to foreign aid, or by enforcing sanctions regimes that have a deleterious effect on national incomes and employment? The reality is that national policy – and the policies of other types of organization – is always a product of a combination of different motives, interests, and normative impulses. We should not, therefore, expect to see R2P cited as an exclusive motive for action but instead look for instances where it forms part of the rationale.

Second, motives are subjective, difficult to discern, and easily disguised by clever political leaders. A better approach is to focus on an actor's intentions – i.e. what does the actor hope to achieve? – rather than its motivations – i.e. why does it want to achieve it? – since the former necessarily gives rise to public manifestations whereas the latter may not. How, though, are we to judge a state's intentions, and the place of R2P considerations within it, when it comes to relations with other states? We can look at the *explanations* offered to justify a particular course of action, paying particular attention not to the normative framework it evinces (since this can be mendacious) but to the outcomes it wants to achieve. If preventing or halting atrocity crimes is among the desired outcomes, then the intent is at least consistent with R2P. Intentions can also be inferred from acts themselves. As Michael Walzer argued in a different context, soldiers that truly intend not to kill non-combatants will take measures to ensure, as far as possible, that they do not.[50] Thus practice allows us to make inferences about intentions. Was practice calibrated to prevent atrocities or protect vulnerable populations, or was it driven by other considerations? Thus, for instance, we can infer from the deployment of French forces during the Rwandan genocide in 1994 that their primary intention was not to stem the genocide. France deployed its forces in areas predominantly populated by Hutus, including the *genocidaires* responsible for the genocide and in a posture that appeared to deter incursions by the Tutsi Rwandan Patriotic Front. Similarly, we can infer from the actual targets of Russian bombing in Syria that the primary purpose of intervention there was to support the regime of Bashar al-Assad and not to protect populations from Islamic State (IS). Although evaluating intentions is a far from exact science, it is possible to achieve at least a proximate view by looking at what actors say they want to achieve and the strategies they employ.

Third, focusing on what motivates an action distracts us from its consequences. There are good prudential grounds for thinking that what ultimately matters is whether atrocities are prevented and populations protected, irrespective of *why*. In domestic life, little time is dedicated to worrying about why a person did not commit a murder on any given day: fidelity to the anti-murder norm, fear of retribution, lack of interest or need, and psychological disposition are all potential explanations. Self-conscious adherence to the norm is only one potential explanation, though of course in the background the anti-murder norm also works to shape the likelihood of retribution, the balance of interests, and subconscious dispositions. The same might be said of the more complex set of norms that comprise R2P. From this perspective, it is the outcome of an action rather than its motivation that is most crucial. This is not to say that motives are unimportant, only that they are not of singular importance to evaluating norms such as R2P. In the final calculation, it is most important that actors fulfill their responsibilities. *Why* they do so and how they articulate and justify their actions is of secondary importance. In the context of R2P, it is more important that states and other actors do what is necessary to support protection than that they ascribe their actions to this particular norm, so that the actions do not themselves undermine the norm.[51] Of course, it is impossible to fully know the outcomes of an action beforehand. By itself, therefore, this approach cannot offer a way of evaluating efficacy because of the wide range of external variables that impact on whether a policy succeeds or fails. That said, if we are to preserve R2P's critical edge, we must keep in mind the question of whether or not populations are in fact being better protected from atrocity crimes.

What we should look for, therefore, in evaluating R2P is evidence of intent to fulfill its requirements (protecting populations from atrocity crimes), practices directed toward the achievement of this goal, and the practical outcomes – bearing in mind the limitations described earlier as well as the wide range of other considerations and factors that impact on decision making and its results. This essentially boils down to a "responsibility to try." As Jennifer Welsh explains, "the norm of R2P is primarily a responsibility to *consider* a real or imminent crisis involving atrocity crimes...; whether international action actually occurs depends on a series of other factors, such as agreement on the facts (and what they signify) and the likelihood that...[the] tools will have a positive effect."[52] This she calls a "duty of conduct" borne by the international community, which comprises duties to identify when atrocity crimes are being committed, or are imminently apprehended, and deliberate on how the three-pillar framework might apply.[53] We think, however, that the "responsibility to try" should be more exacting than this in at least three respects.

First, it should include a peremptory legal obligation to not perpetrate atrocity crimes (Pillar One) and to take active steps to ensure their non-perpetration, including discouraging their incitement. Second, deliberations on how to respond must be undertaken in good faith with a view to examining whatever prudential action might be taken at reasonable cost to strengthen the protection of vulnerable populations. Third, states should furnish whatever political and material support they reasonably can to support collective action in the name of R2P.

Though a noble and lofty goal, R2P does not sit above world politics in splendid isolation. It is a product of world politics and, to the extent that it is impactful, achieves things by operating through world politics. As such, it is subjected to all the forces – power, interest, sovereignty and other competing norms, and conflict – of world politics. Nonetheless, we have shown that although R2P is limited by politics and practicality, it can and does influence behavior and can shape judgments about right and wrong, costs and benefits, in such a way as to make affirmative action on prevention and protection more likely, and idleness in the face of atrocity threats and crimes more costly politically and hence less likely. Because each case of mass atrocity has its own exigencies, which can push the international community to greater or lesser activism, it is to overall trends and patterns of behavior that we must look in order to evaluate the wider impact of R2P. Doing that, we can see clear shifts toward greater international proactivity on atrocity crimes and greater prioritization of protection that are associated with the emergence of R2P. In that context, R2P is best understood as a responsibility to try – a responsibility of actors to do what they reasonably can. Obvious limits to decisive action remain, but R2P must retain its critical edge by shaping expectations about how the world ought to act in order to expose the failings of how it does act and galvanize remedial action.

CHAPTER THREE

Unexpected Challenges and Opportunities

When principles are operationalized, things rarely go as planned. Not only can unforeseen problems arise but new, and unexpected, practices come to the fore or prove to be more influential than anticipated. In its first two iterations (2001, 2005), R2P focused heavily on the responsibilities of states, overlooking the range of other actors that play sometimes decisive roles when atrocity crimes are perpetrated or threatened. When it came time to implement R2P following the 2005 World Summit agreement, it became clear that some non-state armed groups, such as the FDLR and M23 in the Democratic Republic of Congo (DRC), Boko Haram in Nigeria, al-Shabaab in Somalia, the Lord's Resistance Army across southern Sudan, Uganda and the DRC, and more recently IS in the Middle East, posed at least as great a threat to civilian populations as did badly behaved states. Moreover, there had been a history of extreme violence by non-state armed groups against populations in Sierra Leone, Somalia, Uganda, DRC, and elsewhere that predated the articulation of R2P. It was clearly not enough that states accepted obligations under R2P – it was imperative that those obligations extend to non-state actors too. In some theaters, such as the Middle East, this concern stretched to the private companies subcontracted by western states and others to use force for a variety of purposes. This was a point recognized and reinforced in successive reports on R2P by the UN Secretary-General, beginning in 2009.

But there are other grounds for thinking that states alone are incapable of achieving the goals set forth by R2P. Two decades of scholarship on the protracted civil wars that emerged after the Cold War demonstrated how the violent competition for resources, often valuable natural resources, had hollowed out states and replaced (to the extent that they had ever existed) state structures with hybrid forms of authority based on networks of patrimony, economic exchange, and violence. As the struggles to build peace in places such as the DRC and South Sudan attest, the reestablishment and reimposition of state authority is not sustainable in the long term without deeper transformations within civil (meaning outside the state) society. What is more, although there have been some notable successes in the use of state-based diplomacy for atrocity prevention, most obviously in the case of Kenya in 2007–8, there is growing recognition that the most effective sources of escalation prevention and resilience to triggers come from *within* vulnerable societies themselves.[1]

The picture is further complicated by globalization. It is increasingly the case that the options before governments and their capacity to act and shape outcomes autonomously are conditioned and limited by the forces of globalization. All states, including powerful ones, are constrained by the movement of capital, resources, people, and ideas across borders to the extent that very few have a full range of policy options from which to select or the capacity for entirely autonomous action. For a significant number of states – including most of those experiencing chronic risk of atrocities – this means that those with the trappings of formal authority often do not enjoy (if they ever did) what Stephen Krasner labeled "domestic sovereignty" – the practical capacity to exert effective control over territory.[2] What is more, even when states do enjoy formal "control," global forces make it more difficult for them to translate control into desired outcomes. While sovereignty continues to play a powerful constitutional role in the international system, the capacity of sovereigns to autonomously determine their own fate, and that of their people, has been diminished by globalization.

Thus, although R2P was born as an agreement between states, it is an ambition that cannot be achieved by states alone. Not only do the threats and challenges to it extend well beyond the world of states, states are themselves enmeshed in networks and structures that are beyond the control of any one of them. Thus the ability of individual states to protect their own populations and those of other countries is intimately connected to the role played by non-state actors of one form or another.

This chapter will examine the issues and opportunities that have arisen since 2005 as a result of the widening of agency beyond the state. These include – on the challenges side of the ledger – the rise to prominence of non-state armed groups and violent extremists as major perpetrators of atrocity crimes and – on the opportunities side – the emergence of different types of actors involved in the implementation of R2P. The emergence of these challenges and opportunities, and especially of new kinds of politically relevant actors, helps explain why we are in essence calling for a rather different framework for thinking about R2P to those that were current in 2001 or 2005. We will examine some of the unexpected ways in which the practice of R2P has evolved, focusing first on the unanticipated challenge arising from violent extremism and non-state armed groups and then on the multiplicity of actors that have come to the fore in implementing the norm. We will suggest that, generally, the range of actors and tools employed to prevent atrocities has become wider and more nuanced, even as the toughest measures have been seldom used and have proven controversial when employed.

Non-State Armed Groups and Violent Extremists

The scale, brutality and global impact of the acts committed by non-state armed groups like IS, Boko Haram and al-Shabaab represent a powerful new threat to established international norms. Although the commission of atrocity crimes by non-State armed groups is not a new phenomenon, the brazen manner in which certain non-State armed groups seem to have embraced the use of genocide, war crimes, ethnic cleansing and crimes against humanity as a strategy for advancing their objectives is unprecedented.[3]

These words, by former UN Secretary-General Ban Ki-moon, encapsulate the threat posed by violent extremists and non-state armed groups that commit atrocity crimes. As agreed in 2005, R2P focuses primarily on the responsibilities of states, and debates about its implementation have thus far focused almost exclusively on the role of states and the international institutions they comprise. This is in some respects unsurprising given R2P is a principled commitment made by states, that states have specific legal obligations to protect their populations and exercise exclusive sovereign authority within their own territories, authority that has, historically, been associated with responsibility.[4]

The long-term vision and underlying logic of R2P are relatively straightforward. The concept envisages a world of responsible and capable sovereign states that protect their own populations from atrocity crimes as a matter of routine (Pillar One). This vision is to be achieved through a combination of mutual assistance and collective action: assistance (Pillar Two) designed to strengthen the capacity of states to protect their own, and collective action (Pillar Three) aimed at protecting populations and creating the conditions for mutual assistance. Much like the UN's multidimensional peace operations in countries such as the DRC, Mali, and South Sudan, with respect to R2P the international community's goal is to help states in distress to extend their (presumably legitimate) authority and protection over a country's entire territory. Ultimately, though they are also concerned with providing immediate relief to populations in need, R2P's second and third pillars are concerned with helping states fulfill their primary responsibility to protect. It is in this sense that R2P is best understood as an *ally of sovereignty* since the concept as a whole is focused on helping states fulfill the responsibilities attached to their sovereignty.[5]

Things are rarely so simple in practice, however. Though R2P did not explicitly accommodate non-state armed groups, it has become obvious that these groups often play a decisive role in determining whether or not populations are protected from atrocity crimes. Across the world, non-state armed groups, such as those mentioned earlier, have committed significant atrocity crimes. Organizations such as Boko Haram and IS make a point of flouting shared rules about conduct in armed conflict and have perpetrated a wide range of crimes against humanity on a widespread and systematic scale. According to the UN, there are good grounds for suspecting that IS has perpetrated genocide against the Yazidi people of Iraq. Luck explained to the Security Council in December 2015 that, "the rise of violent extremism by groups with highly sectarian agendas … underscores that the inability of states to exercise effective sovereignty over parts of their territory can also contribute directly to the commission of atrocity crimes."[6]

In some cases, where states have struggled to protect their own populations from non-state armed groups, R2P has helped to provide a normative basis and political rationale for international action. As the Secretary-General observed in 2009, "pillar two [of R2P] could also encompass military assistance to help beleaguered States deal with armed non-state actors threatening both the State and its population."[7] In Mali, the UN Security Council explicitly mandated that UN peacekeepers (MINUSMA) "support" the government in fulfilling its primary responsibility to protect (Resolution 2085 [2012]). In practice, this entails helping the government protect civilians from Tuareg rebels. Initially, the UN Mission in South Sudan (UNMISS) had a similar mandate – to "advise and assist" the government of South Sudan in fulfilling its primary responsibility to protect (Resolution 1996 [2011]). Though R2P is not formally part of the African Union's mandate for Somalia, a similar logic can be seen there too – the use of international resources (AMISOM, supported by the UN) to support the extension of state authority over its territory in the expectation that this will establish the foundations for stability, protection, and peacebuilding. As the Netherlands, speaking on behalf of the Group of Friends of R2P, explained at the Security Council Arria Formula meeting on the topic, "there may be circumstances where actions under R2P's Pillar 3 [involvement by the international community] are required to address the threat of non-state armed groups."[8]

But in South Sudan, the logic of assisting the extension of state authority unraveled as government forces themselves were reportedly involved in atrocity crimes, prompting the Council to limit UNMISS's mandate and focus on protection and humanitarian relief. This problem is magnified in Syria where government forces – combating a variety of non-state armed groups, ranging from the pro-democratic to violent extremist – have committed the overwhelming majority of atrocity crimes experienced since 2011. Questions of legitimacy have also hindered international efforts to support the government of Iraq – Prime Minister Maliki's sectarian politics helped stir up support for IS in Iraq and have inhibited a strong and united Iraqi response to the crisis, which began in 2014.

The situation is further complicated by the fact that in these, and other, contexts, non-state armed groups have succeeded in seizing and holding territory. Indeed, in some conflict-affected areas, the nominal state has rarely – if ever – exerted control and authority over its full territory. This raises difficult questions about whether non-state armed groups have the same obligations as states do in relation to R2P. It is clearly not enough that states have accepted certain obligations under R2P – it is imperative that those obligations be clearly extended to non-state armed groups too. Yet conferring responsibilities onto non-state armed groups might inadvertently "legitimize" them by affording them a degree of respectability. Another category of non-state armed groups comprises those that are less formal in their organization and can include militias and organized groups of thugs. These organizations are typically less interested in controlling territory than they are in simply exploiting the civilian population in it.

A further complicating factor is that some non-state armed groups do sometimes comply with IHL and may even provide protection to vulnerable populations. The most recent example is that of the Kurdish peshmerga fighters who defended the city of Kobane from attacks by IS in 2014–15, but there are many other examples of non-state armed groups fulfilling protective roles. Sometimes, such groups claim legitimacy by binding themselves to IHL and not perpetrating atrocity crimes. In other situations, a non-state armed group might be both savior and perpetrator simultaneously – protecting some people from atrocity crimes while subjecting others to them. A less prominent but significant type of actor that can harm civilians are self-defense groups. Here we have in mind groups such as the White Army in South Sudan, which might emerge from noble motives (in this case defending cattle and community property) but soon degenerate into more predatory organizations.

How, then, should we think about the relationship between R2P and non-state armed groups? Although it is relatively uncontroversial to propose that non-state armed groups are obliged to comply with IHL by not committing atrocity crimes and may be subject to international criminal law in cases where they commit violations, things become more complex in situations where international criminal law cannot be applied. In these situations, the prerequisite for achieving compliance with IHL is the consent of armed groups themselves.[9] The NGO Geneva Call has made a significant contribution by persuading several non-state armed groups to commit themselves to IHL through "deeds of commitment." But these arrangements are quite fragile – based, as they are, entirely on good-faith undertakings between non-state entities – and these arrangements are not widely recognized by states. Unsurprisingly, they have not yet been extended to those non-state armed groups with the poorest human rights records.

A further complicating question is whether such groups have R2P-like responsibilities that extend beyond mere compliance with IHL in the conduct of their hostilities to include the prevention of atrocity crimes by others or the protection of populations from incitement. In his role as the UN Secretary-General's first Special Adviser on R2P, Luck suggested that non-state armed groups that control territory have a responsibility to prevent atrocity crimes in the same way that states do: "I made a bigger leap of faith…in proposing to the Secretary-General that he assert that non-state armed groups that control territory as well as national authorities have the responsibility to protect populations by preventing the four specified crimes and their incitement."[10] Supporting this, others have suggested that the "international community" referred to in paragraphs 138 and 139 of the World Summit Outcome Document includes non-state armed groups and that, as such, once these groups control territory, they acquire wider responsibilities to prevent atrocities and incitement and protect populations.[11]

The leap was both political and conceptual. Politically, it remains to be seen whether states might come to accept this proposition. There is concern that assigning responsibilities usually reserved for states to non-state armed groups could legitimize those groups. This could help strengthen their secessionist claims and encourage others to follow suit. Conceptually, it is widely understood – and has been often stated by the UN Secretary-General and others – that the *responsibilities* associated with R2P derive from sovereignty. To say, therefore, that non-state armed groups can have a responsibility to protect could imply – to the mind of many states – that they have sovereign-based responsibilities and would put them on an equal footing with states.[12] Conceptually, the difficulty derives from the fact that unless one cedes notional sovereignty to non-state armed groups that control territory – a proposition hardly likely to win the support of states – it could be difficult to justify the allocation of these wider responsibilities to non-state armed groups.

This may, however, be less of a problem than it first appears. That is because in IHL it is not "sovereignty" that determines applicable law but the empirical condition of "control." The law of occupation (especially the fourth Geneva Convention, 1949) comes into effect as a result of a territory being physically controlled by an armed group and carries with it legal obligations above and beyond the non-commission of atrocity crimes. These include obligations to restore and maintain public order and safety (and thus prevent atrocity crimes), ensure the provision of food and medical care to the civilian population, respect cultural property, and permit the International Committee of the Red Cross (ICRC) to conduct its humanitarian activities. Importantly for our purposes, the law of occupation applies irrespective of whether the occupation is judged lawful or not and is clear in insisting that the occupant does not acquire sovereignty over the territory and that occupation is a temporary condition. Thus, by referring to the law of occupation, we can extend the responsibilities of non-state armed groups that hold territory without undermining the *primary* responsibility to protect which is held exclusively by states. The point here is not to somehow "permit" non-state armed groups to exercise the social functions of the state, much less to furnish them with additional "support." After all, in practical terms they need no such permission when they control the territory in question. Rather, the purpose is to encumber them with additional legal responsibilities for the protection of populations in the territories they control.

A further question relates to the connection between terrorism, atrocity crimes, and R2P. Terrorism and atrocity crimes are connected but not necessarily synonymous. Part of the problem here is that national legislation contains many different definitions of what terrorism is, and there is no agreed global standard. Some factors associated with terrorism are not necessarily components of atrocity crimes. For example, some define terrorism as violence by non-state armed groups, others include an intention to create fear as a defining feature, but neither of these constitutes atrocity crimes. Where there is overlap between them is in the intentional targeting and abuse of civilian populations. Acts of terrorism (bombings, shootings, etc.) targeting civilians are also atrocity crimes. Thus violent extremism, a particular form of non-state armed group that celebrates the killing of civilians, fosters a form of terrorist violence that also constitutes atrocity crimes. As such, it seems clear that:

- First, states have a responsibility to protect their populations from violent extremist terrorism.
- Second, states have a responsibility to prevent the incitement of terrorism and violent extremism.
- Third, states have a responsibility to prevent members of their population from traveling abroad to incite or practice violent extremism.
- Fourth, the international community should assist states to fulfill their primary responsibility to protect their populations from violent extremism.

However, it is important that the different concepts and agendas not be treated as synonymous and some important points of difference should also be noted. Most obviously, terrorism can apply to examples of "lone wolf" violence that are not sufficiently widespread or systematic to constitute atrocity crimes and not all definitions of terrorism involve the incitement or commission of atrocity crimes.

Responding to Violent Extremism: Seven Challenges

Violent extremist groups such as IS, al-Shabaab, and Boko Haram brazenly violate IHL and openly celebrate the perpetration of the most heinous atrocity crimes. As the UN Secretary-General observed in his plan of action to counter violent extremism: "violent extremism is an affront to the purposes and principles of the United Nation. It undermines peace and security, human rights and sustainable development. No country or region is immune from its impacts."[13] These groups deliberately place themselves outside the moral universe of shared norms and principles that guide the international community. What is more, they actively seek to extend violent extremism to other parts of the world. We can identify at least seven specific challenges that violent extremists pose to those responsible for the protection of populations from atrocity crimes.

Challenge 1: Brazen Commission of Atrocities as a Raison d'Etre

Arguably, the most significant challenge posed by violent extremists is the direct threat of atrocity crimes that they pose to civilian populations in places such as Syria, Iraq, Somalia, Nigeria, and, to a lesser extent, the West. Violent extremists are responsible for a growing litany of atrocity crimes that includes the deliberate bombing, shooting, knifing, and beheading of civilians, widespread and systematic sexual and gender-based violence – including forcing women and girls into sexual slavery, torture, kidnapping and forced displacement. What is more, their brazenness in committing these acts – often video-recorded and publicized through social media – constitutes a direct challenge to the international community's shared rules and standards of behavior. Unless this challenge is decisively met, the commission of these acts could weaken or even undermine humanitarian norms themselves. Ending these brazen atrocities and protecting affected populations is the principal challenge.

Challenge 2: Denial of Access to Humanitarian Agencies

The denial of access, besieging of communities, and targeting of humanitarian agencies have become common features of violent extremist practice, making it more difficult and dangerous to provide for the basic survival needs of affected populations. There are a variety of ways in which violent extremists have endangered the lives of communities, including by blocking or stealing humanitarian aid, planting landmines, and targeting humanitarian workers. Part of a trend that extends beyond violent extremism, these groups make a point of showing no respect for international norms and symbols, actively targeting ICRC, UN, and other protected workers. Besides causing further distress to the civilian population, such violent acts have made "humanitarian engagement" increasingly untenable in affected areas.

Challenge 3: Overlapping Response Agendas

Thinking about coherent and effective responses to the atrocity crimes committed by violent extremists is complicated by the fact that it involves multiple policy agendas, institutions, and communities, each with their own particular perspectives, interests, and operating principles. Effective responses require the effective coordination of these different capacities – including R2P, counterterrorism, countering violent extremism, engaging non-state armed groups, and conflict prevention – while recognizing that each individual agenda is separate and distinct. For atrocity prevention and R2P, there are opportunities and risks. In terms of opportunities, the connection between atrocities, terrorism, and violent extremism means the former – atrocity crimes – may be seen as an issue of national security as well as a protection imperative and accorded higher priority within governments. On the risk side, however, the connection has the potential to associate R2P with new political problems and controversies. For example, counterterrorism is sometimes associated with human rights violations and controversial interventions. Moreover, the prioritization of counterterrorism might be used to obscure the commission of atrocity crimes or inhibit international action against governments that use indiscriminate force against terrorist organizations and associated civilian populations, as in Sri Lanka in 2008–9.

Challenge 4: Transnational Networks

As noted in the previous section, violent extremists are increasingly sustained by transnational networks, yet our concepts and practices for responding to them remain largely national. Non-state armed groups are not bound by sovereignty and state borders, and violent extremists often want to redraw or ignore the political map. In particular, violent extremists rely on transnational networks for finances, arms, and recruits. As is now well known, violent extremists in the Middle East rely on transnational networks for the recruitment of foreign fighters (foot soldiers), specialists (such as engineers and medical professionals), and terror cells in third countries. Recruitment often involves a combination of ideological sensitization through social media, distant contact through new communications technologies, and more personal contact through local recruiters. Groups also require physical networks to ensure that recruits can be moved into conflict zones (for example, IS in Iraq initially used bus routes through Syria to bring in foreign fighters). In addition to the theft of assets and money from the civilian populations they control, such groups are financed through transnational networks as well. These include patronage by wealthy foreigners and the sale of raw materials, drugs and stolen assets through criminal networks. Finally, violent extremists rely on the illicit transnational trade in arms and ammunition to sustain their operations. Although individual cells in third countries can commit atrocities with small amounts of arms, the seizing and holding of large swathes of territory requires a significant pool of arms and ammunition, some of which is captured in the field but much of which has to be acquired through transnational networks. As noted earlier, the networked nature of these flows is a key source of their resilience. Targeting one element does not necessarily stop the whole since the network is able to reroute itself. Moreover, these networks have been able to flourish precisely because responses to them have been state based and territorially confined. If they can be identified and tracked, these networks can also be interrupted. At present, the transnational character of violent extremism has been one of its key strengths, but just as regular armies can overreach themselves when their supply lines become too extended, this dependence on transnational networks can become a source of weakness. Reliance on extended networks creates openings to interrupt such processes with significant impact.

Challenge 5: Upstream Prevention

As with atrocity prevention more broadly, there is a widely stated preference for focusing on the prevention of violent extremism. Typically, however, policy approaches to terrorism and non-state armed groups have focused on "countering" violence (i.e. counterterrorism) – that is, reacting to it – rather than preventing it. The challenge here is that although upstream prevention is relatively easy to commit to in rhetoric, it is quite difficult to achieve in practice. There are numerous reasons for this, including the fact that each context is different and requires carefully tailored solutions, the measures required can be both expansive (e.g. "building inclusive communities") and politically controversial (e.g. strengthening human rights, adjusting foreign policies). Moreover, upstream prevention is an inevitably long-term undertaking that may not deliver immediate results and may also be fundamentally undermined by policies that deliver short term results (clampdowns, harsh penalties, limiting freedom of speech, using torture). The challenge here is one of how to turn general appeals for upstream prevention into tangible action and ensure that commitment to prevention is not crowded out by the need to respond to crises.

Challenge 6: To Engage or Not to Engage?

The question of diplomatic engagement is a thorny issue in relation to non-state armed groups in general, but especially so in relation to violent extremists. On the one hand, many governments and the UN prohibit or limit the engagement of their officials with terrorists and non-state armed groups. Individuals may be prosecuted on this basis. UN officials in integrated missions are prohibited from negotiating with some non-state armed groups. This policy of non-engagement has an understandable logic behind it which is that engagement helps to legitimize the group and that engaging with those that are violent encourages others to pursue violence. This approach seeks to isolate and contain violent extremists and other non-state armed groups by blocking all engagement with blacklisted actors. It is also justified on the basis that engagement is unlikely to influence violent extremists to alter their behavior since these groups reject even basic norms. But, while these actions aim to withhold legitimacy and stifle support for violent extremists, they can also foreclose opportunities for negotiating with more moderate elements to secure some concessions and challenge the group's internal cohesion, and they can inhibit proper assessment and analysis that would help states better understand the groups in question. It is also important to bear in mind that social isolation can assist violent extremist groups. By putting social distance between them and their neighbors, isolation can increase group loyalty and reinforce ideologies that reject established norms of behavior.

Challenge 7: Avoiding the Counterproductive

There are many ways in which counterterrorism strategies can prove counterproductive, and it is imperative that these be avoided. Counterproductive strategies can inflame violent extremism and undermine human rights and the very goals of R2P. At its most extreme, counterterrorism has sometimes involved the commission of atrocity crimes or other violations of IHL or human rights. For R2P, the prevention of atrocity crimes committed in the name of countering violent extremism is as important as the prevention of crimes by violent extremists. Second, the use of a state's security apparatus against a section of a population can increase the insecurity of and fear within that group and encourage a violent response. Third, anti-terror legislation can erode human rights and democratic accountability, exacerbating a climate of fear, giving rise to either actual or perceived human rights abuses and instilling the very sort of divisions that the strategy is trying to overcome. Fourth, counterterrorism can create "communities of suspicion" by identifying whole communities as sources of violent extremism and targeting them as such. Policies that set a community apart and create popular sentiment against it will have the effect of making that group more cohesive – as it closes ranks to protect itself from perceived outside threats – and possibly more extreme. Fifth, clumsy strategies can delegitimize moderate voices within an affected community. When counterterrorism identifies specific partners or moderates within the target community and provides resources to them, this can have the effect of delegitimizing them in the eyes of their community, especially if the state has a legitimacy problem.

Counterproductive responses can be avoided by keeping some key principles in mind. These include proportionality of response: the need to avoid over-reaction and repression by security forces. Also important is the need to maintain accountable and transparent government. Additionally, states should ensure civilian and democratic oversight of the security forces. They should also ensure that the security sector has sufficient capacity to conduct its tasks effectively. Finally, it is important that actors show full respect for human rights and IHL in conducting operations against terrorists and violent extremists. It is adherence to IHL that distinguishes legitimate political authorities from violent extremists. When authorities violate IHL in the name of counterterrorism, they become less legitimate and more like those that they claim to be protecting their population from.

In summary, violent extremism represents a new form of pernicious non-state armed group that constitutes a threat not just to the populations it targets but also to the whole system of norms and rules that ensure a basic degree of civility in our common international life. As a key source of atrocity crimes and atrocity crimes risk, it is imperative that the international community develop a comprehensive strategy for combating violent extremist non-state armed groups as part of its commitment to implementing R2P. There is insufficient space here to extrapolate in detail what this would look like, so we will offer just a few points to note.

Countering and preventing violent extremism is so difficult precisely because the problem reaches all the way from complex transnational networks to local communities and sub-groups within them. The ultimate goal is to protect populations from atrocity crimes committed by these groups by supporting the extension of legitimate and protective state authority into areas where violent extremism might take root. As the UN Secretary-General emphasized in his *Action Plan to Prevent Violent Extremism*, a comprehensive approach is needed.[14] It is useful to think of the required response as entailing action across different sectors at three principal levels: global, regional, and national.

The capacity to use transnational networks to secure recruits, finances, and arms and to promote their atrocities is one of the key sources of resilience for contemporary violent extremism. Approaches focused exclusively on the national level fail to reflect the transnational nature of the problem and therefore do not succeed in interrupting or preventing atrocity crimes. What is needed, therefore, is a global partnership able to think and act transnationally and coordinate national actions. As the UN Secretary-General explained, preventing and countering violent extremism "requires international solidarity and a multifaceted approach." Productive partnerships across borders are necessary for the prevention of atrocity crimes by violent extremists and protection of vulnerable communities. Some of these partnerships are most dense – and make most sense – at the regional level. But it is important to recognize that the threats posed by violent extremists are increasingly cross-regional. For example, IS and al-Qaeda franchises reach from the Middle East into North and West Africa, Europe, Southeast Asia and even, potentially, China. What is required, therefore, is a global partnership.

The UN is well placed to coordinate a global partnership. Beyond its unique international legitimacy and inclusive membership, the UN Charter grants the organization the authority needed to play this vital role in the service of peace. Moreover, the UN system already contains the functional capacities, across several sectors, required to marshal a comprehensive approach to violent extremism. These include the Office on Genocide Prevention and R2P, bodies that focus on preventing extremist violence, such as the Global Counter-Terrorism Strategy and Action Plan, the Counter-Terrorism Committee, and the UN Office on Drugs and Crime (UNODC), and organizations more squarely focused on the protection of vulnerable populations (United Nations High Commission for Refugees, (UNHCR), United Nations Children's Fund (UNICEF), United Nations Office for the Coordination of Human Affairs (OCHA) and supporting national capacity building (United Nations Development Programme (UNDP). The UN therefore has a number of capacities that can be brought to bear on the problem. The UN's Global Counter-Terrorism Strategy, shaped by UN Security Council Resolutions 1267, 1373, 1624 and most recently 2178, was unanimously approved by the UN General Assembly in 2006 (Resolution 60/288). This strategy was focused on dissuading would-be terrorists, deterring states from supporting them, denying safe havens and resources, developing state capacities, and defending human rights. It called for a comprehensive approach including prevention, sanctions, law enforcement and legal measures, and a human rights dimension. The Counter-Terrorism Implementation Task Force (CTITF) was established to coordinate implementation. Alongside this, the Security Council's Counter-Terrorism Committee (and Executive Directorate [CTED]) pays particular attention to sanctions and other measures. Security Council

Resolution 2178 highlighted the need for multilateral efforts to respond to transnational threat, especially the issue of transnational recruitment and foreign fighters.

In terms of specific steps that might be taken through the UN, five priorities can be identified:

1 The further development and full implementation of the Secretary-General's guidance on Implementing the Responsibility to Protect, Action Plan for Preventing Violent Extremism, the Global Counter-Terrorism Strategy, and the Human Rights up Front Strategy. This includes ensuring joint action to improve the early warning and assessment of risks stemming from violent extremism and improving coordination in supporting the long-term (structural) prevention of atrocity crimes by violent extremists. The prevention measures identified in all three areas (atrocity prevention, prevention of violence extremism, and counterterrorism) share much in common and are mutually reinforcing. In particular, all three emphasize: (a) strengthening good governance, human rights, and the rule of law; (b) building inclusive governance and communities; (c) the constructive management of difference; (d) gender equality and empowering women; and (e) education. Implementation should also include concerted efforts to control the transnational flows that support violent extremists. These include full implementation of the Program of Action on Small Arms and Light Weapons (dealing with the flow of arms) and ongoing work by the Security Council on controlling the flow of financial assets to these groups. This will require enhancing cooperation with private-sector actors such as banks. The capacities developed by the Security Council's Sanctions Committees would be especially useful in this regard.

2 The UN Secretary-General should consider appointing a high-level representative on preventing and countering violent extremism, who could assist the UN system in setting priorities, developing tangible policies, and implementing these agendas. This appointment could coordinate implementation of the Secretary-General's Plan of Action for Preventing Violent Extremism; provide a focal point in the UN system for action to prevent and respond to violent extremism; and help coordinate action across the various sectors and action plans; help distinguish the prevention and countering of violent extremism from other agendas; help identify capacity-building needs and provide assistance and advice to member states; and, monitor, encourage, and facilitate implementation of relevant action plans.

3 The UN could facilitate the strengthening of transnational partnerships for a strategic approach to preventing and combating violent extremism. As is well known, multiple states and agencies are working on this problem (e.g. UN, Global Counter-Terrorism Forum, EU, OSCE, R2P Focal Points, etc.). The UN could facilitate practically oriented partnerships between them. Such partnerships might be especially useful in marshaling better focused

and resourced approaches to upstream (structural) prevention that supports resilience and builds tailored solutions based on a combination of local and regional insights and international capacities.

4 Ensure greater collaboration across the UN system, for example through sharing information and analysis across departments and agencies; granting a higher profile to the human rights reporting of the Special Rapporteur on the Promotion and Protection of Human Rights (SRPPHR) while countering terrorism and extending this mandate to include countering violent extremism; ensuring a more central role for UN Women to ensure a gender perspective contributes to the development and oversight of strategies; enhanced interaction between programmatic offices and frontline field missions in countries threatened by violent extremism (e.g. Mali, Somalia, etc.) to ensure that the policy settings are right to support the field mission, and that the field mission is configured to address the policy requirements.

5 Ensure that implementation efforts comply with international human rights obligations and IHL. There are a number of useful ways in which the UN could support this goal, including: a greater focus on the reports of the SRPPHR role of the special rapporteur (and that of the Special Rapporteur on Torture) and on the implementation of recommendations; the provision of guidance to member states on good practices, challenges, and priorities. Also, the provision of lessons learned from past practice, containing recognition and analysis of the dilemmas states confront; helping member states identify their capacity-building needs relating to the implementation of the UN's strategies for implementing R2P, preventing violent extremism, and countering terrorism, especially areas where work is needed to ensure compliance and where states struggle to balance the competing demands of protecting populations from violent extremists and protecting human rights; utilizing the UN Human Rights Council's Universal Periodic Review process to encourage peers to ensure that policies intended to protect populations are consistent with human rights obligations and provide guidance on how this might be achieved.

We should not fall into the trap of thinking, however, that combating violent extremists is a job primarily for the UN. Global action is effective only if it is translated into efforts at the regional and national levels. The transnational networks that often help sustain violent extremists are most dense at the regional level. It is imperative, therefore, that states work with existing regional arrangements and, where necessary, new arrangements to assist each other and interrupt the transnational flows that support violent extremism. In particular, regional groupings should facilitate cooperation on identifying, tracking, and preventing individuals from crossing borders in order to join violent extremist groups or commit atrocities. They should also examine what measures might be taken at the regional level to better control financial flows across borders. Regional arrangements can also provide important support to their member states for example by offering technical assistance and capacity-building support to governments in functional areas such as managing diversity in a constructive way, preventing extremism, controlling external flows, and border management. In that vein, regional arrangements could help to review implementation of the Program of Action on Small Arms and Light Weapons and adopt regional processes to strengthen the control of weapons and ammunition and limit their spread across borders. Regional arrangements could also facilitate intergovernmental communication on this issue.

Ultimately, however, individual states have the primary responsibility to protect their populations from atrocity crimes from whatever source, including non-state armed groups. Through the course of the various processes outlined above, a number of steps have been proposed that states could adopt to strengthen the prevention of atrocities by violent extremists and the protection of vulnerable populations. These include: the development and implementation of national plans of action to prevent violent extremism;[15] dedicating time and resources to promoting the constructive management of difference at every level of society; policies and programs directed against extremist ideologies that offer opportunities for de-radicalization and create incentives (such as educational or economic opportunities) for individuals to leave violent extremist organizations; the adoption of national legislation to prevent nationals from traveling overseas to commit atrocities or support violent extremists as required by Security Council Resolution 2178; and the adoption of positive steps to ensure that violent extremists are unable to profit from trade in raw materials, antiquities, hostages, or foreign donations in line with their obligations under Security Council Resolution 2199. As we noted earlier, there is recurrent concern that counterterrorism or countering violent extremism can give way to more militarized and less democratic approaches to national security. In this context, it is especially important to ensure that any use of force or other forms of coercion – which are sometimes tragically necessary – is consistent with the UN Charter, IHL, and international human rights law.

Agency and the Implementation of R2P: Beyond the State

The 2001 and 2005 versions of R2P were focused primarily on the role of states in protecting populations both at home and in other countries. They paid too little attention to the role that regional and sub-regional arrangements and international secretariats, envoys, and high-level figures would play in the implementation effort. The operational track record for these different types of actors has been mixed, of course, but not insignificant. What does seem to be clear, though, is that early, flexible, and effective responses to emerging risks of atrocity crimes require action by a multiplicity of different types of actors. Although it is too early to draw definitive conclusions about what works, what does not, and under what conditions, international efforts to prevent or halt atrocity crimes seem best served: (1) when international engage-ment is early and sustained; (2) when global and regional actors work together; (3) when external actors have some leverage over key players in the situation and are prepared to use it; (4) when civil society in the affected country offers a "moderating voice"; and (5) when the behavior of individuals, as well as institutions, is directly targeted.[16] In short, while states remain pivotal, initial practice suggests that the effective operationalization of R2P depends upon the actions and choices of a wide range of other individuals, institutions, and organizations. Specifically, two critical points have become abundantly clear. These speak to the need for an "early and flexible response, tailored to the specific needs of each situation" as proposed by the Secretary-General in his 2009 report.[17] First, preventive or responsive action is most effective when different actors work together and coordinate their approaches. Second, a flexible approach to agency is needed, both in terms of thinking about which institutions or individuals make the most effective international intermediar-ies and in terms of whether approaches are marshaled best through formal institutional mechanisms or through less formal arrangements.

The principal bearers of responsibility are states and the state that has the greatest responsibility to take early action to protect vulnerable populations is the one on whose territory the threat arises. As a result, international efforts to implement R2P thus far have tended to concentrate on measures designed to encourage and support states to refrain from inciting or committing atroc-ity crimes and/or to fulfill their protection responsibilities. Ultimately, it is the state, and its leadership, that bears the principal responsibility to protect. It is important to emphasize, however, that national leaders exercise a degree of choice in deciding which route they will follow. In recent years, there have been a number of situations in which timely warnings of imminent atrocities, expressions of international concern and effective diplomatic entreaties have persuaded national leaders to think twice about taking their country down the path to atrocity crimes.[18] Most notably, in 2008–9 concerted diplomatic efforts led by Kofi Annan persuaded Kenya's conflicted leaders (Mwai Kibaki and Raila Odinga) to pull back from the brink of civil war and rein in militia responsible for the killing of some 1,500 people. Four years later, in 2013, a comprehensive campaign marshaled by local actors, including private-sector groups, and supported by the international community ensured that Kenya's elections passed peacefully. Likewise, in Guinea (Conakry) in 2009–10, deter-mined action by global, regional, and national actors played a key role in preventing mass violence in the run-up to the country's national elections, but a significant part was played Sékouba Konaté, who headed the country's interim national government. Konaté enjoyed popular legitimacy, served as a useful interlocutor between the conflicting parties, and sent clear signals that he expected the security forces to comply with their R2P obligations, whatever the result of the election.[19]

States are also the principal bearers of international responsibility. When the UN General Assembly refers to the "international community" it means, primarily (though not exclusively), the community of UN member states. As such, the opening of paragraph 139 of the World Summit Outcome Document relates primarily to the responsibility of states to help protect populations from atrocity crimes. States may act "through the United Nations" but the UN is the vehicle for action, not the principal bearer of responsibility. The question of precisely *which* states bear most responsibility in any particular case is one that has vexed moral philosophers.[20] In practice, these will always be fine-grained judgments based on the situation at hand and each state's knowledge and capacity to influence a particular situation. But while figuring out precisely who ought to be doing what in any given situation is important, this should not be allowed to obscure the fact that *all* governments have a responsibility to do what they can to protect populations by peaceful means. In other words, the general responsibility to protect never disappears, even when particular actors take the lead in responding to certain cases and with certain tools.

How individual states should discharge their responsibility to protect populations in *other* countries depends on the situation at hand. But at least three different modes of action ought to be considered. First, outside states often have some form of bilateral relationship with states affected by atrocity crimes and these can be leveraged to support the protection of vulnerable communities from atrocity crimes. When atrocity crimes are committed or are imminent, governments can readjust their bilateral relationship with the affected state in order to better support R2P's goals. For example, diplomatic relations can be leveraged, foreign aid and refugee policy utilized, and a range of other "peaceful" policies relating to trade, travel, and functional cooperation adjusted to support protection goals. But bilateral action can also be taken well in advance of risks becoming imminent. Diplomatic pressure and messaging can be brought to bear in response to the use of hate speech, incitement or the targeting of particular minority groups. Second, states participate in a range of informal or ad hoc groups which might be utilized to support protection goals. These can include informal "groups of friends" established to support peace processes or other goals or informal groupings of like-minded or regional states. These include the global network of national R2P focal points and the New York-based Group of Friends of R2P. States can exploit these networks to coordinate and advocate for early and effective responses to atrocity crimes, apply peaceful pressure on potential or actual perpetrators, support conflict resolution, or leverage other ways of strengthening protection of vulnerable populations. Third, most states are members of one or more international organizations, some of which (such as the UN) have specific responsibilities associated with R2P and others of which have commitments to human rights or principles of non-indifference that support the goals of R2P. States should utilize these formal institutions as vehicles for the peaceful protection of populations. They should also take steps to ensure the proper implementation of the collective decisions taken by these institutions in response to atrocity crimes.

All these actions, of course, require leadership – and the concept of political will that we first mentioned in the previous chapter. A ubiquitous but still somewhat oblique concept, "political will" operates in at least two ways in shaping how national governments respond to atrocity crimes, and their imminent risk, in other countries. The first, and least discussed, is the presence of prevailing interests that can persuade leaders to "will" courses of action inimical to the protection of populations from atrocity crimes. In other words, it is not just that states with the capacity to make a positive difference sometimes lack the will to commit the resources or take the political risks needed to save strangers, but that sometimes the pursuit of their own interests leads them to support or shield the perpetrators. Russia's policy toward Syria, for example, is presumably driven primarily by that country's perceived interest in stemming what it sees as the spread of radical Islam borne by the Arab Spring and preventing these political forces reaching the southern Caucasus. To achieve this, Moscow believes that it must support the regime of Bashar al-Assad which is, incidentally, Russia's last remaining regional ally. In this context, concern for the protection of populations from atrocity crimes lies a distant third – at best – in Russia's list of priorities. Likewise, the link between China's (and to a lesser extent, Russia's) obstinate support for the government of Sudan and its interest in Sudanese oil and arms sales is well known. But the West has also sometimes put its own interests ahead of the protection of populations from atrocity crimes. For example, the UN Security Council's relatively passive response to civilian casualties in Yemen, predominantly caused by indiscriminate attacks by the Saudi-led coalition that intervened in 2015 to reverse a rebellion by the Houthi (Ansar Allah) and groups loyal to former President Saleh, can be ascribed to western (predominantly US) backing for that coalition.

The second, and more commonly discussed, aspect of political will relates to the idea that states consider themselves to be responsible first and foremost for the well-being of *their own* citizens and are reluctant to spend money and risk the lives of their soldiers in order to save strangers from atrocity crimes in other countries. The effects of this lack of will were demonstrated in detail by the 1999 Report of the Independent Inquiry into the UN's failure to prevent and then halt the Rwanda genocide of 1994. The report opened with a damning but general criticism, insisting that the Rwandan genocide resulted from a failure of will across the whole UN system:

> The failure by the United Nations to prevent, and subsequently, to stop the genocide in Rwanda was a failure by the United Nations as a whole. The fundamental failure was the lack of resources and political commitment devoted

to developments in Rwanda and to the United Nations presence there. There was a persistent lack of political will by Member States to act, or to act with enough assertiveness. This lack of political will affected the response by the Secretariat and decision-making by the Security Council, but was also evident in the recurrent difficulties to get the necessary troops for the United Nations Assistance Mission for Rwanda (UNAMIR). Finally, although UNAMIR suffered from a chronic lack of resources and political priority, it must also be said that serious mistakes were made with those resources which were at the disposal of the United Nations.[21]

The "overriding failure," the Inquiry argued, was the lack of resources and lack of will to do what would have been necessary to prevent the genocide and protect its victims. The lack of resources and will was manifested in the UN mission deployed in Rwanda (UNAMIR) not being adequately "planned, dimensioned, deployed or instructed" in a way that would have "provided for a proactive and assertive role" in the face of the deteriorating situation in Rwanda.[22] The mission was smaller than recommended by the UN secretariat, slow to deploy owing to the reluctance of states to contribute troops, debilitated by administrative difficulties, and when troops did arrive they were generally inadequately trained and equipped.[23] Today, the Rwandan genocide is commonly regarded as an exemplar of the failure of international political will.

The key point here is that, even when national governments are well meaning, they may choose to exercise their decision-making sovereignty by not prioritizing the protection of foreigners from atrocity crimes, especially if doing so is likely to incur material or political cost. But neither national interests nor the relative importance of R2P to other priorities are immutable. Instead, they are both intimately connected to national debates about a country's role in world affairs, past experience (whether positive or negative) of engagement with atrocity crimes, the nature and location of the situation at hand, the attitude of civil society toward it, and – crucially – the actions and positions of allied states, regional, and global institutions, and other major powers.

Establishing the will to act begins with national leaders themselves. Ultimately, decisions about whether, and what, a country will contribute to the protection of populations in other countries rests with national leaders, key officials and parliamentarians. This tends to be a relatively small group of people, such that "decisions about whether and how to respond to unfolding atrocity crimes are highly dependent on the values, knowledge and priorities of a relatively small number of officials, as well as on their perceptions of the level of public and parliamentary support for…action."[24] Persuading these people to support measures to prevent or respond to atrocity crimes is therefore often quite significant in determining how a country will respond. In the case of Libya, for example, President Obama's initial skepticism toward intervention was famously changed by forceful moral arguments from his Secretary of State (Hillary Clinton), foreign policy adviser (Samantha Power), and Permanent Representative to the UN (Susan Rice).[25] But very often, external actors also play a significant role in shaping how national leaders respond to crises – not least because governments tend to prefer to act alongside partners or through existing institutions in order to spread the costs and/or enhance legitimacy.

In terms of the range of relevant actors beyond national governments, the UN sits close to the core. Paragraph 139 of the World Summit Outcome Document refers specifically to action being taken "through" the UN (meaning its Charter as much as the institution itself). Relevant UN actors include its Principal Organs (especially the Security Council, General Assembly, and Secretariat) and subsidiary bodies such as the Human Rights Council and Peacebuilding Commission. The measures envisioned by R2P's second pillar and the diplomatic, humanitarian and other peaceful measures identified in the third pillar also encompass actions not specifically mandated by the UN's political bodies. This includes, for example, actions undertaken by the Secretary-General (such as preventive diplomacy, fact finding and reporting, and the provision of good offices), those undertaken by other offices with relevant mandates (such as the Special Advisers on Genocide Prevention and R2P, the Special Representatives on the Prevention of Sexual Violence and Protection of Internally Displaced Persons, and the High Commissioners for Human Rights and Refugees), and those undertaken by departments, funds, and programs (such as OCHA, the Office of the High Commissioner for Human Rights [OHCHR], UNHCR, UNDP, and UNICEF) under the terms of their own mandates. Under the UN Charter, many actions relating to Chapters VI and VIII can be undertaken by the Secretary-General or by regional or sub-regional arrangements without the explicit authorization of the Security Council or General Assembly. Moreover, the Charter places no limit on the range of actions that may be taken with the consent of the affected state.

The idea that the UN system as a whole has a fundamental responsibility to support the protection of populations from atrocity crimes that exists beyond any particular country-specific mandate was first broached by the Secretary-General in his 2009 report on R2P where he called for the principle to be "mainstreamed":

> The United Nations and its range of agencies, funds and programmes have in place critical resources, activities and field operations that are already making important contributions to the elimination of these man-made scourges. They could do that much more effectively if goals relating to the responsibility to protect, including the protection of refugees and the internally displaced, were mainstreamed among their priorities, whether in the areas of human rights, humanitarian affairs, peacekeeping, peacebuilding, political affairs or development.[26]

Since then, the general idea of R2P mainstreaming has been partially advanced under the rubric of "Human Rights up Front" (HRuF), which we first mentioned in the previous chapter, though this initiative's human rights focus is narrower than that required to implement R2P.[27] Framed in response to the organization's failure to protect Tamil civilians in the closing stages of Sri Lanka's civil war in 2009, HRuF calls for the UN system to prioritize human rights protection in all its endeavors. The UN Secretary-General's HRuF action plan declared that: "People, who are at risk of suffering massive and widespread violations of their human rights, look to the UN for action to protect their rights. They must know and be assured that the UN System is doing everything in its power to assist them and to mobilize the efforts of those who can protect them." The plan aimed to achieve this goal through six types of action: (1) integrating human rights into the lifeblood of the UN so all staff understand their own and the organization's human rights obligations; (2) providing member states with candid information about peoples at risk of, or subject to, serious violations of human rights or humanitarian law; (3) ensuring coherent strategies of action on the ground; (4) clarifying and streamlining procedures to facilitate early, coordinated action; (5) strengthening the UN's human rights capacity; and (6) developing a common UN system for information management on serious violations of human rights and humanitarian law.

It is not difficult to see how this list of actions supports the implementation of R2P. In practice, the HRuF initiative has made some progress in terms of redressing some of the weaknesses evident in the UN's approach to atrocity prevention, albeit quietly and in a partial manner. Specifically, it has helped improve the coherence of the UN's response to some crises, improved working relations between the UN's political, humanitarian, and development arms, has empowered early action by regional directors, and through its senior action group has helped the organization identify and coordinate courses of early action.[28] Significantly, it has also led to the development of common criteria to be used across the UN system to assess situations and to elevate those where risks are high or intensifying.[29] However, operationalization remains quite patchy, as does the degree of buy-in across the system, with the initiative relying heavily on the Office of the High Commissioner for Human Rights (OHCHR), while the engagement of other key departments (Department of Political Affairs [DPA], Department of Peacekeeping Operations [DPKO]) and agencies (e.g. UN Development Program) is mixed. Moreover, there remains a disconnect between headquarters and the organization's field missions, where calls to implement HRuF raise more questions than elicit answers. In practice, the HRuF process may have also imposed more distance between the Special Advisers on R2P and Genocide Prevention and the Secretary-General. These concerns notwithstanding, HRuF clearly signals that the UN system's protection responsibilities extend well beyond the implementation of specific mandates handed down by the Security Council.

In practice, there are rarely situations where atrocities are committed in countries where the UN has no presence. At the very least, the UN's humanitarian and development agencies are often present and face difficult questions about whether to speak out about human rights violations or adopt a more conciliatory approach designed to maintain the good relations with local political actors needed to ensure humanitarian access. Indeed, some humanitarian agencies, such as the ICRC, UNHCR, and UNICEF, are specifically mandated by international law to support protection. In the case of Darfur, humanitarian action saved lives immediately at risk from atrocity crimes and other deprivations. So successful was the humanitarian response in 2003–4 that by 2005 the region's average mortality rate had fallen to prewar levels.[30] Humanitarian agencies provide affected populations with both *in situ* life-sustaining support and viable opportunities to flee violence. The relationship between R2P and humanitarian action is complex and challenging but also inescapable for at least two reasons: first, in its commitment to R2P, the World Summit referred specifically to "humanitarian" action as a part of the international community's peaceful response to atrocity crimes; second, in practice humanitarians are often on the front line of efforts to protect populations from atrocity crimes. For example, ensuring humanitarian access has been one of the principal means by which the Security Council has tried to fulfill its responsibility to protect in Syria.

Beyond humanitarian action, with increasing regularity, UN peacekeepers are also deployed with Chapter VII mandates to use "all necessary means" to protect civilians. Indeed, the UN's missions in Mali (MINUSMA) and South Sudan (UNMISS) have explicit mandates to help their host state fulfill their responsibility to protect.[31] In the political space, UN and regional envoys have also played significant roles. We have already discussed Kofi Annan's role in negotiating a cessation of violence in Kenya with UN support and an AU mandate. In Syria, Annan and his successors as joint UN–League of Arab States envoys enjoyed much less success, yet they have nevertheless played important roles in the negotiation of local ceasefires and humanitarian corridors.

These sorts of partnerships, between the UN and regional organizations, have become an increasingly significant part of R2P's operationalization. Experience from the first decade of R2P shows that protection efforts are most effective when individual states, the UN, and regional arrangements work together, as they did in Cote d'Ivoire (2009). What is more, states from all regions agree that regional arrangements should play a critical role in implementing R2P. The precise role that regional arrangements play will differ from case to case depending on the situation, the global response, and the relevant regional capacities, normative settings, and levers of influence. It is important nevertheless to stress the benefits that accrue from engaging regional arrangements in implementing R2P. In particular, it helps foster regional ownership and ensures that the principle is localized in a manner consistent with existing regional practices and cultures; establishes pathways for cooperation between the UN and the region; awards regions a voice in the implementation of R2P; and enhances key national and regional capacities.

If we look closely, we can find that the World Summit Outcome Document specified a number of distinct roles for regional arrangements, several of which relate to the use of peaceful means to protect populations. As key actors in the international community, regional arrangements should: (a) encourage and help states to fulfill their primary responsibility to protect (diplomacy); (b) support the UN in establishing an early warning capability (necessary for rapid responses); (c) help states build the capacity to protect their populations (this can involve immediate boosts to capacity in specifically targeted areas, such as law and order); (d) support the mission of the Special Adviser of the UN Secretary-General on the Prevention of Genocide; (e) utilize peaceful measures under Chapter VIII of the UN Charter to protect populations; (f) cooperate with the UN Security Council in the application of any measures that it adopts (including consensual measures).[32]

In practice, several regional organizations had adopted their own initiatives for atrocity prevention and response prior to the emergence of R2P. Most notably, Article 4 (h) of the Constitutive Act of the African Union (AU), adopted in 2000, gave the organization a right to intervene in the affairs of its member states in matters relating to genocide and crimes against humanity. The AU has also developed its own peacekeeping capacities and adopted a protection mandate for its mission in Darfur (2003) and, subsequently, incorporated civilian protection into its mission in Somalia. The EU established and deployed high-readiness brigades in response to protection crises, and in the mid-1990s the OSCE established its High Commissioner for National Minorities to assist states under stress. NATO also incorporated the protection of civilians into its crisis management work.[33]

This is reflected in recent diplomatic practice where regional and sub-regional arrangements have played a significant role in preventing and responding to crises. Most notably, the AU sponsored Kofi Annan's aforementioned mediation efforts in Kenya (2008), led peacekeeping efforts in Somalia and is a crucial partner in the UN–AU peacekeeping mission in Darfur; the OSCE led international responses to communal violence in Kyrgyzstan; ECOWAS played a key diplomatic role in Côte d'Ivoire and Guinea and is at the fore, alongside the UN and French forces, of international responses to the crisis in Mali; NATO was the principal implementing partner of Security Council Resolution 1973 (2011) on Libya; ASEAN has played a diplomatic role in relation to the situation of the Rohingya in Myanmar; and the League of Arab States and Gulf Cooperation Council played critical roles in Libya, Yemen, and Syria. Each regional and sub-regional arrangement is different. They have different norms, capacities, and interests, which makes it difficult to generalize about the roles they may play in implementing R2P, the approaches they might adopt, or their effectiveness. As with the UN's own efforts, these activities have met with mixed success, suggesting that there is no neat correlation between implementing actor and likelihood of success.

Reflecting on this emerging practice, the Secretary-General's third report on R2P, released in 2011, focused on the role of regional and sub-regional arrangements.[34] The report argued that regional and sub-regional arrangements had important roles to play in helping states implement R2P and in supporting the UN's efforts. Not surprisingly, the Secretary-General argued that regional and sub-regional arrangements could fulfill important functions in relation to all three of R2P's pillars. They could contribute to Pillar One by connecting global standards to local and national action and encouraging compliance, responding to displacement and refugee flows, providing good offices and mediation, supporting conflict prevention capacity, establishing regional norms, resolving existing conflicts, promoting justice, and reducing impunity. Regional organizations could support Pillar Two by building civilian, policing, and military capacity to respond to crises, developing mediation capacity, supporting security-sector reform and strengthening the rule of law, and sharing information for crisis analysis and early warning. Finally, they could support the implementation of Pillar Two by sharing information, developing regional response doctrines, evaluating implementation of targeted sanctions, developing regional tools for cooperating with the ICC.

While it is widely acknowledged that regional organizations have played a constructive role in helping to implement R2P and that global efforts tend to be at their most effective when the work of multiple organizations is coordinated effectively, there have been a number of conflicts amongst organizations, and especially between the AU and the UN. Three conflicts stand out. First, from 2006, the AU and UN disagreed over the composition of peacekeeping in Somalia – the AU (and China and the United States) wanting the UN to take responsibility for peacekeeping, while the Security Council (led on this by its European members) insisted that conditions were not right for UN peacekeeping since there was no viable political process in place and that a multinational enforcement mission would not be viable owing to the insufficient interest of member states. Second, in 2011, the AU and UN Security Council took different positions on the unfolding situation in Libya. In response to the Libyan government's non-compliance with Resolution 1970, and the evident threat posed to the civilian population in Benghazi, the Security Council voted to authorize the use of force to protect civilians. The AU, however, remained opposed to the use of force and continued to pursue negotiations with the Libyan government in the hope (forlorn as it transpired) of securing an agreement that could have challenged the legitimacy of the Security Council's approach.[35] Curiously, however, all three of the African non-permanent members of the Security Council at the time (Nigeria, South Africa, Gabon) voted to support the intervention rather than back the AU's preferred approach. Third, African leaders grew steadily more opposed to the ICC, passing AU resolutions that grant immunity to heads of state and government (2014) and threaten a mass withdrawal from the court (2016) on the grounds that it is biased against African leaders.

The irony, here, of course, is that most of these cases, such as that of the Lord's Resistance Army (LRA), were referred to the Court by African states themselves, and others such as Kenya were taken up by the Court only because the relevant states were parties to the Rome Statute. These points notwithstanding, the political challenge to the Court was led initially by Omar al-Bashir, President of Sudan, who was indicted in 2009 but gathered momentum after the indictment of Kenyan leaders Uhuru Kenyatta and William Ruto for the parts they played in the 2008–9 violence there.[36] At the time of writing, however, only Burundi had actually withdrawn from the Court. Confronting acute atrocity risks of its own, Burundi's withdrawal was widely seen as self-serving. South Africa and Kenya, meanwhile, retracted their own threats to withdraw from the Court, suggesting perhaps that opposition to it had reached a high watermark.

What is more, bitter experience in Syria also suggests that regional institutions may not always be constructive when it comes to atrocity prevention. In that case, the Gulf Cooperation Council adopted a partisan position that was carried over into the League of Arab States and undermined their capacity to negotiate an end to the violence.

Our point here is that it cannot be assumed that global and regional (or regional and sub-regional) organizations will always pull in the same direction and that, just as there has been an unexpected proliferation of actors beyond the state engaging in the implementation of R2P, so too have new challenges risen to the fore.

Finally, we come to the various non-state actors that contribute to protection. These include international NGOs, domestic civil society groups, private-sector actors, researchers and analysts, activists, and other individuals. In relation to diplomacy, international and domestic NGOs play significant roles by setting standards and holding governments to account. This includes not only governments in affected countries, but also those in third-party states where NGOs can ask legitimate questions about what a government is doing to fulfill its R2P and propose ways in which it might do more. Sometimes, prominent individuals – acting unilaterally or as part of a broader group – can support efforts to encourage compliance with R2P and deter atrocity crimes. Non-state actors are also among the principal humanitarian agents whose work can mean the difference between life and death. Civil society groups, private-sector actors, and prominent individuals, especially those found within affected countries and regions, can also play significant roles in helping to protect communities and individuals on the ground, dampening the tensions that can give rise to atrocity crimes. They can also, of course, sometimes have the opposite effect: "neither prevention nor the protection of vulnerable populations can be realized without individuals taking responsibility and assuming risk."[37] Here, we might think in terms of an "individual responsibility to protect" perspective, which aims at developing messages and policies tailored to influence a range of different types of individual that play key roles in preventing – and perpetrating – atrocity crimes, including the vulnerable population, bystanders and the inciters of violence, group and community leaders, national leaders, leaders of influential foreign countries, key officials and decision makers in international organizations, and survivors.

Besides recognizing the sheer range of actors who have come to play a positive role in protecting populations and preventing atrocity crimes, it is also important to understand the connective tissue that binds them and that can make the value of their collective endeavors greater than the sum of its parts. From experience, we know that protection efforts are most effective when different actors work together. While the UN and regional arrangements clearly have important roles to play both as actors in their own right and as coordinators of actions undertaken by a wider range of actors, the central roles played by these bodies could be augmented in different ways. Precisely how these different actors have contributed to preventing and responding to atrocity crimes, and addressing the challenge posed by violent extremists and non-state armed groups that perpetrate atrocities, will be explored in chapter 4.

CHAPTER FOUR

In Search of the
International Community

This chapter addresses one of the most elusive yet critical elements of the responsibility to protect (R2P): the notion that there is, or should be, an international community concerned with preventing or responding to mass atrocity crimes in a timely and decisive manner. As discussed below, as well as in chapter 1, the heads of state and government at the 2005 World Summit assigned important prevention and protection tasks to an undefined international community. So it matters how the scope of that community is defined in theory and how it is activated in practice. That is the central concern of this chapter.

The search for such a community is complicated by the relatively recent emergence and acceptance of R2P principles and of the embryonic development of institutions, at any level, dedicated to forwarding and implementing them. Yet the first step – the coalescing of a knowledge-based epistemic global community of experts and official and unofficial practitioners – arguably has been achieved. It was initially built on the existing networks of specialists on genocide prevention and human security, but the energy created by the enunciation of R2P principles has multiplied the academic and policy interest in stemming atrocity crimes. The next and more ambitious goal of the larger R2P project is to establish and sustain a deeper, wider, and more politically active transnational community, one that would be animated by both commitment and practice.

This chapter contends that the foundations for a transnational R2P community defined by both commitment and practice are being progressively laid, but that it is a work in progress. It is far from being self-sustainable, and there is no reason for complacency. Given regional variances in how far this effort has advanced, the picture differs markedly from place to place. In terms of delineating a community of commitment, the text of the Outcome Document of the 2005 World Summit embodies an unusually broad and high-level statement of common purpose. The universality that is the declaration's strength is also its weakness, however, as the degree of commitment varied enormously among the heads of state and government gathered there. The pledges made were sweeping but general, historic but untested. No institutionalized means of accountability were offered, other than the articulation of standards of behavior that could be subject to peer and public pressure. Building that political pressure was, and is, an abiding purpose of R2P.

A community of commitment that remains at the level of rhetoric – and is not matched by the actions and institutions of a concomitant community of practice – would be a hollow shell that would breed public cynicism instead of confidence. In terms of building a community of practice, the framing of new relationships, doctrines, and institutions is still at an early stage. This chapter finds ample and diverse signs of progress toward these ends, along with reasons to be concerned about whether this progress could be reversible, particularly if there does not continue to be strong leadership from the United Nations and key capitals. The recent ascent of a strain of narrow nationalism in a few key countries, most consequentially in the United States, suggests that progress could be conditioned in the near term by political constraints and financial stringencies. Over the longer term, however, the civil society-led drive to address the scourge posed by atrocity crimes offers some reason for confidence in the sustainability of these concerns. Governments did not create the momentum for human protection. Civil society did; then governments followed. As with the origins of R2P addressed in chapter 1, the future atrocity prevention edifice will be built from the bottom up as much as from the top down.

Given this mixed picture, this chapter looks at the notion of an international community in both theory and practice before turning to ways of reconciling the two conceptions. In doing so, it poses three fundamental questions. One, when it comes to preventing and curbing mass atrocity crimes, what are the shape, form, and dimensions of the international community (and is it so amorphous that we risk not seeing it for what it is and is becoming)? Two, over the still relatively brief life of R2P, what could experience tell us about the existence and nature of the related international community? And three, what lessons could be drawn from practice to date and how should practice reshape the assumptions that motivated and shaped the elaboration of R2P theory?

The International Community in Theory

This book interprets the term "international" in a dynamic and layered manner, encompassing everything from formal relationships among states to informal arrangements among groups that transcend national boundaries. It recognizes both that Chapters VI and VIII of the United Nations Charter impose a hierarchy between the Security Council and regional arrangements when it comes to the peaceful settlement of disputes and the imposition of enforcement measures, respectively, and that these provisions have been interpreted in different ways at different places and times. It does not assume, as some early articulations of R2P seemed to, that global actors are necessarily the most critical ones when it comes to preventing and curbing atrocity crimes. There are three principal reasons why the authors have adopted such an expansive and dynamic interpretation of the international dimensions of R2P: (1) our understanding of the related text adopted by the heads of state and government at the 2005 World Summit when they endorsed R2P by consensus; (2) our understanding of the nature of the international system at this stage of history; and (3) our experience in observing and participating in the implementation of R2P in practice.

First, the R2P text: it is important to recall that the 2005 World Summit that endorsed and redefined R2P was populated by heads of state and government. Employing the first person, they undertook specific and unambiguous commitments both as individual leaders and on behalf of their countries when speaking of the treatment of populations within their borders.[1] They also enumerated a series of responsibilities, though not specific obligations, for the larger "international community, through the United Nations" related to the prevention of atrocity crimes and to "timely and decisive" response "should peaceful means be inadequate and national authorities are manifestly failing to protect their populations" from the four specified crimes.[2] They further invoked the possibility of "cooperation with relevant regional organizations as appropriate."[3] So, with an economy of words (and a concomitant lack of precision), the assembled heads of state and government managed to assert, if not fully articulate, a layered and nuanced set of responsibilities for every level of potential actor, from individuals to global institutions. This 2005 Summit framework implied the coexistence and interdependence of individual and collective responsibilities, whether exercised by civil society or by national and international institutions.

The agreed Summit text on R2P never stated directly or explicitly that the primary responsibility to prevent the four specified mass atrocity crimes and their incitement lies with the state concerned, though that could be inferred by the pledges made by all of the gathered heads of state and government in paragraph 138 that they would protect their populations by preventing the four crimes and their incitement. That declaration constituted an implicit assumption of primary responsibility. Clearly, this is the way the text has been read by officials, diplomats, and scholars throughout the world. Judging by the wording of scores of Security Council resolutions and Presidential Statements since then and by the content of hundreds of member state interventions during the annual informal interactive dialogues in the General Assembly on different aspects of R2P, it is evident that this is the way the representatives of all or almost all member states have understood the text. There has been no dissent on this point.

It is equally clear, however, that primary responsibility is not equivalent to sole responsibility. As chapter 1 related, the impetus behind the initial articulation of R2P principles in 2001 was to find a formulation that would both encourage states to accept and fulfill the abiding sovereign responsibility to protect populations within their territory and simultaneously assert the parallel and continuing responsibility of the international community to assist or, if necessary, to provide such protection itself. The text agreed at the World

Summit did not suggest that states could delegate or cede their sovereign protection responsibilities to the international community at any point. Those responsibilities remain integral to the very essence of sovereignty, even at times and places where national authorities are manifestly failing to fulfill them and the international community has to step in, one way or another, to protect populations from the commission or incitement of the four specified mass atrocity crimes.

What was left unsaid in the Summit Outcome Document, as well as in the UN Charter itself, is which states or other entities – if any – are obligated to step forward and assume the risks and burdens of meeting the collective responsibilities for protection once the Security Council has authorized such action. These collective action dilemmas, of course, have long fueled skepticism about the efficacy of notions of the international community that lack the clear assignment of implementation tasks. This dilemma was not resolved by the establishment of the United Nations, though its Charter takes the critical first step of defining an international decision-making process for authorizing enforcement action, even on subjects, such as genocide and mass atrocity prevention, which are not explicitly addressed in the Charter.

Second, the nature of the international system: in several passages, as has been typical of other multilateral arrangements throughout the postwar era, the Outcome Document made explicit reference to assisting states, in this case to meet their prevention and protection responsibilities. Referring to the responsibility to protect populations by preventing the four mass atrocity crimes and their incitement, paragraph 138 stated that "the international community should, as appropriate, encourage and help States to exercise this responsibility." Likewise, in paragraph 139 the heads of state and government asserted that "we also intend to commit ourselves, as necessary and appropriate, to helping States build capacity to protect their populations from genocide, war crimes, ethnic cleansing and crimes against humanity." In doing so, the Outcome Document reflected well-established international practice. Since at least the nineteenth century, states and civil society groups have formed transnational and international arrangements for addressing common needs and challenges.

Under the principles of functionalism, as espoused by David Mitrany in the 1930s, the United Nations, like the League of Nations before it, was to provide a means of facilitating collaboration across borders to resolve problems of a transnational character that individual states could not handle efficiently and/or effectively on their own.[4] With the end of the Cold War, the functionalist drive to create new institutions and norms to address a wider range of common problems – including atrocity prevention – accelerated. Whether the policy challenge involved development, security, resources, governance, human rights, or the environment, the prevailing assumptions were – and largely remain – that collaboration (1) would naturally transcend borders; (2) would as likely be horizontal as vertical; (3) frequently would involve non-state as well as state actors; and (4) would be undertaken as a matter of choice or reciprocity more often than one of obligation. Despite the current pushback from a narrow brand of nationalism, as noted above, the momentum of this centuries-old movement toward broader and deeper international cooperation appears strong.

The articulation of R2P principles, in that sense, could be considered to be one product of the multifaceted efforts to give policy expression to the more general notion of human security popularized in the mid-1990s and discussed in chapter 1. The assistance dimensions of R2P, as captured under Pillar Two of the Secretary-General's 2009 implementation strategy, also reflected a widespread but seldom voiced concern that weak or "failing" states might otherwise be unable to prevent armed groups from committing atrocity crimes, sometimes across borders. Before the advent of R2P, in Sierra Leone, Somalia, Uganda, the DRC, and elsewhere, international military intervention had been required to protect populations threatened by violent armed groups when governments were unable to control all of the national territory. Both the African Union, in Article 4 (h) of its Constitutive Act, and ECOWAS, in its armed interventions in Liberia and Sierra Leone, had recognized the possibility of regional or sub-regional enforcement action to protect populations from atrocity crimes well before the World Summit endorsement of R2P. Indeed, these steps occurred before the ICISS commission first coined the phrase "reponsibility to protect."

As addressed in chapter 6 below, strategies for atrocity prevention, much like those previously enunciated for conflict resolution, put great emphasis on local, national, sub-regional, and regional actors, as well as civil society, in supplementing and complementing efforts at the global level. Both atrocity prevention and conflict prevention doctrines stressed subsidiarity and the bottom-up flow of information and analysis. This was consistent with the UN Charter's clear preference for having local parties, neighbors, and sub-regional and regional arrangements try to resolve disputes and conflicts before refer-ring them to the Security Council.[5] Yet, as Lise Morjé Howard has observed in reference to peacekeeping, most of the attention and resources have gone to reform and renovation at the global, headquarters, level rather than to enhancing local, national, and field-based capacities.[6]

The text of the Outcome Document outlines and advocates certain patterns of voluntary assistance and collaboration in preventing and responding to the four mass atrocity crimes and their incitement. It provides, as well, some general rules, procedures, and standards to guide these international efforts, most directly in the case of coercive and/or enforcement action under Chapter VII of the Charter to protect populations. It does not, however, articulate any specific course of action that member states would be compelled or obligated to undertake, even in the face of unfolding atrocity crimes. It does not attempt to offer a collective human security commitment any more than the Charter embodies a collective security undertaking among the member states. To have done so, in our view, would have been a bridge too far in terms of the current stage of the evolution of the international system. It is worth recalling, in this context, that the Charter was drafted to give the members of the Security Council maximal leeway in determining what constitutes a threat to international peace and security and how the world body should respond.

Third, the R2P experience: the way in which the heads of state and government articulated R2P principles at the 2005 World Summit envisioned strategies for R2P implementation that would involve efforts at every level, as appropriate and necessary, to prevent mass atrocity crimes and protect populations. In our view, practice has confirmed that these actors will typically range from individuals to communities to governments and from the private sector to interstate institutions on the sub-regional, regional, and global levels. The 2005 text featured actions and results, not actors and protocols. R2P, in other words, was to be all about prevention and protection by whichever actors could make a difference. The concept was, from the outset, much more flexible, even agnostic, about who would need to do what, where, and when to protect the vulnerable.

On the one hand, this preference for flexibility reflected a recognition that action on many levels would be needed when weak or misguided national authorities failed to do their part. Which actors would have the capacity and the will to make a difference would inevitably vary from case to case. This essential pragmatism was echoed in the Secretary-General's 2009 implementation report, which laid out a strategy that called for an "early and flexible response tailored to the specific circumstances of each case."[7] On the other hand, this preference also meant that essential prevention and protection tasks remained unassigned, adding to the accountability and collective action problems noted above that have always haunted international efforts at atrocity prevention and human protection.

As our opening chapters have underscored, distinctions among the individual, group, national, sub-regional, regional, and global dimensions of the responsibility to protect tend to fade in practice. When massive atrocity crimes appear to be imminent in a given situation, effective prevention requires timely, concerted, and mutually reinforcing action at multiple levels by a diverse collection of actors. A range of credible incentives and disincentives may be needed. All hands should be on deck, each doing its part to convince would-be perpetrators to choose another way forward. If there are dissident voices among would-be responders, then messages get confused and more room opens up for spoilers and their divisive splitting tactics. Even when influential international actors see the situation in similar ways, there is a premium on translating common purpose into complementary, even joint, practice. This may not be a simple task, including when burden-sharing questions arise, given the asymmetrical distribution of power and capacity among concerned countries. Such asymmetries may be more pronounced when a coercive military response or economic sanctions are being contemplated than when preventive steps are being considered. The asymmetries of capacity may be less apparent in prevention efforts, but the greater sense of equality in those endeavors may also lead to situations where there are too many actors at various levels seeking to serve as mediators, intermediaries, and/or messengers. As noted in chapter 7, that tendency became a real obstacle to progress in the post-election crisis in Côte d'Ivoire.

These matters of capacity and collaboration, though central to the implementation of R2P principles, have been under-explored in both scholarship and policy. Concerted international efforts to prevent and curb mass atrocity crimes are of relatively recent vintage and are still few in number. So neither scholars nor practitioners have yet to develop a keen understanding of how an intelligent, concerted, and layered international response should work in practice, particularly when each crisis presents a new mix of factors, players, and circumstances. Both the actors on the ground and the interests and capacities of potential international players present differently in each situation. But in almost all situations, those closest to the violence have the greatest stake in seeing it either perpetrated or curbed. Distant actors have less intimate, personal, and existential motivations. This helps explain why global actors may have more capacity than will, and local ones the opposite. These asymmetries in degrees of commitment and quality of interests, though unquantifiable, should be given greater attention in both policy making and policy analysis.

So when this chapter addresses the "international" dimension of R2P implementation, it does so with a keen recognition that success at the international or global level rarely, if ever, comes without simultaneous and mutually supportive efforts by local and national actors, reinforced by those in neighboring countries. The bottom-up aspects of R2P implementation are just as evident when it comes to containing and curbing the early exercise of violence against populations. Distant decision makers, whether in powerful capitals or international organizations, would do well to track and evaluate more closely the dynamics on the ground and the motivations of those actors in closest proximity to the situation at hand. This is particularly true when the risks and costs of intervention appear to be high and/or the engagement on the ground is likely to be prolonged.

It has been our experience that R2P works best when the key actors on these disparate levels recognize their common determination to protect populations through every means possible and when the messaging loop flows from the top to the bottom and, simultaneously and seamlessly, from the bottom to the top. Global decision makers need to be ready to adjust their preconceived perceptions and assumptions as feedback from the ground level requires. Too often, the most damaging errors have stemmed from faulty, incomplete, and/or inflexible assessments, not from a lack of early warning. That was a painfully clear lesson from the UN's three mea culpa reports on its failures in Rwanda, Srebrenica, and Sri Lanka. In each of these situations, moreover, the bottom-up flow of information within the UN system was blocked, suppressed, and/or distorted at crucial points. Top international policy makers viewed developments on the ground through selective prisms that twisted information to fit their preconceptions and assumptions about the nature and causes of the violence.

Such distortions in international decision making may be tempered by mechanisms designed to insure that diverse viewpoints are heard and taken into account. But a diffuse decision-making process may not be a coherent one. In such an environment, R2P can provide a helpful framework for disciplined decision making. When diverse actors decide, individually or in concert, to take action to prevent or curb further atrocity crimes, R2P principles can, and often do, provide a degree of coherence in developing a common message and course of action. R2P principles and standards, as articulated in the 2005 Outcome Document and elaborated in the 2009 implementation strategy of the Secretary-General, lead policy makers to ask a set of questions and to put a premium on a range of factors that differ from those for other policy disciplines, such as conflict resolution, peacekeeping, humanitarian assistance, and even human rights. This can be an important – if sometimes contentious – asset in the policy realm, which necessarily involves trade-offs among a range of distinct but interactive perspectives and mandates. This asset has been underappreciated by R2P advocates and critics alike. Too often, scholars and practitioners seem to believe that it would be better to address curbing mass atrocity crimes through other policy disciplines rather than the more direct route offered by R2P.

Having a multiplicity of voices can serve to reinforce R2P messages by magnifying their resonance and bolstering their credibility among a wider range of political actors on the ground, where it matters most. In delivering messages of tolerance, accountability, and responsibility, players at the individual, local, national, and sub-regional layers may be more persuasive and harder to ignore than more distant or global ones, while the latter may be more authoritative arbiters of international legal and normative standards. It is not a matter of favoring one level over another but of finding better ways of integrating the advantages that each level brings into a more layered and nuanced understanding of policy options and their consequences.

Questions of capacity and legal authority matter much less at an early stage of initial engagement than when responses to mass violence are being weighed once prevention has failed. Then, the range of relevant tools and actors may narrow dramatically. As responses become more globalized, questions of law and authority tend to come to the forefront as notions of consent and sovereignty become contested. So it is understandable that, for those who have seen R2P as just a more palatable version of humanitarian intervention, the critical choices are made by global players in the Security Council or major capitals, not by neighbors or peers. In such a conception of R2P, those with military capacity become the ultimate decision makers when it comes to curbing atrocity crimes.

We take a broader view of R2P and its application. In our conception, the bottom-up dynamics of R2P implementation are every bit as critical when international responses are being weighed. Global decision makers need the candid input of local, national, and regional actors and stakeholders in order to make informed and nuanced choices. This is not because actors on the ground are necessarily going to have better instincts or be less partial – indeed the opposite may be the case – but because they may offer unexpected insights. Besides, they are the ones who will have to live with the results of whatever actions international actors may or may not take. Timely bottom-up feedback matters immensely when it comes to assessing how an engagement is faring, how conditions are developing on the ground, and whether mid-course corrections should be considered. Neither exit strategies nor post-atrocity rebuilding could sensibly proceed without input from those most affected.

This brings us to what may be the biggest gap in R2P theory and practice: an understanding of how post-atrocity rebuilding ought to proceed. This lacuna is ironic for two reasons. One, the original ICISS commission report had identified rebuilding as its third policy basket, though the assembled heads of state and government at the 2005 World Summit left it out of their formulation of R2P. Two, in addition to their endorsement of R2P, a second prominent product of the Summit was their call for a Peacebuilding Commission (PBC). Its mandate, however, was to advise the Security Council and the General Assembly on assisting countries emerging from armed conflict, not mass atrocity crimes.[8] In practice, the PBC has served neither as an effective advisory body nor as a bridge between the Council and Assembly.[9] There has been at best modest interplay between the R2P and peacebuilding mandates, either on the intergovernmental or secretariat levels. The country-specific configurations of the PBC have not focused on situations where atrocity crimes have occurred and where victims and perpetrators remain on the ground, side by side, even as the issues that fueled the violence remain unresolved, and international mediators, peacekeepers, and peacebuilders begin to withdraw.[10]

This R2P peacebuilding gap is troubling for several reasons:

1 The long-observed tendency is for mass atrocity crimes to occur in places where they have previously occurred.
2 Because of these patterns, prevention needs to be addressed after a round of atrocities with as much focus, urgency, and seriousness of purpose as beforehand. Sequencing models, therefore, may be misleading or counterproductive, as there is no downtime for prevention in societies under stress.
3 Rebuilding strategies may well need to be cast differently in places that have experienced atrocity crimes than in those recovering from more conventional conflict. When it comes to peacebuilding, it seems doubtful that one size would fit all. For instance, it may be particularly critical to take

into account intergroup effects of economic, political, and institutional rebuilding steps in the former case, so as to avoid perpetuating or exacerbating ethnic, ideological, or sectarian differences, whether real or perceived.
4 We do not have a keen understanding of what kind of rebuilding measures would be most appropriate and productive under distinct sets of circumstances, as there has been remarkably little study or analysis of rebuilding after atrocity crimes under any conditions.

As conceptions of R2P have evolved, so should notions of related peacebuilding. As discussed in chapter 1, the ICISS approach to rebuilding seemed to be based on the premise that coercive military intervention would cause wide societal damage that should be addressed by those undertaking such interventions or others in the wider international community. Rebuilding plans, it was asserted, should be in place before the decision to use force is taken. In practice, of course, most engagements to prevent atrocities and/or protect populations have not involved the coercive use of force. Either force has not been employed or it has been used with the consent of the local government, so the question arises of how rebuilding plans and strategies might differ depending on whether consent had been obtained and/or other tools for prevention and protection had been utilized.

The International Community in Practice

As noted at several points in this volume, the international track record in anticipating, preventing, and responding to atrocity crimes has been mixed at best. As expected, the advent of R2P has not yet fundamentally altered the cost/risk/benefit calculations in major capitals about undertaking armed interventions for human protection purposes. But the efforts to implement R2P principles have demonstrated that there are a wide range of prevention and protection tools. Some entail the employment of military assets, but many do not. In some situations, both military and non-military steps may be needed. Responsibility demands agility, not rigidity, when it comes to looking for the tools and actors who could make a difference in each unique situation To that end, expanding and altering the terms of domestic and international political debates about whether and how to offer greater protection to vulnerable populations should remain a core goal of R2P. Arguably, the attention generated by R2P has led to a much broader and more sustained search for practical means to prevent and curb mass atrocity crimes, as well as to understand their origins and motivations. Indeed, the persistence of long-standing inhibitions to armed humanitarian intervention has encouraged a more creative exploration, in practice as much as in theory, of alternative means of discouraging the occurrence or escalation of such crimes. It has also spurred a more inclusive understanding of who should be considered to be part of the international community.

This heightened flexibility and adaptability has been evident at the United Nations, which remains integral to the development of R2P as a concept and as a driver of policy. As chronicled in chapter 1, the world body has played an absolutely central role in the inception, development, and diffusion of R2P as a global norm. It has been the locus for the articulation and continuing refinement of international doctrine about how R2P should be implemented in practice. The deliberations of the General Assembly, the Security Council, and, to a lesser extent, the Human Rights Council have shaped the contours of R2P doctrines and strategies, as well as public expectations about the possibilities for preventing mass atrocity crimes, protecting vulnerable populations, and making perpetrators at least sometimes accountable. The unprecedented and unrivaled authority of the world body under international law put it at the center of the conception of R2P that emerged from the 2005 World Summit, itself a gathering of international leaders under UN sponsorship and oversight. Secretary-General Kofi Annan was the most exalted norm entrepreneur and one of the most energetic advocates for R2P in its formative years. Secretary-General Ban Ki-moon followed with a determination not only to give life to R2P by applying it in practice and by giving it an institutional home in the world body, but also to refine it through an ongoing series of annual reports and dialogues in the General Assembly.[11]

Here, as in many other endeavors, however, the world body's unique qualities for producing and disseminating norms are not matched by comparable assets for implementing them. The physical capacities of the United Nations system to ensure that R2P principles are put into practice are as thin as they are broad and varied. In terms of dedicated personnel, as of this writing the post of Special Adviser for the Responsibility to Protect remains unpaid (one dollar per year) at the level of Assistant Secretary-General. He/she shares an office suite with the Special Adviser for the Prevention of Genocide, a full-time, paid position at the higher Under Secretary-General level. Almost all of the small staff of the Joint Office was hired to do genocide prevention, not the much more expansive R2P mandate. Each set of Special Advisers has done its best to foster a collaborative spirit and maintain a united front in dealing with specific situations, but whatever success the office has achieved has been in spite of, not because of, these glaring asymmetries. Beginning in 2008, the Special Advisers initiated several practices that have become standard operating procedures for the world body.

1 Regularly engaging in quiet dialogue with key actors and/or issuing joint statements when mass atrocity crimes appeared imminent or had begun to be committed in specific situations. Public statements by the Special Advisers have become standard features of the UN's response to such circumstances, as the bully pulpit can be one of the UN's primary preventive measures, especially when the Security Council is divided or unengaged. Non-public messaging has often been employed by one or both Special

Advisers as well, though that has not been feasible or useful in all circumstances given questions of proximity and diplomatic rank.

2 The effort to insert R2P or atrocity prevention language into statements by the Secretary-General, Special Representatives assigned to the situations in question, or other ranking officials. The matter of who should say what and when – and sometimes where and to whom – became a subject of sharp debate on some occasions, given how integral the use of language and signaling was to the UN's conflict resolution as well as atrocity prevention efforts. For those engaged in delicate diplomacy with difficult governments, whether for purposes of conflict resolution or humanitarian access, the pointed messages generally favored by those focused on human rights abuses or preventing atrocity crimes were often considered to be too provocative or untimely. As chronicled in the Report of the Secretary-General's Internal Review Panel on UN Action in Sri Lanka and addressed in chapter 7, R2P and genocide prevention perspectives were not welcome in high-level Secretariat deliberations about how to respond to the growing threat of violence against civilian populations there in 2009.[12] Specifically, the crisis had been framed at the highest levels as a humanitarian emergency in which access to the government and to threatened populations was given priority over messaging about potential war crimes or crimes against humanity. Whether a more assertive stance on potential mass atrocity crimes and the R2P responsibilities of the government and the LTTE rebels would have led to a diminution of the violence cannot be known. At the very least, however, it would have put the world body more firmly and publicly on the side of human protection over a span of weeks in which the course that both sides in the conflict were taking was so painfully evident. It also would have shown a more consistent commitment to R2P principles.

3 The ongoing work of the Joint Office staff to collect information from a wide range of sources on developments in situations of potential concern, to meet with the two Special Advisers at least weekly to review the direction and nature of change in each of those situations, and, through that process and other consultations, for the Special Advisers to reach a joint assessment of situations of concern. As helpful as streams of early warning could be, the more essential step was to make a sound, fully informed, and dynamic assessment of the situation at hand. This conclusion was reflected in the report to the General Assembly that the Special Adviser prepared for the Secretary-General in 2010 on "Early Warning, Assessment and the Responsibility to Protect."[13]

4 Site visits undertaken by one of the Special Advisers and/or the staff of the Joint Office. Each of the three Special Advisers on the Prevention of Genocide have been quite active in that regard, despite the awkwardness of that title for the purpose of opening doors. In several situations, staff of the Joint Office have made fact-finding and evaluation visits to gain a

closer and more nuanced understanding of the local dynamics. In some cases, internal reports were prepared afterward and the Secretary-General was briefed on the results.

5 The preparation of internal memos laying out possible strategies for approaching certain situations from an R2P/atrocity prevention perspective. Generally, these were not mandated by higher authorities, but sometimes such self-generated assessments found a place in the wider Secretariat-led policy-making process and occasionally gained the informal interest of members of the Security Council. The Joint Office – either the staff or the Special Advisers – participated on a regular basis in a number of inter-office consultations on individual situations, as well as on more generic policy matters.

6 A meeting of the two Special Advisers at the beginning of each month with the incoming President of the Security Council – a practice initiated by Francis Deng – to compare notes on expectations and plans for the month ahead, including brief exchanges on situations of possible concern. One or both Special Advisers would often meet with members of the Security Council, with representatives of countries concerned about developments in their own country or in neighboring countries, or with officials from regional and sub-regional organizations to discuss matters of mutual concern. The large and growing Group of Friends of R2P would meet regularly with the Special Adviser for R2P and the heads of the major R2P civil society groups based in New York. The friends would negotiate common statements for the annual General Assembly dialogues on R2P and occasionally express common positions on specific issues.

7 A continuing effort to find ways of bringing situations of imminent concern to the attention of the Secretary-General and, through him/her, to the attention of the Security Council, as the mandates of both Special Advisers specify, above and beyond the informal contacts just noted. For the Special Adviser on R2P, access to the Secretary-General was initially relatively easy and frequent. Both recognized that policy judgments could be enhanced by personal exchanges and the input of R2P perspectives in situations of serious concern. In addition, the Special Adviser was permitted to participate in relevant meetings of the Policy Committee, a group of about a dozen high-level UN officials chaired by the Secretary-General, who would generally invite the Special Adviser on R2P when the latter believed that a situation under discussion had a high risk of mass atrocity crimes. (The one case in which this was not allowed was Sri Lanka.) After mid-2012, the Secretary-General placed less reliance on the Policy Committee, whose operation was subsequently terminated. Many of its functions were absorbed by the Senior Action Group, chaired by the Deputy Secretary-General. In part, this shift reflected lessons from the Sri Lanka debacle and the resulting Human Rights up Front initiative within the Secretariat. The new

arrangements, however, have had the effect of lessening contact between the Special Adviser for R2P and the Secretary-General.

8 The ongoing dialogue with the General Assembly and, to a lesser extent, the Human Rights Council and the Peacebuilding Commission on the content, scope, and implications of R2P. As noted in chapter 1, the reference to "continuing consideration" in paragraph 139 of the 2005 Outcome Document was taken by the Special Adviser for R2P as a golden invitation to an intensive and ongoing exchange of views with the 193 UN member states. The annual cycle he initiated of reports from the Secretary-General, as prepared by successive Special Advisers, and informal interactive dialogues with the member states has allowed the kind of opportunity for building understanding and a sense of ownership from the New York diplomatic corps that genocide prevention never experienced, since that subject has never been addressed by the General Assembly. With the help of civil society partners, particularly the Global Centre on R2P, the Geneva-based Human Rights Council is becoming more engaged in these matters, though it still lags far behind the General Assembly in terms of the depth and sophistication of its R2P dialogue.

9 An effort by the Joint Office to contribute to the expanding field of atrocity prevention studies, including through the preparation and publication of a *Framework of Analysis for Atrocity Crimes*, available through the Joint Office website. Originally developed only for genocide, it was reworked when the Joint Office was formed to encompass all four R2P crimes. It is widely used around the UN system and thus is helping to bring attention to and better integrate the work of the Joint Office. However, in typically expansive UN fashion, it includes 14 risk factors of potential concern, along with 143 indicators under them, making it an unwieldy instrument. The factors, moreover, are not weighted, so they serve more as a checklist than as a set of clear priorities.

10 A determination to mainstream R2P in the wider work of the UN system. This work began in 2008 but has accelerated in recent years. In 2016, Secretary-General Ban declared that "the United Nations must redouble its own efforts to mainstream the responsibility to protect. Faced with mounting challenges on multiple fronts, business as usual will not be sufficient."[14] Over the long term, these efforts offer substantial promise, given the extraordinary breadth of the world body's mandates and work, its unusual combination of normative and operational dimensions, and its far-flung presence in different parts of the world, including in areas of particular concern. This has, however, been tough sledding. Officials charged with other mandates – whether they be in political affairs, peacekeeping, humanitarian affairs, development, legal affairs, or even human rights – may see R2P claims as disruptive and unhelpful in forwarding their responsibilities. This task is made no easier by the small size of the Joint Office. So personal leadership by the Secretary-General and/or a push by

influential member states is needed to make a lasting difference in making this a system-wide priority for an organization that has more than its share of urgent priorities.

11 An ongoing effort to encourage, work with, and learn from the research, analysis, and policy advocacy on R2P issues that has been going on in the NGO, academic, and think-tank communities since the advent of R2P at the turn of the century. The sheer volume and diversity of the R2P literature have been nothing short of overwhelming. The growth of academic and policy interest in R2P has permitted the publication of a quarterly journal – *Global Responsibility to Protect* – devoted to the subject, along with innumerable books, chapters, reports, dissertations, and gatherings of scholars, policy analysts, and practitioners. The Joint Office has had a wide range of NGO and think-tank partners on both the global and regional levels. Among these have been the Global Centre on R2P, which has worked closely with the member states on situations of concern, on the development of the norm, and on ministerial events during the Assembly's general debate in September, as well as providing staff support for the establishment of national focal points in more than sixty governments; the Asia Pacific Centre for the Responsibility to Protect, which has sponsored extensive research projects and fostered high-level dialogue throughout the region on implementing R2P norms; the International Coalition for the Responsibility to Protect, which has focused on building international civil society support for R2P; the Kofi Annan International Peacekeeping Training Centre that conducts Africa-wide education and training programs; the Auschwitz Institute for Peace and Reconciliation, which organizes global training courses and staffs the Latin American Network for Genocide and Mass Atrocity Prevention; the Jacob Blaustein Institute on a range of legal questions; and the Stanley Foundation, which has sponsored policy research and international dialogues on these matters since the inception of R2P.

As these snapshots of the work of the Joint Office suggest, its role is much more catalytic than autonomous or definitive. It succeeds to the extent it can help convince others with greater capacity and/or closer proximity to act. Like much of the rest of the United Nations, the Special Advisers largely work through partnerships, some ongoing and others time, situation, and project specific. Their small office lacks the resources and capacities of larger departments, agencies, and programs. To make a difference, its occupants have to rely on access, messaging, and an ability to pose questions that others may not be asking, particularly in inherently cautious and silo-driven international and national bureaucracies. Preventing atrocity crimes and protecting vulnerable populations is a compelling subject, one that has the promise of awakening broad public, parliamentary, and media concern. For the UN, and especially for the Secretary-General, avoiding another systemic failure of the magnitude of Rwanda, Srebrenica, Sri Lanka, and now Syria should be a high priority.

This imperative – the very purpose of R2P – is the Special Advisers' greatest strength.

The 2001 ICISS report, as noted in chapter 1, paid remarkably little attention to the potential role of the UN Secretariat, as its attention – as that of most observers – was squarely on the Security Council. The prospects for protection, it was widely believed, rested largely on its unreliable shoulders and, most especially, on the unity of the five permanent members. There is much to this, of course, but experience has shown that unity among the five is neither a sufficient nor necessary condition for effective prevention and protection. In the worst cases of the UN's failure to take timely and decisive action in the face of mounting evidence of unfolding atrocity crimes – Rwanda, Srebrenica, and Sri Lanka (and earlier in Cambodia) – the preference for a unified front among the five permanent members actively discouraged individual or collective action. Indeed, there seemed to be a joint determination among the five to look the other way or to downplay reports of very serious human rights violations or warnings of possible atrocity crimes. In each of these cases, Council engagement came too late and was too modest. It sought to clean up after the atrocity crimes had occurred rather than trying to anticipate and prevent them. At times, a lowest common denominator tendency among the five works against timely action and bold initiatives. There is reason to believe, as Simon Adams has argued, that the commission of atrocity crimes by the Syrian government and its supporters escalated following the vetoing of draft resolutions in the Council by Russia and China.[15]

The legitimate but not legal debate over the use of force in the Kosovo crisis in 1999 – addressed in chapter 1 – that spurred the work of the ICISS commission that invented R2P has not been repeated, as states have since generally avoided humanitarian interventions without the authorization of the Security Council.[16] (Military interventions for other reasons, particularly counterterrorism, have, of course, not gone out of style.) In the R2P era, the Council has authorized Chapter VII military enforcement measures at least in part for human protection purposes in six situations: Côte d'Ivoire, Libya, Mali, Central African Republic (CAR), the Democratic Republic of the Congo (DRC), and South Sudan.[17] All six situations have been in Africa and five of the six have proven to be relatively successful from an R2P perspective.

This modestly positive track record has largely been overlooked as attention has focused instead on the controversies surrounding the intervention in Libya. There, where support from a number of major and emerging powers in the Council was tepid at best, the immediate atrocity prevention goals were achieved by the NATO air strikes, but the interveners added regime change objectives that were not explicitly authorized by the Council (though neither were they explicitly forbidden, the resolution mandating that "all necessary" means be taken to protect civilians). The requisite political and material support for post-intervention peacebuilding in Libya was not sustained and the longer-term outcomes remain uncertain at best.

On the other hand, there have been a number of situations in which the Council did not act in a timely or decisive manner, but a combination of local, sub-regional, regional, and UN Secretariat efforts – often undertaken in explicit or implicit collaboration – served prevention and protection objectives well. This was the case in the crises in Kenya, following the disputed December 2007 elections; in Guinea (Conakry) in 2009–10; and in Kyrgyzstan in 2010. Given that the geopolitical interests of several permanent members were implicated by the events in the latter case, it was striking that they kept a relatively low profile and did not seek greater Council engagement. That reticence, plus the cooperative attitude of the government, may, in fact, have helped to foster the relatively quick resolution of the immediate crisis. It may sound ironic, but if there is ever a silver lining to the lack of Security Council engagement in situations in which atrocity crimes appear imminent, it would be the added freedom of maneuver it could allow other actors. It may, for instance, serve deterrent purposes for others to be able to invoke, in their interactions with would-be perpetrators, the possibility of Security Council enforcement action, whether in the form of referrals to the International Criminal Court, the establishment of an ad hoc tribunal, sanctions of various kinds, or military intervention. Sometimes, the threat of such action may be most credible when the Council has not yet addressed the situation and the positions of various Council members are not yet known. Spoilers are often tempted to try to exploit perceived differences among Council members. In such circumstances, uncertainty and unpredictability may be useful components of an atrocity deterrence strategy.

Clearly, the Secretary-General and his/her Special Advisers should take the attitudes of Security Council members into account when conducting public and private diplomacy in R2P situations, but they should also strive to maintain a degree of flexibility and adaptability that may be difficult for the Council, as a collective and highly political body, to sustain. There may be times and occasions when key members of the Council will see the relative autonomy of the Secretary-General and his advisers and envoys as an important asset, even if that means that they will explore avenues of conversation and messaging that do not conform strictly to national positions. At the same time, the Secretary-General, when employing his/her authority under Article 99 "to bring to the attention of the Security Council any matter which in his opinion may threaten the maintenance of international peace and security," should be sure to include the risk of mass atrocity crimes. As Special Adviser, Luck advocated this stance when addressing the Security Council's Ad Hoc Working Group on Conflict Prevention and Resolution in Africa in December 2008.[18] Since then, it has become common and generally accepted practice. This evolution of practice parallels the greater comfort that Council members have displayed when it comes to employing R2P language on a regular basis in resolutions and Presidential statements and to welcoming the views of the Special Advisers. These trends also reflect a growing understanding within the Council of the utility of R2P tools and perspectives in preventing atrocity crimes, even though individual members remain reluctant to openly embrace R2P in its entirety for political or ideological reasons.

We detect signs of an emerging, if yet amorphous, community of commitment and, to a lesser extent, of practice. Across a range of international institutions, the combination of peer pressure, secretariat inputs, public expectations, and precedent may well be having at least a marginal influence on how individual delegations address some decisions and texts related to human protection challenges. In the Security Council, the influence of collective culture and mentality on such issues appears to have been more than negligible, especially given the disproportional interest that non-permanent members have tended to have in such matters and the need to acquire a super-majority of nine votes in the Council to pass non-procedural resolutions and to gain consensus on Presidential and press statements. Nevertheless, it is equally critical to recall the extent to which the decisions and actions of such bodies are shaped by the preferences of the individual members, particularly the five permanent members in the case of the Security Council. This pattern of peer pressure within the Council is fueled in part – but not only – by the strong inclination to seek consensus, reflected in the fact that more than 90 percent of Security Council resolutions are adopted unanimously even in these contentious times. It also reflects how highly dependent such bodies are on the will and capacities of individual member states and coalitions to carry out and, if necessary, enforce their collective decisions. To a large extent, the most critical implementation decisions are undertaken in national capitals, not in international headquarters. Any apparent gains for R2P in international organizations cannot be sustained without parallel progress in domestic politics, which has not been an area of strength for R2P advocates to date.

The Security Council has not been the only intergovernmental body that has been paying increasing attention to protection norms, including R2P. This has been true in the Human Rights Council and the General Assembly, as well as in any number of regional and sub-regional arrangements. The Human Rights Council has mandated Commissions of Inquiry (COI) on the Democratic People's Republic of Korea (DPRK) and on Syria, both of which have addressed mass atrocity crimes extensively. The detailed and candid report on human rights conditions in the DPRK emphasized the violation of R2P principles.[19] On Syria, the General Assembly, with no veto to be concerned about, has been far more outspoken on atrocity crimes than has the Security Council. For instance, in December 2016 it authorized the establishment of a mechanism to investigate atrocity crimes allegedly committed there.[20] In October 2016, the Assembly took the unusual step of voting down the Russian Federation's bid to become a member of the Human Rights Council, apparently over widespread concerns about the commission of mass atrocity crimes in Syria.[21]

The active engagement of regional and sub-regional bodies has been critical for both normative and operational reasons. As noted above, under the

Charter local, sub-regional, and regional efforts to address disputes and resolve conflicts are to precede, not follow, Security Council engagement. The latter's involvement is necessitated when the former efforts fall short. Though the Charter does not make reference to atrocity crimes, the same logic should apply to atrocity prevention as to conflict prevention. Ethnic, sectarian, and ideological divides have a tendency to cross borders, whether through the media, group, and political ties, the actions of armed groups, and/or the flow of money, resources, arms, and refugees. Diaspora in neighboring countries can be either helpful or unhelpful in terms of healing wounds or fueling conflict.

As chapter 7 chronicles, regional and sub-regional actors are always part of the picture when it comes to preventing or abetting atrocity crimes. As it suggests, perhaps the most consistent predictor of success or failure in international efforts to prevent and/or curb atrocity crimes in recent decades has been the nature and extent of engagement by neighbors and sub-regional and regional arrangements. On the plus side, the active involvement of sub-regional and regional actors was a significant asset in Kenya, Guinea (Conakry), Kyrgyzstan, Côte d'Ivoire, Mali, Central African Republic, and Burundi, as well as earlier in Liberia, Sierra Leone, and East Timor. Neighbors tended to be part of the problem in Rwanda, the Democratic Republic of the Congo, Srebrenica, South Sudan, Syria, and Yemen. The lack of helpful neighbors or a competent regional arrangement hampered responses in Sri Lanka, as differences in African Union and Arab League approaches complicated attempts to handle the crisis in Libya, and those between ECOWAS and the African Union produced contradictory messaging on Côte d'Ivoire.

In that regard, it is worth noting that the three cases of humanitarian intervention, cited by Secretary-General Kofi Annan in his memorable series of addresses in 1998 and 1999, were all South–South interventions by neighboring countries: India in East Pakistan (now Bangladesh); Vietnam in Cambodia; and Tanzania in Uganda. All three interventions, in his view, were legitimate but not legal.[22] When he presented his probing questions about humanitarian intervention to the General Assembly in September 1999, however, this South–South history was lost and the debate focused, in typical General Assembly fashion, on possible intervention by northern, including former colonial, powers in the global South. This North–South dynamic has hindered and, at times, distorted the dialogue on R2P within the world body. Until Secretary-General Ban and his Special Adviser began to stress the African origins of R2P in their interactions with the member states and civil society groups in 2008, this critical part of the narrative had not received the high-level attention in the world body that it deserved. This neglect, reflected in the mandate for the 2001 ICISS report, had pernicious effects both politically and substantively. This distortion fed the assumption by many that R2P was just another brand for northern-led humanitarian intervention.

The reliance on the United Nations as the primary venue for developing and disseminating R2P principles and practices had another consequence as well. Though the publication of a number of detailed case studies is beginning to broaden perspectives and enhance understanding of the local, sub-regional, and regional dimensions of R2P, the UN-centric origins and development of R2P have tended to prize global actions over those of actors who are closer to vulnerable populations and those who threaten them. At this stage in R2P development, we would do well to assign a premium on looking at R2P through other lenses, including the individual one that is featured in this volume. No single perspective has all the answers, so the test is how well analysis and strategy manage to integrate multiple perspectives in a broader understanding of the origins of mass violence, of the forces that propel such crimes, of the multiple avenues for trying to prevent them and to protect populations, and of the conditions most often associated with the relative success or failure of external engagement.

Peacekeeping can provide one such lens for viewing R2P in practice. In many – though certainly not all – situations since 2005 in which the threat of atrocity crimes has appeared to be acute, international peace operations were already underway, usually with a mandate to protect civilians. Over these years, the UN Security Council has included civilian protection clauses in most peacekeeping mandates and, as noted above, has referred to R2P in these resolutions with increasing frequency. In such cases, the policy debates have generally been about tactics and messaging, not about whether the international community has a responsibility to try to protect populations. The expansion of Security Council efforts to integrate civilian protection (POC) into peacekeeping mandates preceded the advent of R2P, as the challenge of providing some degree of protection to threatened populations had been a long-running problem for peacekeeping doctrine and practice, whether or not mass atrocity crimes were being threatened or committed. To many in the peacekeeping community, the addition of atrocity prevention responsibilities was not entirely welcome, as it appeared to add new and uncertain tasks to already overburdened forces with ever-growing mandates.[23] Within the United Nations, whether among Security Council members, between them and troop- and police-providing countries, or within the Secretariat, the evolving and uncertain relationship between the demands of R2P and the expectations of peacekeepers and the countries that supply them remains unsettled and, at times, contentious.

In any case, having international peacekeepers on the ground, not unlike having Security Council engagement, has not provided assurance that human protection will succeed in all situations. UN peacekeepers were deployed in Rwanda at the time of the genocide and in Srebrenica at the time of the massacre, but both forces, outnumbered, insufficiently armed, and with ambivalent signals from the UN leadership, were overwhelmed by the determined actions of the perpetrators. Through an extended series of internal reviews, blue-ribbon commissions, reports of the Secretary-General, and independent studies, important lessons have been learned. Some studies have concluded that properly trained, equipped, led, and mandated peacekeepers have been doing better at human protection.[24] The Council now includes protection of civilian (POC) or broader human protection mandates regularly in most peacekeeping mandates. Direct references to R2P remain relatively infrequent in resolutions mandating peacekeeping operations, though the Council's mandate for the UN peacekeeping mission in South Sudan contained a specific reference to the second – assistance – pillar of the Secretary-General's 2009 R2P implementation strategy.[25]

The routinization of human protection mandates could pose additional risks, however.

1 These references will be included so regularly in Council mandates that an understanding and recognition of the special, volatile, and sometimes subtle mix of factors that are likely to lead to true atrocity crimes – which fortunately are still a relatively rare phenomenon – could be lost.
2 Policy makers might come to see atrocity crimes and their prevention as largely matters to be settled through military means. Again, this is sometimes the case, but quite often atrocity crimes occur in situations where there is no armed conflict, as discussed earlier. In a number of situations of potential atrocity crimes – Kenya, Guinea (Conakry), and Kyrgyzstan come to mind – successful preventive steps were taken with no peacekeeping component.
3 There have been a range of situations in which horrific crimes have been committed – Sri Lanka, Syria, and Yemen among others – but there has been no possibility of international peacekeeping deployments. If effective prevention and protection are to be undertaken in such places, then admittedly colossal task, then other means will have to be found to try to influence the choices and actions of the parties.
4 Despite pledges to develop Africa-wide forces for such contingencies, peacekeeping is still largely conducted by UN-led or mandated forces. The experiments with UN–African Union hybrid or joint forces have had mixed results, so peacekeeping remains a largely asymmetrical enterprise when other atrocity prevention and protection lessons are pointing to greater reliance on sub-regional and regional actors.

The asymmetries are even greater when it comes to the potential use of military enforcement measures, given the concentration of force projection capabilities in a small handful of northern countries. This compounds perceptions that R2P – at least when a large and technologically sophisticated military response is required to protect populations – is inherently biased toward powerful countries. But, as we have argued throughout, these are the least likely R2P contingencies and there is little reason to believe either that major military powers are eager to intervene militarily for R2P purposes or that they have been especially receptive to embracing R2P principles and responsibilities.

As underscored at the outset of this chapter, the quest to build R2P communities of commitment and practice is still in its early stages of development. But the direction is clear. R2P is gradually becoming a more inclusive and global phenomenon. Its core principles remain inviolable, but the means to forward them have become more diverse and layered. The critiques from the global South were largely taken on board both at the 2005 World Summit and in the Secretary-General's implementation strategy of 2009. Despite continuing controversies, R2P is becoming less of a North–South issue as countries large and small, wealthy and poor, seek to find better means of preventing mass atrocity crimes and protecting vulnerable populations. This is coming to be appreciated as a global challenge. Just as importantly, the efforts to put R2P into practice in scores of situations since 2007 have tended to confirm and reinforce the recasting of R2P concepts and principles to make them more workable in practice, not just more politically palatable in the debating halls of the United Nations.

Bringing Theory Into Line with Practice

This chapter's search for an international community of commitment and practice has led to several tentative conclusions that would seem to be inconsistent with the way some aspects of R2P were first introduced in 2001. These lessons from experience would also raise doubts about some widely held assumptions about the nature of mass atrocity crimes, the circumstances that foster them, and the range of policy responses available to the international community. As detailed in chapter 1, the ICISS commission had been tasked at the turn of the century with finding policy responses to a series of questions relating to sovereignty and international intervention and stemming from the controversies surrounding NATO's use of force in the Kosovo crisis in 1999. Much has happened since, not least the attacks of 9/11 that occurred at the time the ICISS report was about to be released and the emphasis on counterterrorism in much of the world over the years that followed. The geopolitical context has shifted markedly. Policy priorities have been recast, more than once, in many capitals. Yet, the core principles of R2P have survived, even prospered, as the strategies, doctrines, and tools to implement them have been modified to respond better to changing conditions and needs.

Territorial sovereignty has not turned out to be the all-consuming, make-it-or-break-it, issue for R2P which early advocates and critics alike had expected it to be. True, contending views of the nature and limits of sovereignty have been at the center of scholarly and political debates about R2P from its earliest days. They have been critical to the inception and development of R2P as a norm, as discussed in chapter 2. Somewhat ironically, however, these national–international distinctions have been less central to the actual implementation of R2P in practice than they have been to its theoretical and normative development. This may sound counterintuitive, but that has been the experience in a number of real-life situations since the 2005 World Summit, several of which are addressed in chapter 7. As noted above and chronicled in chapter 6, this is partly explained by the increasing emphasis on prevention, as experience has shown that the best chance of protecting populations in high-risk situations has been to prevent atrocities in the first place. But there are other explanations, as well. For instance, the original theory did not take account of the substantial proportion of mass atrocity crimes committed by armed groups. Governments facing such threats and unable to control all of their territory may welcome international security assistance and even armed intervention aimed at the armed groups committing the atrocities on their national soil.

Moreover, as noted in chapter 1, though the initial conception of R2P in 2001 stressed the need to rethink the limits to territorial sovereignty, the two most prominent and tragic failures to protect populations in the 1990s – Rwanda and Srebrenica – had actually been due much more to questions of decision-making sovereignty in foreign capitals reluctant to intervene in a timely and decisive manner. Concerns had been secondary about the territorial sovereignty of countries, such as Rwanda and Bosnia-Herzegovina, which were in the midst of civil wars and in which UN peacekeepers were already deployed. Decision-making sovereignty remains the single greatest obstacle to R2P implementation today. As suggested earlier in this chapter, the community of commitment appears to be much wider than it is deep. In that regard, member-state governments have the capacity to make international institutions look remarkably good or bad, competent or incompetent. They may, for the purposes of public diplomacy and/or domestic politics, agree to all sorts of norms that they have little intention of making any real sacrifices to carry out, especially in places where the risks and costs of implementation are high and the chances of success uncertain. They may, even more cynically, delegate to international institutions tasks that appear doomed from the start, as such organizations may be well placed to perform a scapegoat function for their members when all else fails. That, too, may be a contribution to shaping an international community, be it an ambivalent and uncertain one.

Where efforts to implement R2P and protection policies on the ground have been relatively successful since 2005 – such as in Kenya, Kyrgyzstan, Guinea (Conakry), Côte d'Ivoire, and Mali – there usually have not been major barriers imposed by claims to territorial sovereignty. (Burundi may be an exception, though it had been a site for a preventive peacekeeping deployment at an earlier point.) In Sri Lanka, the government was vociferous in asserting its sovereignty, but the main obstacle to effective engagement was ambivalence across the international community due, in part, to the government's effective deployment of a counterterrorism narrative. In terms of protecting populations, the picture has been mixed in Libya, Iraq, the Democratic Republic of the Congo (DRC), the Central African Republic, Somalia, and Nigeria. Immense difficulties have been encountered in Sudan, South Sudan, Yemen, and Syria, with larger geopolitical and/or historical factors part of the volatile mix. In none of these calamities, however, have simple questions of territorial sovereignty been the primary explanation for the failure to protect.

When governments refuse or are highly reluctant to consent to an international presence on the ground, such as in Sri Lanka and Syria, foreign capitals and international organizations may well be more reluctant to take decisions to intervene given the costs and risks that a lack of consent may well entail. Nevertheless, there have been several situations in which protection and R2P concerns appear to have motivated the deployment or expansion of an international military presence despite reluctant, qualified, or coerced consent, such as in Sudan, the DRC, South Sudan, and Burundi or, at an earlier point, in East Timor. Moreover, international secretariats may – and often do – take a range of preventive actions, involving quiet diplomacy, collaboration with civil society, and/or public messaging, without either the consent of the government in question or the explicit authorization of intergovernmental bodies, whether on the sub-regional, regional, or global levels. Preventive diplomacy, in fact, may have the highest likelihood of success if undertaken before the government decides either to refuse consent to international engagement or to commit itself to a course of atrocities against elements of the population.

All of this underscores the essentially political nature of R2P, in that its ultimate success will depend on the extent to which it inspires a shift in priorities and attitudes within national capitals and political discourse, not just within the confines of international debating halls. It needs to affect the decisions that powerful states, as well as societies under duress, make about when and how to engage when populations are at risk. And it needs to convince them that there are multilateral policy options that can make a difference in a timely and decisive manner and that others share a commitment to meeting their R2P responsibilities through the United Nations and regional and sub-regional bodies whenever possible. Over the years, it has become increasingly evident that the glue that ties the R2P communities of commitment and practice to each other is composed of politics, both domestic and international. This – the capacity to affect political choices, even if marginally, imperfectly, and inconsistently – remains the most important element of R2P's added value.

Practice has also raised questions about which models of military action are most appropriate for the purposes of prevention and protection. The initial conception of R2P seemed to envision interventions involving ground forces capable of providing immediate physical protection, such as better armed peacekeepers with more robust mandates. This was certainly the kind of force that critics saw most clearly missing in Rwanda and Srebrenica. As chapter 1 pointed out, the rebuilding phase of the original, 2001, version of R2P appeared to be needed as a result of a coercive armed intervention by ground forces that would inevitably produce widespread damage and social disruption, particularly if they had to engage national military forces, non-state armed groups, or armed mobs that had been engaged in mass killings. That model would have fit, to some degree, the pre-R2P situations in Rwanda and Srebrenica, or earlier in Cambodia. Yet the most immediate trigger of the humanitarian intervention debate had been Kosovo, a situation in which NATO was unwilling to commit ground forces to provide immediate protection and chose to undertake the strategic bombing of Serbia instead.

As noted above, since the acceptance of R2P at the 2005 World Summit, the Security Council has authorized armed enforcement measures for human protection and other purposes in six situations, all in Africa. The only one carried out primarily from the air – and the only one that was highly controversial – was in Libya. Though the "just war" criteria for the use of force elaborated in the 2001 ICISS report retain their validity, they have not been included in any formulation of R2P accepted by the member states or put forward by the Secretary-General. The Brazilian responsibility while protecting (RWP) initiative, undertaken in the wake of the use of force in Libya, tried to revive consideration of similar criteria and of how they might be incorporated into the Council's working methods, but to no avail.[26] It initially attracted wide interest but eventually foundered politically, in part because of deep aversion among members of the Security Council to having others try to impose limits on its decision-making competence beyond the provisions of Article 24(2) of the Charter. This also helps explain why subsequent efforts by France and Mexico and by the wider-based Accountability, Coherence and Transparency (ACT) group of states to promote codes of conduct for members of the Council in such situations have fallen short, despite wide support from the UN's general membership.

In the R2P community of practice, it has become generally accepted that the use of coercive force for protection purposes should be a measure of last resort, as asserted in the Secretary-General's 2009 implementation strategy, meaning that it should not be undertaken lightly or without proper authorization. Relegating coercive force to a last resort in a chronological sense, however, would unnecessarily exclude deterrent or protection options that could be essential to protect populations under imminent threat. Such a chronological interpretation would also be inconsistent with the spirit of Article 42 of the United Nations Charter, which permits the Security Council to authorize military action when it considers that other measures "would be inadequate" not just "have proved to be inadequate."[27] In some dire situations, there may be no other feasible options. Keeping all options open would seem to have been the intent of the "timely and decisive" phrase in paragraph 139 of the Outcome Document. Preventive, consent-based, deployments, such as those that bolstered stability in Sierra Leone, the Former Yugoslav Republic of Macedonia (FYROM), and Burundi, might be excluded under a last-resort rule. The first of these was coercive, the other two were not. But the essential point is that all three were undertaken with the consent of the government. In an era with so many atrocities being committed by non-state armed groups, some with terrorist intent, it would make more sense to feature consent, not coercion, as the critical criterion.

The ICISS report properly recognized the destructive and often unpredictable consequences of the use of force. What it did not address was what kind of use of force would make the most sense under which circumstances. This remains a critical and unsettled question, whose importance has been underscored by the uneven practice in terms of the use of force since 2005. As a general proposition, it would seem difficult to protect populations from the air for any length of time. Unless air strikes are followed up with some sort of military or police presence on the ground, as well as with broader efforts at social and political reconciliation, security-sector reform, and respect for human rights and democratic values, their value would seem at best temporary and transient. In Libya, the lack of a sufficiently sustained and intensive effort to help create longer-term governance institutions and social stability may have undermined the results of the bombing campaign. These, too, cannot be created from the air. But the preference of powerful states to try to make a difference from above the fray is understandable. Nor have UN efforts to refine its peacebuilding strategies, as noted above, fully incorporated R2P and mass atrocity prevention perspectives. In these respects, experience has not yet provided compelling answers to these dilemmas, but it has underscored the importance of these lingering questions about the utility of different models for the use of force to protect populations.

According to chapter 7, below, practice has also highlighted the importance of understanding the players on the ground: who is contemplating, inciting, or committing such crimes, why are they doing this, how deeply committed are they to this path, and what might dissuade them? As noted above, it is likely that they are more determined to commit such crimes than the international community is to stopping them. The variance from one situation to the next, however, has been substantial. It may be a tautological assertion, but the only times since 2007 that coercion was not required to curb the ongoing commission of mass atrocity crimes was when the leadership in question demonstrated a degree of flexibility and willingness to compromise. In Côte d'Ivoire and Libya, coercive force was required to compel a change of course, but not in Kenya, Guinea (Conakry), or Kyrgyzstan. In the latter situations, public and private diplomacy on several levels made a difference because there were political actors on the ground willing to listen to international entreaties. In those situations, the community of practice included both national and international actors. Making such global, regional, and national connections is critical to building effective communities of practice.

Better tools of assessment are needed to make more tailored and refined choices about the mix of tools that should be applied in different situations, based in part on an understanding of the personalities and political dynamics involved. For instance, it is widely asserted, and properly so, that elections can trigger domestic violence, often along ethnic or sectarian lines. The record to date, however, also suggests that these situations may be more prone to peaceful resolution than are other cases of atrocity crimes. Questions of political control and power may often be associated with some of the worst crimes, as in Sudan, South Sudan, Syria, Nigeria, Central African Republic, Srebrenica, and Rwanda, but these cases of extreme and prolonged violence have not revolved around elections per se. On the other hand, it was possible, in part through R2P-motivated engagements, to end election-related violence in Kenya (twice), Burundi, Guinea (Conakry), and Kyrgyzstan, among others. In part, this pattern may reflect selection effects, in that the very fact that a society holds regular and contested elections may be a positive sign. But, as chapter 7 suggests, it also may be that the stakes in election disputes are more amenable to non-violent solutions if the latter are presented and pressed by credible external figures. In some other situations, however, the stakes may appear to be or are manipulated publicly to seem to be more existential in nature, with the viability and sustainability of one group or culture presented as being threatened fatally by another.

The international community, of course, does not always get it right. Mistakes of judgment occur for a variety of reasons. Lessons are not learned. Perceptions are flawed. Information is distorted, ignored, or misread. Indeed, another counterintuitive lesson from practice has been that assessment matters, in most cases, more than early warning. It would obviously be better to have both, but experience reveals that there have been situations in which early warning was lacking but the international community got the assessment right and prevention and/or rapid engagement worked. That was the case in Kenya, Guinea (Conakry), and Kyrgyzstan, for instance. There have also been a number of cases in which early warning led neither to correct assessments nor to early and/or effective action. In each of the UN's most egregious failures to prevent atrocity crimes or protect populations – Rwanda, Srebrenica, and Sri Lanka – there was adequate warning but not a concomitant will to act. People have a striking capacity to ignore or reinterpret information that does not match their mindset or preferences. Officials, in particular, may resist messages about imminent mass violence because it runs counter to their mandates. And, as discussed above, those charged with conflict resolution, peacekeeping, or humanitarian assistance may find R2P warnings and the disruptive and unsettling rhetoric that comes with them to be especially hard to integrate with their mandates. That, too, has been the UN experience.

In practice, when Luck served as Special Adviser, he often found it difficult to draw clear lines between prevention and response, as so many academic models do, including the 2001 ICISS report. Upstream or structural prevention can be differentiated from response because it is not triggered by particular actions or developments in the society in question. Its generic quality sets it apart. But as one moves closer to operational or direct prevention – i.e. when the possibility of violence appears to be growing, even if not yet imminent – then the way in which international engagement is defined or carried out will begin to look and feel more like a response predicated on specific developments or triggers within that society. On the response side of the equation, actions that are taken by international actors will also have a preventive purpose. The goal is to prevent an escalation or intensification of the violence and/or to prevent or forestall its repetition. So while it may make sense for analytical purposes to draw lines between prevention and response, one should take care not to think of these categories as discrete steps along a chronological continuum.

The most consequential lesson from experience, however, has been the growing recognition that armed groups are among the most determined perpetrators of mass atrocity crimes. This point, though addressed in chapter 3 and earlier in this chapter, bears repeating at this juncture because of its broad implications for how R2P is defined and practiced. The 2001 and 2005 versions of R2P missed this point and, in retrospect, appear much too state-centric. Putting territorial sovereignty at the heart of the R2P dialogue reflected this overly narrow view, as discussed above. It was when Luck was developing the three-pillar R2P implementation strategy, as outlined in the 2009 report of the Secretary-General, that it became obvious to him that R2P theory had to be adjusted to encompass non-state as well as state actors, whether as perpetrators or potential protectors. Today, there is little dissent on this point, yet how to integrate state and non-state actors into R2P doctrine and practice remains a challenge. The next chapter, by considering the domestic dimension of R2P, adds to a more layered understanding, not only of where R2P is today but also of where it is going.

CHAPTER FIVE
The Domestic Dimensions

In May 1998, UN Secretary-General Kofi Annan gave a speech in Kigali, Rwanda, in which he underscored an undeniable – if uncomfortable – truth about the genocide there four years earlier. For all that the international community could be condemned for failing to confront the mass slaughter, the genocide itself "was a horror that came from within."[1] Atrocity crimes do not emerge from nowhere but arise out of deep-seated fear and practices of discrimination, marginalization, and conflict. On most occasions, both the forces that drive societies toward the abyss and those that inhibit such moves are driven not by international actors focused on R2P but by national governments, civil societies, and private sectors animated by a complex array of more local concerns. As Scott Straus has argued, international actors can play a "supporting role" but "it is very difficult, if not impossible, for international actors to impose new political narratives or to impose peace on ruling elites who do not want to compromise."[2] As such, the actors primarily responsible for determining whether or not a country will experience the horror of atrocity crimes are those within the country itself.

R2P recognized the centrality of domestic actors to the prevention of atrocity crimes by assigning the *primary* responsibility to protect to the state itself. Indeed, as we observed earlier, R2P aspires to a world of responsible sovereigns that protect their own populations from atrocities as a matter of habit. International institutions – so long the focus of political and scholarly attention with respect to R2P – play secondary roles either by encouraging and supporting states to fulfill their responsibility (Pillar Two) or by serving as protector of last resort when states manifestly fail to protect their own (Pillar Three). Yet it is somewhat more challenging, analytically and politically, to address the domestic sources of risk and resilience to atrocity crimes than it is the international institutions. Politically, these questions go to the heart of issues concerning national sovereignty, culture, social practices, and historical memory. In other words, it involves deep questions about relations within states and societies themselves. Analytically, it is more challenging to identify precisely the distinct added value of R2P or atrocity prevention or a causal relationship between specific actions and the occurrence or non-occurrence of atrocities. However, wherever we see states and societies establish institutions or practices intended to inhibit violence or pull back from the brink or manage major political crises peacefully, we see the effects of prevention at work, whether or not it is consciously labeled as such. But despite the political and analytical challenge, it is imperative that domestic actors – states, civil society, the private sector – are situated at the heart of thought and practice on R2P, not only because the primary responsibility to protect rests with the state but also because it is often true that the most consequential actors are domestic ones.

This chapter starts with the presumption that one of R2P's principal goals is to encourage and support states to protect their own populations from atrocities. Naturally, we recognize that states are often the primary perpetrators of atrocities against their own populations, exemplified by the systematic campaign of atrocity crimes unleashed by the Syrian government against its own people since 2011. Questions of state culpability for atrocity crimes and international responses to these crises are further considered in the following two chapters. In practice, the picture has become quite complex. States are rarely the only protagonists and, in situations in which non-state armed groups are committing the atrocities, the vulnerable may include state structures and institutions as well as targeted groups. In some cases, therefore, R2P has to support efforts to enable populations to protect themselves from sectors of society that would commit atrocity crimes against them. The picture is made more complex still by the fact that states are not singular "black boxes" but comprise individuals and institutions with different interests, values, perspectives, sources of authority, and material power. Nor do they operate within a domestic vacuum but are situated alongside people, groups, other institutions, and organizations as well as the societies they populate. In many cases each of these types of actor is also attached to transnational civil society – which serves as an important transmission belt for the diffusion of norms and makes significant practical contributions especially through its connections with domestic civil society. Of course, transnational connections are not inherently virtuous and can also operate in the other direction. For instance, diaspora groups can sometimes inhibit prevention efforts by inciting and instigating violence. These connections, as well as that between "national authorities" and the wider public in states under stress, are central to the core notion of responsibility. As such, the chapter will underscore the need for the assumption of individual responsibility across all of these sectors if collective responsibility is to be achieved.

We proceed in three stages. The first briefly amplifies our opening point that, when it comes to atrocity crimes, the horrors usually come from within. It identifies some of the principal forces that can drive societies toward atrocity crimes. Our intent here is to demonstrate the rootedness of atrocity crimes within their specific context. The second section examines the steps that some states have taken to fulfill their primary R2P and other measures that might be adopted. The third section turns to the role that civil society and private-sector actors can and do play in order to inhibit (or sometimes drive) atrocity crimes. Our purpose is to demonstrate that the decisions that actors take in each of these spheres are consequential and that atrocity prevention requires the assumption of individual responsibility across society as well as by individuals within states. It is not enough for anonymous institutions to make rhetorical commitments; those commitments have to drive the actual behavior of individuals which, in turn, will influence how institutions themselves behave.

The Horrors Within

Individual decision making is shaped by the social context in which it occurs. As Christopher Clark observed in his magisterial account of the origins of World War I, structural forces such as nationalism, racism, capitalism, or liberalism matter only insofar as they influence the choices of individual decision makers.[3] R2P's first pillar – the state's primary responsibility to protect its population – rests on the premise that by changing social and political contexts to make them less permissive of atrocities and by establishing frameworks for the positive management of difference, it is possible to alter individual decisions about whether to perpetrate these crimes. To understand the role that states and other domestic actors can play in fulfilling R2P, therefore, we need to have some sense of the types of context and factor that can give rise to these crimes. That is the purpose of this section.

Because atrocity crimes are products of their historical, political and social context, and are – to return to Clark – "saturated with agency," analytical models can never perfectly identify their general causes or predict their coming with complete accuracy.[4] However, as UN Secretary-General Ban Ki-moon maintained, atrocities are processes and not singular events.[5] As such, though each case is different in important respects, not least in the configuration of relevant actors, we can identify the broad landscapes that push states and societies toward atrocities. It is important, though, to understand that conditions that increase the risk of atrocities do not make them inevitable. There is no simple causal pathway between risk and actualization. As the Secretary-General pointed out in 2013:

> The presence of risk factors does not directly or inevitably cause atrocity crimes. Societies can exhibit multiple sources of risk but not experience atrocity crimes. The absence of atrocity crimes can stem from sources of resilience within a given country or simply from the absence of a triggering or driving factor. Although it is impossible to draw a direct causal connection between the presence of specific risk factors and the occurrence of atrocity crimes, they are rarely committed in the absence of those risk factors.[6]

These conditions, which may or may not be the result of conscious policies and decisions, create the structural possibility that atrocity crimes may be committed and elevate the risk that they will be. Although the existence of these conditions does not always result in atrocities (in fact, they generally do not), these crimes have rarely occurred in their absence.

One of the effects of the emergence of R2P has been the proliferation of studies on the factors associated with heightened risk of atrocity crimes. Where we once had limited understanding driven by a relatively small number of studies, we now have a much sharper understanding based on a wide range of studies. These risk factors were recognized and put to good use by the UN's Office on Genocide Prevention and R2P in its *Framework of Analysis for Atrocity Crimes*, which identified several of the most significant underlying sources of risk, including: long-standing patterns of human rights abuse, the weakness of state institutions, and entrenched discrimination against defined groups.[7]

Further clues as to the contexts that tend to give rise to atrocity crimes can be collected from past cases. Most of the major episodes of atrocity crimes since the early twentieth century fall into one of six broad types:

1 state repression where atrocities were used to maintain state power, usually in the context of relatively weak and authoritarian states (e.g. North Korea);
2 counterinsurgency where atrocities are employed in order to defeat an insurgent organization by denying it access to a civilian population (e.g. Syria, 2011–12, Darfur, Yemen) in contexts where armed forces are incapable of prevailing through more discriminating strategies;
3 the support of radical social transformation where atrocities are employed by state or non-state actors to impose radical change on a society, usually by eliminating a particular ethnic, religious, political, or socioeconomic group (e.g. Khmer Rouge, Rwandan genocide, IS). This is commonly associated with violent extremism or revolutionary leadership;
4 insurgency and rebellion where atrocities are employed as a strategy by non-state actors against states and hostile societies, sometimes through insurgency or terrorism (e.g. Boko Haram, al-Shabaab). Non-state armed groups will typically employ atrocities either because they are insufficiently strong to target the enemy's forces, to instill fear amongst the targeted population, or to enforce its political program;
5 sometimes actors will employ atrocities as a strategy for winning a major war at the lowest cost (e.g. Syria, 2012–present);
6 intercommunal strife where ad hoc groups attack sections of their community (e.g. Kyrgyzstan, 2010).

Although not synonymous with armed conflict, because atrocities can occur in its absence, a majority of atrocities are perpetrated during armed conflict. Indeed, around two-thirds of the atrocities committed since 1945 occurred in the context of armed conflict, a figure rising to more than three-quarters if we consider only the post-Cold War era.[8] As a result, it is fair to posit armed conflict itself as one of the principal sources of risk of atrocity crimes.

A prerequisite for atrocities is the existence of established divisions between identifiable groups, be they of an ethnic, political, socioeconomic, or religious nature. As the Secretary-General observed in 2013, it is not the differences themselves that matter, but rather discrimination "based on such differences that creates unequal access to resources and exclusion from decision-making processes and leads to a denial of economic, social, cultural, civil and political rights."[9] Discrimination can take different forms, and the Secretary-General pointed specifically to the denial of basic political rights (such as the right to a fair trial, the right to vote, freedom of speech, freedom of association), denial of citizenship, freedom of religion, self-identification, and limitations on basic social or civil rights (such as freedom from discrimination on grounds of race, ethnicity, religion, etc.), unequal access to economic opportunities, land and other resources, employment, food, shelter or health care, and denial or inadequate protection of basic rights relating to physical security and the status of women, compulsory birth control and unequal access to services and property.[10]According to the Secretary-General, discrimination is an especially important problem because it sows the seed of discord between groups. From the perspective of atrocity prevention, however, he observed that discrimination is

> especially disturbing when it stems from patterns of deliberate exclusion. Persistent discrimination establishes divisions within society that serve both as a material cause and as a perceived justification of group violence…Discrimination is often accompanied by violence and additional human rights violations, such as arbitrary detention, enforced disappearances, torture and killing, against specific members of a community or a community as a whole.[11]

Indeed, so significant are patterns of discrimination that the Secretary-General observed that without them, even deep-seated grievances were "unlikely to transform into patterns of abuse that give rise to atrocity crimes."[12]

Where identities are politicized and discrimination is entrenched, ordinary political battles over the allocation of resources or justice concerns become conflicts *between groups* – setting out parameters for future conflict. These practices of discrimination are, as the Secretary-General recognized, associated with deeply ingrained, often widespread and systematic, violations of fundamental human rights. In his 2013 report on R2P, the Secretary-General pointed out that entrenched discrimination is often evidenced through the use of "exclusionary ideology" that constructs identities in terms of "us" and "them," rather than in inclusive terms. He also observed that such ideologies give rise to hate speech and propaganda which not only reinforce divisions by seeking to justify discrimination, but also lay the groundwork for incitement to violence and atrocity crimes.[13]

Often related to aspects of discrimination, some economic factors are associated with heightened risk of atrocity crimes. Although overall levels of wealth (measured in terms of GDP per capita) matter, it is the relative economic position of groups within a country that is especially important for atrocity crimes. These are *horizontal* inequalities (across groups) rather than the more commonly measured *vertical* inequalities (referring to relative wealth of rich and poor measured by Gini coefficients).[14] These economic inequalities increase risk indirectly by raising the stakes of intergroup competition. Moreover, disaffected groups may have a lower commitment to peace.[15] Sometimes, however, the causal path can be unusually direct, for instance when atrocities are perpetrated as a result of competition between groups for scarce resources. The mismanagement of income secured from natural resources, for example, can become a key point of dispute between groups. The role that the increasing scarcity of water and grazing land, both necessary for survival in Darfur, played in sharpening the conflict there is an example. These more specific causal paths raise questions about the role of economic elites and private-sector actors in driving or inhibiting atrocity crimes, a question we return to later.[16]

Now we come more explicitly to the role of the state since social practices of discrimination, intergroup conflict, and economic inequality can be either mitigated or exacerbated by the state. State institutions and political leadership can be constructed in order to mitigate even serious social cleavages. Conversely, the weakness and partiality of state structures and institutions can themselves exacerbate crises, whether because they fail to mitigate the problem, become a source of conflict in themselves, or are utilized as a tool to support atrocity crimes.

Perhaps the most fundamental institution of the state is the rule of law since political stability, human rights, and economic prosperity are all premised upon it. When the rule of law breaks down, civilian populations become subject to the arbitrary exercise of power in which the absence of an impartial judiciary allows for impunity in acts of discrimination and violence against vulnerable groups by an arbitrary power or by non-state armed groups that operate beyond the law. Adherence to the rule of law provides accountability even in the face of discriminatory policies from governments, ensuring a safety net for targeted groups. Thus, while most major crises do not result in atrocities, one decisive factor that heightens the risk of them doing so is the existence of an unaccountable political elite.[17] Regimes that espouse or permit "exclusionary" ideologies are especially pernicious.[18] What is more, weakness in the rule of law reinforces cultures of impunity that are especially important for persuading would-be perpetrators to commit atrocity crimes. Ensuring legal accountability for past crimes through transitional justice, and guarding against impunity in the present, are deterrents to the perpetration of future atrocity crimes. However, their absence can significantly reduce the perceived costs associated with committing atrocity crimes. When impunity is permitted, atrocity crimes can even be "normalized" to some extent.

An accountable system of government contains institutional and ideational deterrents that impede political elites from attacking their own populations.

Even semi-democracies – regimes in the process of developing a democratic political system – are less likely to commit atrocity crimes than autocratic regimes. Although transitions to, and away from, democracy can often result in political instability – such that transitions themselves are a significant source of risk – major crises in autocratic states are much more likely to give rise to atrocities than similar crises in democratic or semi-democratic states.[19] However, "rollback" in new democracies is not uncommon, and several episodes of atrocities have occurred when former or fledgling democracies have experienced a reversion.[20] Among the most obvious examples are those of Croatia, Bosnia, and Burundi in the 1990s, where atrocities were immediately preceded by experiments in democratization.

Unaccountable government is related to atrocity crimes in two main ways. First, various types of autocratic regime might advocate atrocities as a matter of stated policy, either by denying a particular group's right to exist or arguing that groups that oppose particular policy programs act illegitimately and make themselves targets. The types of regime that have harbored violent extremist ideologies which provide the justificatory logic of mass killing include Marxist-Leninist, extreme anti-communist, Islamist, racist, and extreme nationalist. Many non-state armed groups operate in similar ways – combining unaccountable decision making with violent extremist ideology. Second, it is often the case that in autocratic governments and non-state armed groups, the executive leadership exercises arbitrary power, increasing both the likelihood of its using extreme violence to protect itself or achieve its goals and that of it attracting domestic armed opposition. South Sudan's civil war, characterized by atrocities on all sides, arose out of a personal dispute between the president and vice-president, both of whom commanded sizable personal militias.

Finally, states sometimes have the will but not the capacity to protect their own populations. As we observed in chapter 3, one unexpected development since 2005 has been the rise of non-state armed groups capable of operating beyond state control and perpetrating atrocities. Even if it wanted to protect populations beyond Baidoa and Mogadishu, Somalia's transitional authorities would find it difficult to do so. The same had been true in Iraq, where the Iraqi government had long proven simply incapable of protecting its population from IS atrocities. Fulfilling the responsibility to protect is not just therefore a matter of achieving the right mindsets within governments and societies; it is also a question of backing those mindsets with material capability.

Collectively, these different domestic conditions can increase the risk of atrocity crimes. Indeed, such crimes may be impossible in their absence. But they do not make atrocities inevitable. Far from it. Most countries and societies exhibit some risk factors but very few experience atrocity crimes. That is because atrocities require individuals and groups willing to perpetrate them. There needs to be a *reason* to commit atrocity crimes. Typically, perpetrators select atrocities as a rational strategy for pursuing their objectives, such as countering a serious existential threat, when there are either no viable alternatives or when the costs of alternative strategies are prohibitively high.[21] Whether committed as part of an armed struggle, to suppress a challenger, or to realize a program of radical social transformation, atrocities are a means to an end, not an end in themselves. Unless there is reason to think that their use might serve some purpose, even actors strongly predisposed toward committing atrocities will be unlikely to do so. This reason is usually provided by an acute crisis but it can also be generated by an elite's (exclusionary) ideology. Perpetrators also require the *opportunity* to commit atrocity crimes which may result from the weakness of institutional restraints and/or the support/ acquiescence of external actors.

The State: Potential and Practice

We observed earlier that there are significant limits to what outsiders can do to prevent atrocity crimes. To date, excessive attention to the "rescue fantasies" of outsiders has drawn attention away from the role of states, civil societies, private sectors, and individuals in affected countries in protecting themselves, mitigating risk, or driving communities over the abyss.[22] To fully understand the implementation of R2P, and make use of all available resources, our focus needs to be placed squarely on those domestic capacities that help societies reduce underlying risk and navigate peacefully through difficult times – much as the Nobel prizewinning National Dialogue Quartet did in Tunisia in 2013. The concept of "resilience" – a core theme in development and humanitarian circles that has not yet penetrated atrocity prevention – puts the focus squarely on the capacity of states and societies to prevent atrocities themselves. Within this context, the forging of trusting relations both between groups and between individuals, groups, and the state's formal institutions is crucial for the establishment of sustainable peaceful relations.[23]

In this section, we focus on the role that states play in facilitating the prevention of atrocity crimes and emphasize that political leaders and members of the wider community have choices about the type of political, institutional and economic relations that they want to establish and that these choices are consequential. We know this because states with similar structural conditions can experience wildly different trajectories owing to the decisions their leaders make. To give one example, given conditions of authoritarian government, deep social fragmentation, economic decay, and a history of civil war, Zimbabwe from the early 2000s contained all the elements necessary for internal conflict and atrocity crimes. That it has not suffered the same fate as many of its neighbors owes much to the conscious decision of opposition leader Morgan Tsvangirai to avoid armed resistance in the face of considerable pressure pushing in that direction. R2P works by instilling a sense of individual responsibility across states, political leaders, national communities, and civil societies. In this section, we examine the role of states and their societies in five key areas: the management of diversity; the exercising of legitimate and capable authority; the securing of livelihoods; the vibrancy of civil society; and – in conditions where atrocities were committed in the past – the guaranteeing of non-recurrence. Before we move onto these in more detail, two points are especially important to bear in mind. First, as we have argued throughout, there is no "one-size fits all" template to atrocity prevention. Each state and society needs to chart its own path, and there are multiple ways in which the goals set out here can be achieved. Second, we should recognize that periods of intense political transition or transformation can heighten the immediate dangers of violent conflict and atrocity crimes. As such, they need to be monitored closely and managed carefully

Management of Diversity

Because atrocity crimes are, in effect, extreme forms of identity-related conflict, the cornerstone of prevention is the building of an inclusive, non-discriminatory form of politics capable of managing diversity constructively.[24] There is much evidence to recommend the constructive management of diversity as a key part of structural prevention. States and societies imbued with multiple risk factors (diversity, histories of violence, weak institutions, and/or poor economies) that have adopted a constructive approach to managing diversity have tended to avoid atrocity crimes.

For example, post-independence Tanzania was founded on an inclusive ideology supported by strict policies to ensure equality between the country's main religious and ethnic groups, especially in the military and public sector. Although far from democratic, Zambia under Kaunda followed a similar path. Botswana adopted a consultative model of governance that blended the traditional with the modern and shared power through a Council of Chiefs. Following decades of military rule, Uruguay established a national human rights institution to address issues of accountability and impunity.[25] All of these countries have thus far escaped atrocities despite having many of the preconditions for them. Similarly positioned countries that embraced exclusionary ideologies have proven less capable of preventing atrocities. For example, successive Sudanese governments promoted an exclusionary Islamist ideology, both Tutsi- and Hutu-led governments in post-independence Rwanda enacted policies that clearly favored one group over the other, and Côte d'Ivoire's path to civil war and atrocity crimes began with the spread of *Ivoirité* – an ethnic ideology that intentionally marginalized immigrant groups and their descendants.

At the most abstract, the constructive management of diversity requires state ideologies and constitutions that pay respect to difference and incorporate different identities into the project of the state/society itself. As Scott Straus argues, "the long-term best asset against the risk of genocide and mass categorical violence is to craft a political vision that incorporates a role for multiple identities as fundamental to the project of the state."[26] The key to this, Straus argues, is for national leaders to "articulat[e] a nationalist narrative of pluralism and inclusion [which] provides the greatest source of restraint."[27] In practice, the constructive management of diversity requires laws and institutions designed to promote equality between individuals and groups and protect them against discrimination. In particular, it requires constitutional and legislative protections for human rights and the rights of groups as the principal bulwarks against discrimination. These protections should be overseen effectively by independent judiciaries and national human rights institutions or ombudsman's offices, with vibrant civil societies capable of holding authorities to account. The establishment of formal institutions and ombudsman's offices demonstrate a state's commitment to protecting diversity, while creating spaces through which populations can hold authorities accountable. For example, after the end of apartheid, South Africa built a comprehensive system of rights for minorities into its national constitution, supported by relevant institutional guarantees. Dealing with diversity also involves the prioritization of equality across groups in fields such as education, employment (especially public sector), and health.[28] In addition, comprehensive strategies for tackling exclusionary ideologies, combining coercive and persuasive approaches, are often needed, yet it is sometimes state authorities themselves that are responsible for the articulation and dissemination of such ideologies.

Finally, to avoid communal conflicts escalating to the point of atrocities, states need to ensure that potential disputes between groups have a means of peaceful resolution. Recognizing that where there are different identities there are likely to be conflicts connected to group loyalties and contending visions of justice, states and societies require means for managing (and ideally resolving) conflicts in a peaceful and constructive fashion. Most obviously, there is a need to prioritize the termination of any armed conflicts and beyond that a need for institutions to facilitate the peaceful management of disputes.[29] A good example is Ghana's National Peace Council, which promotes and facilitates the non-violent resolution of conflict, conflict prevention, and sustainable peace.[30] Another comes from Kenya, where after the violence of 2007–8, the government established a National Cohesion and Integration Commission to facilitate good relations between groups and peaceful dispute resolution, and to promote the principles of equality and peaceful coexistence, as well as to advise government on the steps it could take to advance national cohesion and eliminate discrimination.[31]

Legitimate and Capable Authority

Preventing violent conflict between groups is what stable, legitimate and effective states do, consciously or unconsciously, every day. As we have already argued, R2P aspires to a world of states that protect their own populations from atrocity crimes habitually. However, where governance and security sectors are unaccountable and rule of law is weak, the apparatus of state authority can be captured by sectional interests and utilized to further the goals of one group, often at the expense of the others, eroding the legitimacy of the state and sowing the seeds of future conflict. The capturing of state institutions by sectional interests – namely the Alawis and the Shi'as – lay at the heart of the conflicts that gripped Syria and Iraq from 2012, for example.

Arguably, the most basic condition in relation to this is the rule of law that upholds and sustains fundamental human rights. The UN's *Framework of Analysis* recognized this when it described atrocity prevention as an ongoing process "that requires sustained efforts to build the resilience of societies to atrocity crimes by ensuring that the rule of law is respected…"[32] According to former UN Secretary-General Kofi Annan, the rule of law:

> refers to a principle of governance in which all persons, institutions and entities, public and private, including the State itself, are accountable to laws that are publicly promulgated, equally enforced and independently adjudicated, and which are consistent with international human rights norms and standards. It requires, as well, measures to ensure adherence to the principles of supremacy of law, equality before the law, accountability to the law, fairness in the application of the law, separation of powers, participation in decision-making, legal certainty, avoidance of arbitrariness and procedural and legal transparency.[33]

Understood this way, the rule of law can help states and societies achieve a number of goods related to atrocity prevention, including inclusive, transparent, and accountable governance and protections for basic human rights. In practice, strengthening rule of law capacity for atrocity prevention calls for action in three main areas.

First, access to justice. The principle of equality before the law finds its meaning in the equal capacity of individuals and groups to access justice. This means that states must have sufficient judicial capacity, spread throughout their territory, to ensure that complaints can be brought before them, but also that people have equitable opportunities to bring matters to courts, knowledge about their basic rights, and sufficient information about the relevant justice institutions. It also requires that the justice dispensed be fair, impartial, and governed by transparent rules. Amongst other things, access to justice is improved by expanding the capacity of judicial institutions, ensuring judicial independence, the provision of education and training on rights and institutions, the lowering of financial obstacles to accessing the law, and the provision of legal support.

Second, effective and legitimate security forces are crucial for the rule of law. On the one hand, discriminatory and abusive security forces can either be the instruments of atrocity crimes or the catalysts for violent conflict. On the other hand, ineffective and corrupted security forces are less capable of protecting populations from atrocities perpetrated by non-state armed groups than professional forces. Broadly speaking, Security Sector Reform initiatives focus on three dimensions: (1) ensuring transparent and accountable civilian control of security forces (which may entail processes of disarmament, demobilization, and reintegration (DDR) in situations where there are multiple paramilitary and non-state armed groups); (2) ensuring the effective, transparent, and accountable management of security forces; and (3) ensuring the professionalization of the security forces so that they are capable of discharging their duties effectively and legitimately. But these are issues central to the daily functioning of states and their security sectors, and there tends to be significant resistance to change. Indeed, there is little indication as yet that states have considered R2P relevant to questions of internal security sector management.[34]

The third principal rule-of-law consideration relates to the need for transparent and accountable governance – simply put, ensuring that the political authorities are subjected to the same laws, and level of scrutiny, as everyone else. This might start with constitutional guarantees that government will be subject to law but needs to be reinforced with judicial institutions and security forces that are sufficiently independent to enforce the law equally and with other practices that promote transparency and accountability, such as a free press. It also involves systems of governance that are representative, inclusive, and accountable.

One of the most effective ways of making governments more accountable to their population is ensuring that they raise revenue from their citizens through taxation. Governments in resource-based economies, or those that are heavily dependent on foreign aid, tend to be less responsive to their citizens because they are not dependent on them for their income. Likewise, citizens have less invested in the state. Establishing taxation as a principal source of income gives the state an economic interest in protecting the population (it needs them to be productive) and gives the population an economic incentive to demand services and accountability from the state. Establishing a financial relationship between states and their populations, through taxation, contributes to atrocity prevention in a number of ways – by promoting accountability, inclusiveness, protection, and more effective service delivery.

A country's rule of law is typically correlated with the state's capacity to provide basic services, equitably, to its population. Independent and rule-governed institutions tend to be more professional and effective when it comes to the delivery of basic services such as health, education, and physical security. Moreover, effective institutions support societal resilience and adaptive capacity, address inequalities, reduce corruption, and mitigate tensions between groups.

Secure Livelihoods

Poorer countries are significantly more likely to experience violent conflict than wealthier countries, and countries with pronounced horizontal inequalities between groups are more likely to experience atrocities than those without. Economic shocks – and their impact on livelihoods – are among the triggers that drive societies toward violent conflict and atrocities. That there is a connection between economic well-being, equality, and proneness to atrocity crimes is widely accepted. Precisely what that connection is and how it operates is less clear. But it is no coincidence that, for example, the massive decline of atrocity crimes in East Asia between 1978 and today has accompanied an equally massive increase in that region's economic well-being responsible for lifting hundreds of millions of people out of poverty. Nor is the connection between the presence of lootable natural resources, weak or captured state institutions, and increased likelihood of civil war and atrocity crimes coincidental.[35] All this suggests that there are direct and indirect pathways between structural economic factors and the risk of atrocity crimes. It also suggests that policies and measures that enhance secure livelihoods indirectly contribute to a society's resilience to atrocity crimes.

Indirect connections between economic factors and atrocity crimes can be found in the correlations between wealth and violence and in the role of horizontal inequalities. Socioeconomic inequalities are not only a source of tension and conflict themselves, they can also limit a society's capacity to withstand and forestall atrocity crimes. For example, horizontal inequalities and poverty cycles help to fuel violence and atrocity crimes in different parts of Nigeria.[36] Arguably, the most important set of economic policies for the prevention of atrocity crimes are those aimed at reducing socioeconomic horizontal inequalities. These include antidiscrimination laws, ensuring balanced regional investments, and monitoring both government contracts and public-sector employment to ensure equality across groups – and the adoption of positive discrimination policies to address inequalities.[37]

Economic measures more directly related to preventing conflicts that give rise to atrocities include those designed to reduce corruption and those aimed at improving the management of natural resources. As noted earlier, the presence of lootable natural resources is related to a heightened risk of civil war and atrocity crimes. There are a number of reasons why this might be, but two stand out: (1) they help *cause* violent conflict between groups locked in zero-sum competition for the wealth generated by natural resources; and (2) they help *sustain* violent conflict by giving non-state armed groups access to tradable resources which they can transfer for weapons and ammunition. Preventing this entails the adoption of policies and strategies to ensure the legitimate and transparent management of natural resources and tackle corruption and practices of neo-patrimonialism that help reinforce social divisions.

Vibrant Civil Society Supporting a Plurality of Views

Although governments, non-state armed groups and international actors are often the key players whose decisions determine whether a situation escalates into atrocity crimes or not, it is important to recognize the wider range of actors that relate to these organizations and perform important functions, whether to support prevention or drive a country toward violence. Of course, civil society groups are not, by definition, virtuous since they can also play a key part in enforcing discrimination, articulating exclusionary ideologies, supporting hate speech and incitement, and providing material support to perpetrators. Indeed, civil society can have an especially pernicious effect when it squeezes out diversity and is captured by extremists. What we want, therefore, is for states to support civil society that nurtures a plurality of different views and that defends the right of groups to hold and express alternative perspectives while protecting the population from hate speech and incitement. In the past few years, non-state actors have occasionally played crucial roles in the prevention of imminent conflict and atrocity crimes. For example, the Nobel prizewinning Tunisian National Dialogue Quartet, comprised of civil society organizations representing organized labor, the private sector, the legal profession, and human rights advocates, navigated the country peacefully through a political transition that contained all the portents of violence and atrocities. Similarly, in 2013, KEPSA – the Kenya Private Sector Alliance – played a pivotal role in supporting atrocity prevention activities that helped the country avoid a repeat of the violence resulting from elections in 2007–8.

Vibrant civil societies that hold authority to account and create spaces for the resolution of disputes, along with active and free private sectors that reinforce the connections between peace, stability, and economic well-being, are therefore crucial – yet often overlooked – sources of resilience. Building societies resilient to atrocity crimes involves paying attention to the roles of actors beyond the state. It should be recognized that civil society groups and private actors are not innately positive and can also play pernicious roles. That is all the more reason why cultivating positive action within the non-government sector should be an important element in the implementation of R2P.

As the Secretary-General recognized in his 2009 report on R2P, vibrant civil societies can be a powerful source of resilience to the underlying risks of atrocity crimes. His second Special Adviser on R2P, Jennifer Welsh, explained in 2013 that "civil society...is often present in places where the government is not," and its representatives are often "the only witnesses when atrocities are committed."[38] In particular, the Secretary-General noted their capacity to correct abuses in the justice system; reduce the chances of would-be perpetrators avoiding international criticism; help survivors cope with the trauma of their experience; facilitate the learning of lessons from survivor networks; provide early warning of atrocity crimes; resolve, mediate and manage conflicts; support the rule of law; advocate for preventive action; support the normative consolidation of R2P; and support research, training, and education on atrocity prevention.[39]

At least three of these roles are especially crucial. First, civil society is a crucial partner in the establishment of the sorts of "inclusive processes" for atrocity prevention judged necessary by the Secretary-General in his 2014 report on R2P. Ghana's National Peace Council stands as a particularly good model for bringing different sectors of society – traditional leaders, women's groups, youth groups, and faith-based groups – together to resolve tensions and prevent violence. Second, civil society groups – sometimes working in partnership with government – can play important roles in defusing local tensions. Such groups tend to have broader coverage than the government and can be seen as being impartial in ways that governments cannot. Third, because civil society groups are rooted in their local communities, they are particularly well placed to monitor risk factors and provide early warning.[40]

Yet far from fostering more vibrant and open civil societies, several major states have moved to further curb their freedom of action and in particular their capacity to challenge the state. Since the outbreak of the Arab Spring in 2011, for instance, both Russia and China have introduced new laws designed to restrict the capacity of civil society to fulfill the aforementioned roles and in particular to question the government. Transnational civil society groups have been especially targeted, with legislation in Russia prohibiting the foreign funding of organizations deemed to be politically active by the state, while legislation passed in China in 2016 requires that all foreign non-state groups register their financial affairs with the state. Such clampdowns are common in states confronting instability since governments tend to view independent civil society as a threat to their authority. And while that might often be true, it is also the case that by limiting civil society's freedom of action, governments significantly inhibit a key source of resilience against atrocity crimes.

Guarantees of Non-Recurrence

Few questions are more sensitive – or more important – than that of addressing historical cases of mass atrocity. The question goes to the very heart of sovereignty, national and political identities, and contested understandings of the past. Opening up past issues is painful and potentially dangerous, yet one of the principal sources of risk of future atrocities is a recent past of atrocity crimes not properly dealt with. It is therefore important to pay close attention to those countries that have recently experienced atrocity crimes and to examine any additional efforts to prevent the recurrence of those crimes. Two interrelated issues are especially important in this regard: first, the need to ensure effective peacebuilding, which includes measures aimed at addressing the sources of past atrocity crimes; and second, the need to address issues of truth, justice, and reparation relating to crimes from the past. The first points to the need for a closer relationship between atrocity prevention and peacebuilding. The second points to the need for more attention to be paid to the UN Human Rights Council's thematic agenda on the promotion of truth, justice, reparation, and guarantees of non-recurrence.[41]

Within these rubrics, there are a number of discrete areas relevant to the structural prevention of atrocity crimes. First, in post-conflict settings, requirements for DDR and security sector reform (SSR) are especially pressing. Second, in order to break past cycles of impunity that could encourage past perpetrators to reoffend or past victims to commit reprisal atrocity crimes, it is imperative that perpetrators of past atrocities be held legally accountable for their crimes. There are a number of ways in which this might be achieved, including referrals to the International Criminal Court, special international tribunals, hybrid courts comprising national and international elements, national processes including the exercising of universal jurisdiction, and processes that combine formal prosecutions for senior leaders with more traditional forms of restitution for lesser offenses. Third, attention needs to be paid to the promotion and protection of human rights, and especially to combating forms of discrimination that may have given rise to atrocities in the first place.

According to the UN Human Rights Council's Special Rapporteur on the promotion of truth, justice, reparation, and guarantees of non-recurrence, guaranteeing non-recurrence requires a comprehensive strategy, which should be adopted by states in partnership with the international community in the aftermath of atrocity crimes. Core elements of such a strategy would include ensuring security for all and the ending of violations, especially against the most vulnerable; recognition of the legal right to identity for all, so that members of all groups can be legal persons before the law and access their rights through established institutions; ratification of relevant instruments of international human rights and humanitarian law and the passage of enabling legislation; legal reform aimed at de-incentivizing the perpetration of atrocity crimes; judicial reform to ensure judicial competence and independence; constitutional reform to remove discriminatory provisions, incorporate international human rights standards, regulate the security sector, ensure separation of powers, and facilitate judicial oversight of constitutional law; ensuring that education promotes critical thought and peacefulness by emphasizing different perspectives, international standards of human rights, and the resolution of disputes; utilizing cultural initiatives – museums, exhibitions, monuments, and theater – to memorialize past crimes, recognize victims, and build empathy and understanding; and ensuring that survivors are provided psychosocial support and trauma counseling.[42]

The record thus far is mixed, not least because R2P and post-conflict peacebuilding have generally been treated as distinct domains. On the one hand, significant strides have been taken toward achieving the non-recurrence of atrocity crimes in West Africa, especially Sierra Leone and Liberia. In both of those countries, a combination of state-led prosecutions and civil society-driven reconciliation processes has supported the embedding of peace. On the other hand, the UN and NATO and its allies failed to prepare for the peace in Libya, leaving the country badly fragmented and without a legitimate central governing authority. Elsewhere, successful transitions from atrocities to peace have been achieved precisely, in part, by avoiding questions of historical memory. In Indonesia and more recently Myanmar, peacebuilding has been based upon the idea that past crimes should not be confronted until peace has been well embedded. In both cases, the key to transition has been the capacity of reformers to persuade the military to accept reform in return for implicit guarantees that individual officers will retain their social and economic status. Myanmar's transition remains at an early stage and the ethnic cleansing of the Rohingya suggests that there is a long road ahead., Reform in Indonesia, in contrast, has proven highly successful, transforming the state from a serial perpetrator of atrocity crimes into a functioning democracy while steadfastly avoiding many of the historical memory issues described above.

Beyond the specific examples mentioned above, what steps have states taken to address these challenges? Most of what states do nationally to address discrimination, economic inequalities, or intergroup conflict is done without reference to R2P, atrocity prevention or even, more broadly, conflict prevention, so it is difficult to gauge precisely what states have and have not done. One useful source of record is the annual reports of the UN Secretary-General, which include numerous examples of situations in which states have taken steps to address atrocity crime risks. These examples are especially useful as they are sourced directly from the states themselves, showing that, even where policies are adopted without specific reference to R2P, the states adopting them understand them in terms of their responsibility to protect. Several states have, however, taken concerted steps to begin to integrate R2P into national policy.

The Obama Administration in the United States led the way in terms of incorporating atrocity prevention into foreign, defense, and aid policy, going so far as to include a section on R2P in its 2010 National Security Strategy.[43] Its activism in this area was partly a product of earlier initiatives, such as the Genocide Prevention Task Force, chaired by Madeleine Albright and William Cohen, and the Harvard University/Department of Defense (Peacekeeping and Stability Operations Institute) project on Mass Atrocity Response Operations, which produced a policy-planning handbook in 2012.[44] In 2010, President Obama appointed David Pressman as Director on War Crimes, Atrocities and the Protection of Civilians within the National Security Council. Two years later, the President announced the establishment of an Atrocity Prevention Board (APB) charged with assisting the government in identifying and addressing atrocity threats and overseeing institutional reforms designed to make the United States better able to respond. The APB includes representatives from the Departments of State, Defense, Treasury, Justice, and Homeland Security, as well as the Joint Staff, USAID, the US Mission to the UN, the Office of the Director of National Intelligence, the CIA, and the Office of the

Vice-President. These officials meet monthly at the level of Assistant Secretary (with individuals designated by name by the Principals), with a twice-yearly Deputies-level meeting and an annual Principals-level meeting to review the Board's work. Among its specific early tasks were monitoring preparation of the first National Intelligence Estimate on the global risk of genocide and atrocity crimes, working with the Director of National Intelligence to include information about the risk of genocide and atrocity crimes in his intelligence estimates to Congress, and establishing "alert channels" to facilitate the supply of information directly to the APB – if necessary, outside the usual chains of information flow.[45]

Although the realist scholar Stephen Walt complained that the APB would push the United States toward more foreign entanglements, the first few years of the Board's life suggests that the larger challenge may be in mainstreaming its atrocity prevention goals within the relevant departments so that this approach succeeds in changing practice across the foreign policy sector.[46] One recent study of the Board's work found that it may be necessary for the President to periodically remind senior foreign policy advisers of the importance attached to atrocity prevention in order to avoid the agenda's marginalization in the face of other pressing foreign policy concerns.[47]

The US has not been alone in incorporating atrocity prevention considerations into national policy. In 2013, Australia commissioned an independent assessment of its performance in implementing R2P and moved to fulfill two of its central recommendations: that diplomatic staff and aid workers receive training on R2P and atrocity prevention and that an atrocity prevention lens be incorporated into the reports that embassies feed back to the capital. Denmark and Germany have undertaken similar studies, and the UN Association in the United Kingdom published a report covering similar terrain for the United Kingdom.[48]

States have also developed networks to facilitate information sharing, mutual encouragement, and policy coordination. The most significant of these is the R2P Focal Points Network. More than a quarter of the UN's member states (55 by July 2017) have appointed a senior official as national R2P focal point, most – though not all – based in their foreign ministry. The R2P focal points initiative was launched in May 2011 by the governments of Denmark and Ghana (Australia and Costa Rica subsequently joined the facilitating group) and is administered by the Global Centre for R2P based in New York. An annual meeting of focal points has become a regular event. Unsurprisingly, given different systems of government and bureaucratic cultures, there is no single template for the role of a national focal point or uniformity on where within the government a focal point should sit. At the most basic level, the focal point is a senior official who is "responsible for the promotion of R2P at the national level" and for supporting "international cooperation on the issue through participating in a global network."[49] Additional roles that some (though not all) focal points have taken on include leading on the integration of atrocity prevention concerns into national policy (early warning and assessment, provision of atrocity-specific advice to other departments, etc.) and developing the capacity to convene departments and ministries to consider "whole of government" responses to actual or imminent protection crises.[50] One critical issue that continues to animate discussion is the question of whether the focal point should be primarily outward looking (focused on prevention externally) or inward looking (focused on domestic prevention). Ideally, the focal point should have both orientations but, given the configuration of most states into domestic and externally focused institutions, this is difficult to achieve in practice.

In April 2012, the Auschwitz Institute for Peace and Reconciliation (AIPR) established the Latin American Network for Genocide and Mass Atrocities Prevention in cooperation with Argentina's Ministry of Foreign Affairs and Ministry of Justice, Security and Human Rights. The Network has 18 member governments[51] and "was conceived as a capacity-building mechanism for the region, as well as a forum to support the development of more effective policy to prevent genocide and other atrocity crimes." Its members are expected to appoint a national focal point to "coordinate policy and share information" with each other. The AIPR has developed a training curriculum that will be used, when approved by the member governments, to train selected officials on the prevention of genocide and atrocity crimes.[52]

R2P also has Group of Friends networks based in New York and Geneva. Initially established by Canada to promote R2P prior to its adoption by UN member states in 2005, today the Group of Friends comprises around forty member states (there is no formal "membership" and attendance at meetings varies widely; the EU delegation to the UN also participates). The group describes itself as "an informal cross-regional group of UN member states that share a common interest in the responsibility to protect and advancing the norm within the UN system."[53] Thus the Group of Friends is primarily a network of diplomats based in permanent missions to the UN and is designed to assist with the coordination of strategy at UN Headquarters in New York. Chaired by the Netherlands and Rwanda (since 2010), the Group of Friends meets four times a year at ambassadorial level and occasionally at the working level to discuss matters related to the concept's political and conceptual development and situations of concern. Meetings often focus on specific country situations or developments within the UN. The Group has coordinated diplomatic strategy on the inclusion of R2P in Security Council statements and General Assembly deliberations and has coordinated support for the Secretary-General's proposals to the Fifth (Budget) Committee. The Group of Friends also works closely with the UN, inviting briefings from officials in the Department of Political Affairs and inviting the Special Advisers on Genocide Prevention and R2P and the working-level experts from the Office of Genocide Prevention and R2P to meetings as a matter of routine. The co-chairs also participate in an ongoing informal dialogue with the UN's office.

There are four key points here. First, that preventing atrocity crime requires concerted state-led action across a number of different sectors. In each country, the precise configuration of risks, sources of resilience, and institutional capacity and authority is different, lending credence to the view that there is no one-size-fits-all approach to implementing R2P, and that each country needs to develop its own approach. Second, that implementation of Pillar One responsibilities is difficult to measure precisely since it touches on many areas of government policy and many, if not most, relevant initiatives are not consciously associated with R2P. A practice or policy need not, however, be labeled R2P in order to be making an important contribution toward fulfilling it. After all, fulfilling their domestic R2P is what legitimate and capable states do every day as a matter of habit. Third, when we canvas what has been done by states to fulfill their responsibility to protect, the record is mixed. This is partly because states are sensitive about embracing R2P in domestic policy and remain deeply reticent about seeking, and taking, advice from outside parties since it implies both that they have a problem (which most states would rather not admit to) and that they are incapable of addressing it themselves.[54] That is hardly surprising, given that such guidance depends upon detailed understandings of specific contexts. Fourth, leadership and individual responsibility is crucial. Political leaders get to make choices about the rhetoric they employ, the institutions they craft, and the policies they pursue, and these choices are highly consequential. We have seen, for example, how in postcolonial Africa, leaders confronting similar sets of structural issues adopted different approaches to them with vastly different effects. Some pursued their own personal interests and those of their political tribes and patronage networks at the expense of the national interest and dragged their countries into civil wars; others embraced diversity and attempted to forge polities representative of the whole community. These countries tended to experience far fewer atrocities, despite confronting many of the same structural challenges. A further point is that, even within their domestic contexts, states do not operate in a vacuum. Instead, they act within a society that comprises other types of actors, such as civil society groups and the private sector.

Civil Society and the Private Sector

In chapter 3, we pointed out that, while states bear the primary responsibility to protect, they cannot alone achieve the goals of R2P. Non-state armed groups, civil society organizations, and the private sector all have a role to play if the goal of preventing and ending atrocities is to be achieved. This point, about the important role of non-state actors, was recognized by the UN Secretary-General in his 2009 report, *Implementing the Responsibility to Protect*. But while research has burgeoned on non-state armed groups as perpetrators of atrocity crimes and sometimes as facilitators of protection, the potential and actual roles played by civil society organizations and the private sector in atrocity prevention remain relatively obscure.

Thus, although R2P was born as an agreement between states, it is an ambition that cannot be achieved by states alone. Not only, as we noted in chapter 3, do the threats and challenges extend well beyond the world of states, states are themselves enmeshed in networks and structures that are beyond the control of any one of them. Thus the ability of states to protect their own populations and those of other countries is intimately connected to the role played by various types of non-state actor.

Civil society groups, private-sector actors, and prominent individuals, especially those found within affected countries and regions, can also play significant roles in helping to protect communities and individuals on the ground and in dampening the tensions that can give rise to atrocity crimes. The "individual responsibility to protect" perspective can help us here by illuminating different types of individuals acting in different sectors of the community.

Beyond this, there are a number of reasons why we should pay attention to civil society and the private sector. First, R2P is universal and enduring: that is, it applies everywhere, all the time.[55] The responsibilities of protection always exist; what differs is the best way of exercising them in any given context. With that in mind, whether civil society and private-sector actors accept their part or not, they do have a moral responsibility to do what they can, one entailed by the individual R2P. It is always, therefore, legitimate to ask whether these groups are contributing to the prevention of atrocity crimes or to their commission.

Second, actors beyond the state are effectual. Whether for good or bad, consciously or not, they influence the course of events in countries at risk of genocide and atrocity crimes. Non-state actors are not aloof from the forces that drive and inhibit atrocity crimes and should not be treated as such. Instead, they shape and are shaped by those forces and can influence decision makers in myriad ways. They can also play a role in determining the extent to which "leaders" find willing "followers."

Third, the forces of globalization are eroding the distinctions between public and private, national and international, spaces. On the one hand, advanced liberal states are turning increasingly to public–private partnerships and subcontracting to non-state actors as ways of delivering services more effectively, including services associated with security. On the other hand, many postcolonial states are essentially hybrid political orders that combine formal state institutions with a variety of less formal, non-state, practices and institutions.

Fourth, the disruption of distinctions between the public and the private can be heightened when atrocities are perpetrated, especially when this occurs in contexts of civil war or state fragility. In such situations, where there are "extremely violent societies," the state might be dysfunctional, its authority spatially limited, while private actors might assume more responsibility for basic functions such as governance and security.[56]

To better understand the different roles that civil society and private-sector actors play, it is useful to conceptualize them along a spectrum of action ranging from "perpetrator" at one end, to "protector" at the other and to think about the function of these roles at different stages of the atrocity cycle. At one end of the spectrum, civil society and private-sector actors can be the *direct perpetrators* of atrocity crimes, though this is quite rare since perpetrating is usually done by non-state armed groups. Nevertheless, there are situations where civil society groups or private-sector business are directly and knowingly involved in the commission of these crimes or provide material support to such acts. Prime recent examples include Radio Libre de Milles Collines, which played a crucial role inciting and directing violence during the Rwandan genocide of 1994. At the beginning of Indonesia's anti-communist massacres in 1965–6, in which some 650,000 people were killed, Nahdlatul Ulama (NU) was an Islamic party fiercely opposed to communist ideology. Under the tutelage of the Indonesian army, however, NU became one of the principal perpetrators of mass killing, often using agricultural implements to behead victims en masse.[57] Although there are no modern examples of private-sector actors constituting the primary perpetrators of atrocity crimes, there are innumerable historical examples.[58] For example, in 1623, the Dutch East India Company tortured and beheaded 20 people it suspected of plotting against its spice trade in Amboyna. Indonesia. There are, however, recent cases in which private-security personnel have been responsible for the commission of crimes which, in some circumstances, could be described as war crimes or crimes against humanity. This includes the well-documented abuses by personnel working for Blackwater in Iraq. More recent history has also provided examples of private companies engaged within systems of mass extermination. Perhaps the most obvious example is the dozens of German companies that operated civilian-worker camps to exploit the labor of Jews and other imprisoned groups prior to their extermination in the Holocaust. As the story of one of those involved in this practice, Oskar Schindler, shows, private-sector actors were fully aware of the system of extermination of which they were a direct part.

More commonly, civil society and private-sector actors have aided the perpetration of atrocity crimes through the provision of *direct or indirect assistance.* Direct assistance involves the provision of services or other resources to actors known to be perpetrators of genocide or atrocity crimes. For example, in October 2004 a Canadian mining company, Anvil Mining, transported members of the Congolese Armed Forces (FARDC) to Kilwa in the DRC, where it had a mine, to suppress a rebellion. The FARDC forces committed atrocity crimes including extra-judicial executions.[59] There are numerous examples of the provision of indirect assistance – the provision of goods or services that provide material assistance to the perpetrators of atrocity crimes. Vesselin Popovski, for example, describes how Talisman Energy and other multinational companies aided the Sudanese government's campaigns in Darfur and elsewhere through the transfer of royalty payments.[60] Other examples include the foreign companies that supplied Rwanda with the machetes used to perpetrate the 1994 genocide and the companies that helped Saddam Hussein amass a massive stockpile of chemical weapons, which he then employed against Kurdish civilians.[61]

As we observed earlier, some civil society groups get their hands dirty in support of the perpetrators of atrocity crimes. Indeed, it is very difficult indeed for perpetrators to sustain large campaigns of atrocity crimes without a significant degree of support from civil society. At the most general level, extremist civil society groups play a role in creating the social contexts that appear to make atrocities permissible – employing hate speech to dehumanize targeted groups, valorizing violence against them, and creating a supportive environment for the commission of atrocities against them. This goes some way to explaining why countries transitioning to democracy are especially vulnerable to atrocity crimes – the easing of authoritarianism creates space for the airing of long-suppressed radical views and the gathering of extremists into organized groups. All too often in such contexts, democratization is confused with "majority rule" and civil society helps legitimize and reinforce the majority's new tyranny. There are countless examples of civil society organizations helping to create conditions conducive to atrocity crimes and then supporting the perpetrators. Indeed, we would be hard pressed to find a case where this *did not* happen to some extent. For example, radical Serb nationalism was first given a voice by the Serbian Academy of Sciences and Arts (SANU), whose infamous leaked memorandum in 1987 set out a radical Serb nationalist vision that set in train Yugoslavia's demise and crystallized the objectives of other Serb nationalists, which were actively pursued through violence and atrocity crimes. More recently, IS has profited from the support of civil society groups who operate through the internet to spread the organization's propaganda, raise funds and secure recruits. Indeed, much like Serbian nationalism which originated from within civil society, radical Islamism was fermented within Egyptian civil society in the 1970s and 1980s.

Most common of all, though, is the role of bystanders. This is a morally and legally ambiguous role that in general demands greater understanding and explanation and is a function that the concept of the "individual R2P" can shed useful light upon. A bystander is commonly defined as "one who is present [in the sense of having knowledge about what is happening] but refrains from involvement," though it should be noted that bystanders occasionally cross the line into being perpetrators or rescuers, albeit temporarily.[62] Although often portrayed as passive, bystanders are crucial to the perpetration of atrocity crimes. Bystanders are not neutral in situations of mass atrocity – their decisions not to obstruct perpetrators or help victims facilitate the commission of these crimes. Indeed, for atrocities to occur at anything beyond a modest and selective level, it is *necessary* that the vast majority of private actors "stand by" and do nothing. As Laurel Fletcher points out, "those who orchestrate mass violence are aided by the failure of spectators to intervene. In this context, 'doing nothing' is 'doing something' – bystanders are thus an integral part of the killing apparatus."[63] Bystanders can be usefully further delineated into internal bystanders – those within the perpetrating society – and external bystanders, those with knowledge but who sit outside the perpetrating society itself. The list of groups and organizations that fit into the bystander category is enormous and extends to major transnational organizations. The Catholic Church as an institution chose not to take a stand against the Holocaust. Although some individual clerics aided the Jews and other victims of Nazi terror, others assisted and supported the bloodshed, while the institution itself remained largely mute. During the Khmer Rouge genocide in Cambodia, the human rights organization Amnesty International dismissed allegations of human rights abuse as nothing more than US propaganda. Over more than three years of Khmer Rouge rule, in which a quarter of Cambodia's population died or was killed, Amnesty did nothing to report on the country's plight and was thus complicit in the veil of secrecy that surrounded it.[64] Because R2P aims to prevent atrocity crimes from occurring in the first place, more attention needs to be given to the role of bystanders – large and small, domestic and transnational – and further thought given to the diffusion of responsibility to these groups.

Beyond "bystanders," we move into the positive roles that civil society private-sector actors can play in supporting R2P. One of the principal objectives of engaging with bystanders is to understand how, through the diffusion of responsibility, they might be encouraged to take positive steps to protect populations from atrocity crimes. These need not involve taking risky action to rescue vulnerable populations from imminent harm, though in some cases it might. As *indirect sources of prevention and protection*, civil society and private-sector actors stop short of taking conscious steps to prevent atrocities or shield victims, but through their everyday actions challenge would-be perpetrators, their legitimacy, and their support networks.

For example, the Alternative ASEAN Network on Burma (Altsean) works to document human rights abuses against vulnerable populations and ensure that their legal rights are respected. It thus uses the country's own constitution and human rights legislation to challenge extremist groups. Likewise, the West African Network for Peacebuilding (WANEP) established an early warning network to monitor and report on situations that could give rise to atrocity crimes and support grassroots efforts to resolve tensions before they escalate. Private-sector actors too can fulfill these roles in a number of ways. For example, they can facilitate positive and mutually beneficial interactions between groups through "gentle commerce."[65] Or companies might resist ethnic, religious, or gender discrimination by pursuing an inclusive and non-discriminatory approach to recruitment and promotion for entirely self-interested reasons (because hiring and promoting on merit produces the most efficient outcomes).

Civil society and private-sector organizations might foster the constructive management of difference within their organizations and thus set an example for the wider community. In these ways, they can help challenge the politicization of difference that can lead to atrocities and reinforce a sense of shared humanity. By doing so, they help reduce general and horizontal inequalities through their investment and employment decisions, making it more difficult for political agitators to stimulate conflict by aggravating economic grievances. When they behave this way, civil society and private-sector actors help reinforce the norms and cultures that challenge atavistic ideologies and practices of hate speech and incitement.

Civil society and private-sector actors can also be *direct supporters of prevention*. That is, they might make a more direct and conscious contribution to preventing atrocities than those outlined above. For example, civil society organizations might support mediation between groups to prevent conflict between them. In 2014, for example, the Dutch group PAX facilitated peace negotiations between the government of South Sudan and the "Cobra Faction" of the South Sudan Democratic Movement/South Sudan Defence Army (SSDM/A). PAX personnel mediated between the parties and provided logistical support to negotiations that resulted in a ceasefire agreement between the two parties.[66] Elsewhere, nationally based NGOs played a significant role in conflict transformation in Indonesia, the Philippines, and Thailand, especially through their grassroots and community work.[67] Private-sector actors can also provide logistical support to help prevention efforts and can offer pro bono services to support the various needs of those charged with atrocity prevention. One recent example of a comprehensive and joined-up approach to active atrocity prevention is that of the Kenya Private Sector Alliance (KEPSA), an industry association comprised of some 200 organizations that took active steps to prevent violence during the country's 2013 election. In the year immediately preceding the election, KEPSA implemented a campaign aimed at promoting peaceful elections and a peaceful transition of power, which included private meetings with key political actors, the promotion of peace in the wider community through initiatives such as a theme song for peace and a network of peace ambassadors, and a series of public events designed to reinforce the message. Individual members utilized their own capabilities to support the endeavor. For example, a mobile-phone provider, Safaricom, issued guidelines on how to block hate messages and took steps to prevent the spreading of messages inciting violence through the mobile-phone network.

Having been insufficiently organized to play an active role in prevention in 2007–8, KEPSA played an important role in the successful effort to prevent violence during Kenya's 2013 election. Its experience carries with it some important lessons, not least relating to the capacity for non-state actors to foster positive norms and encourage actors to adopt certain types of behavior. Not only did KEPSA actively promote peace within the wider Kenyan society, it also created powerful norms that identified certain types of behavior as appropriate or inappropriate. In particular, it promoted a politics of non-confrontation and created a powerful social incentive for actors to move beyond being bystanders.

This brings us to the final role – that of *rescuer*. As rescuers, civil society private-sector actors do whatever they can to protect civilians from harm, including by providing safe havens, facilitating escape, containing perpetrators, providing early warning, or maintaining a steady flow of information to the outside world. Often improvising in the face of great adversity, these actors have helped save thousands of lives through their direct – indeed, heroic – actions. There are countless examples of individual heroism that saved lives, including Oskar Schindler during the Holocaust (immortalized in the film *Schindler's List*) and Paul Rusesabagina during the Rwandan genocide (immortalized in the film *Hotel Rwanda*). Less well-known is Khushdeva Singh, a Sikh doctor who ran a refugee station during the bloody 1947 partition. Singh refused to allow Hindu militia to enter his camp to seek out Muslims and used a combination of bribery and deft diplomacy to smuggle all the Muslims in his care (more than 300) to safety. In our own time, the White Helmets – mostly Syrian civilian volunteers – were organized to respond to attacks on civilian housing during Syria's civil war, a job that mainly entailed pulling people – and bodies – from the rubble of buildings destroyed by indiscriminate fire (an atrocity crime). According to one source, by mid-2016, these civilian volunteers had saved as many as 60,000 lives.[68]

Past experience shows that humanitarian agencies (NGOs and others, including UN agencies) sometimes play a critical role in keeping people alive when populations are subjected to genocide and other atrocity crimes. As we mentioned earlier, when the storm of atrocity crimes breaks, humanitarian agencies – often locally based NGOs – are often the only international presence on the ground. This was true even of Darfur. At the beginning of the Darfur emergency in 2003, there were very few agencies present in either Darfur or in Chad and no peacekeepers or military observers. It was not until May 2004 – approximately 18 months after the killing and displacement began – that international agencies began arriving in significant numbers.[69] More often than not, in practice the task of protection is left to local communities themselves, sometimes with the assistance of humanitarian agencies. In these contexts, humanitarian NGOs can act as rescuers in at least four wars: by delivering life-sustaining assistance; by providing sanctuary for displaced people and refugees; by using their influence to support individuals and groups within government that promote respect for civilians; and by bearing witness to atrocity crimes in the hope that this will deter prospective perpetrators.[70]

Integrating these different non-state actions more fully into the practice of atrocity prevention and human protection essentially requires shedding light on the roles that they already play and demonstrating that being a bystander or a supporter of perpetrators is a positive choice that affects people's lives. Actors beyond the state can make critical contributions in at least three areas. First, norm diffusion: they can diffuse norms relating to inclusiveness, non-discrimination, equality of treatment, the rule of law, and rejection of violence through their everyday practices. They can help instantiate global norms and reinforce the unacceptablity of incitement, hate speech, discrimination, and violence as socially unacceptable. Evidence from social psychology tells us that social pressures such as these that define the limits of appropriate behavior exert a powerful influence on human behavior.[71] Second, non-cooperation: by moving beyond "bystanding" to non-cooperation, non-state actors can make it more difficult for perpetrators to secure sufficient legitimacy or material support for their actions. Third, active prevention and protection: as we have detailed above, there are multiple ways in which non-state actors can make a tangible difference by saving lives when atrocities are perpetrated or threatened. All this requires steps to diffuse responsibility for atrocity prevention and response across society through the notion of an *individual* responsibility to protect which expects everyone to do what they can to protect people from atrocity crimes.

Preventing, and responding effectively to, atrocity crimes requires determined action by states and non-state actors in the affected areas. States have the primary responsibility to protect their own population. Ultimately, R2P envisages a world of capable and responsible sovereigns that protect their own populations as a matter of habit. But states do not operate within a vacuum, they exist alongside a range of civil society and private-sector organizations. Nor are they unitary "black boxes." Instead, states comprise a range of institutions and individuals with different capacities, values, and intentions. As such, individual responsibility needs to be diffused throughout society if collective responsibility is to be achieved.

As the case of Kenya in 2013 (in contrast to Kenya 2008–9) shows, there is immense value in the development and implementation of national strategies to prevent violence that seek to meld the complementary efforts of state, civil society, and private-sector actors together in a common undertaking to prevent and protect. Yet the roles they can and do play are still not as well understood as they ought to be. More must be done to utilize domestic opportunities for prevention and protection where they exist and to support local endeavors to prevent violence. By forging key relationships with domestic actors in advance, international actors can build them into their networks of action. Through this, it may be possible to develop more comprehensive responses to atrocity crimes that make better use of human and material resources already *in situ*.

CHAPTER SIX

The Challenge of Prevention

As part of their commitment to the responsibility to protect (R2P) principle at the 2005 World Summit, heads of state and government pledged themselves to the *prevention* of genocide, war crimes, ethnic cleansing, and crimes against humanity and their incitement. Since then, governments, UN officials and analysts have repeatedly maintained that prevention is the single most important element of the R2P because it is morally, politically, financially, and prudentially better to prevent atrocity crimes than to react to stop them once underway. But despite this consensus about the abstract *merits* of prevention, it has proven difficult to make the prevention of atrocity crimes a "lived reality" in practice. Policy makers and analysts have tended to focus instead on timely and decisive responses to atrocity crimes. But if the past is anything to go by, waiting until the bodies begin to pile up before acting produces reactions that are often too little too late.

In November 2013, the Secretary-General announced the "Human Rights up Front Action Plan," which aimed – among other things – to make the Organization better able to fulfill its responsibility to prevent atrocity crimes. In announcing the action plan, the Secretary-General noted that the General Assembly, the Security Council, the Human Rights Council, and other UN bodies had further defined the human rights responsibilities of member states and the UN system, "with a special emphasis on their role to prevent armed conflict and to protect people from atrocities and egregious crimes." He continued, "when people face such risks they expect the UN to act, and the Organization's performance is rightly measured by this benchmark."[1] But despite some clear signs of progress, it has proven difficult to translate principled commitments to the prevention of atrocity crimes into effective international action. During the closing stages of Sri Lanka's civil war, for example, the international community was slow and confused in its response to civilian destruction, despite advance warning from the UN about the potential for atrocity crimes that accompanied the resumption of conflict.[2] The Secretary-General acknowledged this "systematic failure" to protect in Sri Lanka.[3] In Syria, clear warnings issued by the UN and others at the start of the crisis in 2011 failed to galvanize collective action to stem the tide of conflict, which resulted, ultimately, in atrocities on a massive scale. In the Central African Republic (CAR), the presence of a UN peacebuilding support office (BINUCA) did not prevent the UN being criticized for responding too slowly and timidly to the onset of atrocities in 2013. And, more recently, in Iraq and Syria it appears that relatively little was done to prevent the Islamic State's onslaught, characterized by widespread attacks on the civilian population, despite the widely acknowledged general threat of violent conflict and atrocities.

This chapter will set out the imperative for prevention, examine the challenges of making prevention a lived reality, and assess prevention in practice, including efforts to build preventive capacity, to link to peacebuilding, and to avoid recurrence. The chapter will emphasize how interrelated prevention and response are in practice. This connection suggests the need to treat prevention and response as fully integrated pieces of our overall strategies for curbing atrocity crimes in particular situations. It will show that the natural tendency to think of these as two distinct policy challenges organized along a chronological continuum of response has hurt our efforts in a number of cases. What is required, we will argue, are policy responses driven by fine-grained and dynamic assessments of situations at hand, where a premium is placed on the flexible tailoring of policies to specific situations.

We proceed in four main parts. The first examines the place of prevention within R2P. The second considers the practice of prevention since 2005 and highlights some of the key challenges that have emerged. The third part focuses on the role of peacekeepers in preventing atrocity crimes. The fourth focuses on the battle against impunity as a deterrent to atrocities and evaluates the complex relationship between R2P and the International Criminal Court.

The Prevention Imperative

Since the Carnegie Commission's landmark report on the prevention of deadly conflict in 1997, it has been common to separate prevention into two components: *operational* prevention, aimed at preventing violence that is imminently apprehended, and *structural* prevention, aimed at reducing or mitigating the underlying risks of violent conflict.[4] In practice, however, the lines between the two are quite blurred. This is also the case when it comes to the three pillars of R2P, since aspects of prevention can relate to all three depending on the context. In what follows, we will show how prevention can be both a consensual measure designed to encourage or support the state (Pillar Two) or be part of a set of policies designed in response to violence (Pillar Three). For example, multidimensional UN peace operations typically comprise elements of both. This reflects the fact that effective prevention entails activities aimed at both the underlying sources of risk and the more imminent triggers of violence. What is more, even when violence erupts, R2P calls for ongoing efforts to prevent atrocity crimes. It is also important to emphasize the relationship between R2P, prevention, and post-conflict peacebuilding. Countries are at their most vulnerable as they emerge out of violence. As such, effective peacebuilding is a crucial part of the prevention, and the two should be seen as overlapping agendas.[5]

We should underscore at this point that the international community has only a limited capacity to prevent atrocities. As Scott Straus has argued, international actors can play a "supporting role" but "it is very difficult, if not impossible, for international actors to impose new political narratives or to impose peace on ruling elites who do not want to compromise."[6] International action to prevent atrocity crimes is therefore best understood as an exercise in *supporting* certain actors, institutions, and capacities and *influencing* behaviors. An effective partnership with global, regional, national, and local actors is key to both of these aspects.

Another point to recognize is that, although they are related, atrocity prevention should not be viewed as being synonymous with conflict prevention. A question commonly posed is whether atrocity prevention simply duplicates work already undertaken under the rubric of conflict prevention. Proponents of the view that it does maintain that sophisticated approaches to conflict prevention already take account of atrocity prevention considerations to such an extent that the latter ought simply to be understood as a subcomponent of the former.

The most obvious reason why this should not be the case is that not every atrocity crime is perpetrated within a context of armed conflict. As such, while conflict prevention may contribute to the prevention of atrocity crimes, most obviously in response to crises in places such as South Sudan (2014–16) and Yemen (2011–12), it does not cover the full spectrum of situations in which atrocities occur. Recent examples of atrocity crimes committed outside a context of armed conflict include post-election violence in Kenya (2007–8), riots in Osh, Kyrgyzstan in 2010, intercommunal violence in Rakhine state, Myanmar, in 2012, and the early atrocities in Syria, committed *before* the crisis there became a fully-fledged armed conflict. Around one third of the major atrocities perpetrated since 1945 occurred *outside* a context of armed conflict.[7] What is more, not every armed conflict triggers atrocities as the decade-long civil war in Nepal demonstrated. As such, preventing armed conflict between groups or states may be insufficient to prevent atrocity crimes.

More fundamentally, however, conflict prevention and atrocity prevention have different *purposes*. While the former tries to find a mutually agreeable settlement, the latter is focused on dissuading actors from committing atrocities.[8] As a result, conflict prevention strategies are sometimes unsuited to the prevention of atrocity crimes, as they proved in Bosnia (1992–5), Rwanda (1994), and Darfur (2004–). In these cases, perpetrators and victims were treated similarly by international mediators, and the international community stopped short of deterring or coercing actors for fear of inhibiting the chances of a negotiated resolution. In some other situations, conflict prevention undertaken without a view to deterring atrocities may encourage atrocities by groups wanting to "earn" a seat at the table, as was apparent in the DRC.[9]

With these in mind, the key purposes of atrocity prevention might be summarized as entailing three main components. First is the building of local and national resilience by supporting efforts to mitigate risk and strengthen the "inhibitors" to atrocity crimes. Described at greater length in the previous chapter, this aspect of atrocity prevention is sometimes associated with "structural" conflict prevention, as it involves helping states and societies reduce the factors that constitute underlying risk of atrocities and build resilience both to these sources of risk and to the "shocks" that can trigger the escalation of conflicts. It specifically includes measures to challenge ideologies and hate speech that lay the normative foundations for atrocity crimes.

The second involves influencing behavior so that political leaders are less likely to allow or instruct their followers to commit atrocity crimes. As the field of international criminal justice well recognizes, atrocities occur because military and political leaders *choose* to authorize or permit them and armed individuals *choose* to commit them. At its most basic, atrocity prevention – as distinct from conflict prevention – is about persuading them to choose not to. This implies measures along the full range between the entirely consensual and the utterly coercive. At one end of the spectrum, leaders might be dissuaded by genuine efforts to resolve a dispute or recognize their legitimate grievances. International actors might promote compliance by socializing or diffusing international norms, or by reporting in detail on the situation so that local actors know that their violations will not go unrecorded. Or they might induce good behavior by offering rewards, including political recognition and support and financial incentives. At the other end of the spectrum, non-consensual measures might be utilized to either *deter* leaders from committing atrocities or *coerce* them into changing course. Measures might involve the use of coercive diplomacy, targeted sanctions and embargoes, threats of legal accountability, non-recognition or conditions on negotiations, promises of support to adversaries, threats of military force or other measures, or the use of lawful but covert actions, all with the intent of increasing the cost of committing atrocities relative to the cost of not doing so. If groups commit atrocities primarily because they are cost-effective ways of achieving an objective, measures designed to increase those costs may inhibit perpetrators and encourage them to adopt an alternative course.

The third requires denying perpetrators the means to commit atrocities. Also a form of cost raising, international actors can sometimes prevent atrocities by making them more difficult to execute effectively. The most obvious measures include embargoes on arms and ammunition, financial sanctions, measures to prevent foreign fighters joining the cause, and jamming communications and incendiary media. Other approaches involve putting space between the would-be perpetrators and their victims by, for example, deploying peacekeepers with mandates to protect civilians, establishing safe zones, and facilitating flight into safer regions or third countries. On the ground, direct measures include seizing weapons and ammunition, seizing shipments, and employing tactical level force to protect civilians under immediate threat.[10] One aspect of this is recognition of the specific sets of circumstances that "trigger" atrocity crimes. These are not limited to the outbreak of armed conflict but can also involve other forms of political violence, protest movements under authoritarian regimes, contested elections, and intercommunal disputes, among other things.[11] A society can endure high risk for many years, but it is not until there is a triggering event that precipitates violence that atrocities occur. Anticipating triggers and understanding how societies themselves anticipate and respond to the "shock" of potential triggers is critical.

From this brief discussion, it should be clear that prevention cuts across the three pillars of R2P (state responsibility; international responsibility to assist the state; international responsibility to take timely and decisive action in response to atrocity crimes). Tailored to meet individual circumstance, prevention might entail measures that involve a combination of all three pillars. What is more, as Jennifer Welsh points out, preventive action can be both intrusive and controversial. It should not be assumed, therefore, that prevention is a "safer" policy option than the "response" element of R2P, in part because in practice the two are closely related and in part because prevention may sometimes require action that is every bit as controversial (if not more so) as actions taken in response to atrocity crimes.[12] As such, political boldness is needed if atrocity prevention is to be turned from theory into lived reality.

Prevention in Practice

In some situations, such as Darfur (2003), Sri Lanka (2008–9), and more recently Libya (2011) and Syria (2011), atrocities erupt in places where the international community has only a limited field presence. Often, in these situations, the in-country efforts of the UN, regional organizations, or bilateral partners are focused on humanitarian or development issues and are not necessarily configured for responding to the rapid onset of a protection crisis. In these situations, the international community's capacity to directly influence events on the ground is generally limited to: (1) employing diplomatic means to persuade the parties to refrain from committing atrocities; (2) providing humanitarian assistance and safe-passage options to vulnerable populations; and (3) encouraging individual states or political bodies such as the UN Security Council to adopt or support measures to prevent atrocity crimes (either direct measures targeted at the parties or indirect measures to protect populations). In this section, we focus on the third of these elements for two main reasons. In the first place, the success or failure of diplomatic entreaties depends mainly on the willingness of the parties themselves to reach an agreement and abide by it. When the parties are not willing to resolve their differences through negotiation, there is relatively little that outsiders can do in the short term to force them into this position. Sometimes external pressure might encourage or coerce compliance, but this then becomes more a function of the exercise of influence by states or international organizations than of their peacemaking skills per se. Secondly, we examined the role of humanitarian actors in the previous chapter. Moreover, the main challenges in relation to humanitarian assistance are the enduring problems of access, security, and protection that plague the sector as a whole.

The international community's recent record in this area is mixed. At one end of the scale, the UN joined the AU in supporting successful diplomatic action to prevent the escalation of atrocities in Kenya in 2007–8. At the other end, events in Sri Lanka in 2008–9 marked "a grave failure of the UN to adequately respond to early warnings and to the evolving situation during the final stages of the conflict and its aftermath, to the detriment of hundreds of thousands of civilians and in contradiction with the principles and responsibilities of the UN."[13] In that case, very little was done by the UN to prevent atrocity crimes until the final stage of the crisis when the Secretary-General intervened directly. More recently, the horrors of Sri Lanka have been surpassed by Syria. With the UN Security Council divided and deadlocked on how to respond, the international community has managed only a series of ineffectual diplomatic initiatives and a humanitarian effort that has failed to reach many of Syria's besieged communities for long periods and that has itself become a target.

In most cases, performance has fallen somewhere between these extremes. For example, in South Sudan and CAR, UN officials tried – and largely failed – to persuade the parties to comply with their legal obligations. They succeeded, however, in persuading the UN Security Council to adopt a wider set of measures, though in the case of South Sudan even the significant reinforcement of the UN mission (UNMISS) there has fallen well short of what may be necessary to prevent atrocities, and in the CAR many judged that the international response to the crisis came too late and was too limited. The UN also succeeded in marshaling significant humanitarian responses to both crises – though responses to the plight of South Sudanese civilians have been plagued by access problems, and humanitarian action in the CAR has been criticized for its timidity in the face of the escalating crisis.

One of the critical issues to emerge in a number of cases is the international community's inability to translate concerns and analysis about the likelihood of atrocity crimes into clear warning and action. This is a derivative of the "prevention dilemma" noted earlier: the difficulty of persuading governments and publics to commit attention and resources (political and material) to addressing crises that have not yet arisen and, thus, about which considerable uncertainty remains. As former New Zealand Permanent Representative and President of the Security Council Colin Keating points out, governments are predisposed to be risk averse owing to concerns about the opportunity costs and political dangers associated with preventive action.[14]

Arguably, the clearest example of this was provided by the Internal Review Panel's report on the UN's response to the crisis in Sri Lanka. The Panel found that the UN system generated ample evidence and analysis to predict that a militarized crisis in the Wanni region of Sri Lanka would pose serious dangers to the civilian population. There was also evidence to suggest that this risk included the danger of war crimes, ethnic cleansing, and crimes against humanity. These signals were not translated into clear early warning assessments and were not systematically incorporated into policy planning. In the opinion of the Review Panel, that was because "the analysis and understanding of the conflict within the UN as a whole was inadequate."[15] There are times when officials do not want to hear facts and analyses that do not fit their assumptions and that would imply courses of action that they do not want to pursue.

Although Sri Lanka offers one of the most clearly documented cases of the difficulty that the international community confronts in translating early warning analysis into effective policy, it is not the only example. Annan's diplomatic efforts to resolve the crisis in Kenya in 2007–8 were widely lauded, but some analysts have pointed out that there were clear warning signs of likely communal violence, signs that were identified before the event by some foreign officials based in Nairobi, but that these were not picked up or acted upon until *after* atrocities were committed.[16] Likewise, although the UN had an Integrated Peacebuilding Office (BINUCA) with conflict prevention and human rights components in the CAR, which identified the risk of atrocity crimes associated with the escalation of conflict between the anti-Balaka militias and those loyal to the government as early as late 2012 (prompting a decision to withdraw non-essential staff), it was not until September/October 2013 that the UN's Special Adviser on Genocide Prevention and High Commissioner for Refugees began to publicly discuss the commission of atrocity crimes and risk of genocide. By that stage, the anti-Balaka militia had already embarked on a systematic campaign of ethnic cleansing and crimes against humanity that resulted in the forced migration of approximately 80 percent of the country's Christian population. As in Kenya, the UN adopted policies and messaging about preventing atrocities in the CAR only *after* atrocities had been perpetrated. The same was also true in Libya in early 2011. Before violence erupted there, nobody suspected that Libya would experience atrocity crimes. More recently, threats of atrocities by jihadist extremists in Iraq were also predicted, yet there was little discernible effort to prevent them until atrocities were perpetrated and the Yazidis were confronted with genocide.

As noted above, the biggest barrier to effective early warning is often political, in that key decision makers do not want to know. But there are also mechanical and procedural shortcomings. For instance, at times analysis pointing to the risk of atrocity crimes has not been translated into credible warnings and preventive action because of a gap between the collection and analysis of data that could warn of future atrocities and its proper assessment and utilization for atrocity prevention purposes at UN headquarters and amongst individual states. This gap derives from the multiplicity of agencies and departments that have mandates relating to protection and other atrocity considerations, the devolved nature of the UN's engagement with individual states where field presence is limited, and the lack of a defined focal point within UN headquarters capable of collecting and assessing information and analysis from the field and providing authoritative advice to the organization's senior leadership and its member states. The UN's lead agency on human rights (OHCHR) has a direct role in monitoring and assessing situations only when it is specifically tasked and its mandate does not relate directly to risks associated with atrocity crimes. Although the UN's Office on Genocide Prevention and R2P has strengthened its analytical capacity, it has not yet developed the sort of analytical capacity or operational networks necessary to fulfill this role – nor is such a role widely envisaged for the office. The nub of the problem here is that across these different cases there was little consolidated and credible assessment of available information with a view to providing early warning of atrocity crimes and no process by which atrocity-specific analysis might inform the UN and international community more broadly. To be sure, individual states, such as the United States in the case of the Middle East or France in the case of the CAR, may have had access to detailed intelligence about unfolding events, but it is likely both that intelligence reports did not utilize an atrocity prevention lens, so that particular risk was not fully appreciated, and that these reports were not shared sufficiently.

This brings us to the fact that, despite commitments to the prevention of atrocity crimes, the UN and most of its member states still lack a systematic institutional focus on this issue. Indeed, one of the concerns raised with regards to the UN's "Rights up Front" initiative noted earlier was that although its purpose as articulated by the Secretary-General was clearly focused – in part – on atrocity prevention, its approach is directed exclusively to human rights and does not include a specific focus on atrocity prevention. How this manifests in practice is that atrocity prevention is usually only one among a "mosaic of considerations" guiding how the international community responds to emerging situations that include a risk of atrocities.[17] As mentioned earlier, when crises emerge in situations where the UN has a limited field presence, the organization's engagement with the host country is usually guided by agreements with the government relating to development and humanitarian operations. This can pose acute problems, especially in situations where the government is responsible for creating some of the atrocity risks or is (as is often the case) unwilling to acknowledge the presence of risk, because the UN's operations depend on the cooperation and goodwill of that same government. In this context, the perceived need to preserve existing programming, including the delivery of urgently needed humanitarian aid, can sometimes override atrocity prevention considerations. As former Emergency Relief Coordinator Sir John Holmes argues, field missions need to take difficult decisions about what to prioritize in a context where promoting atrocity prevention might backfire, resulting in a loss of host-state cooperation or humanitarian access without delivering commensurate gains in the form of protection. This, in his view, would leave vulnerable civilians worse off overall.[18] This dilemma is especially acute in a context where the UN's Country Team has no specific mandate relating to atrocity prevention or where the UN as a whole has no identifiable framework for addressing these risks.

The devolved nature of UN engagement with individual countries and the absence of an atrocity-specific focus, either within the UN or within the external policies of most states and regional organizations, compound the problems of early warning described earlier. It means that, while warning of future atrocity risks might be generated, it is difficult, politically and institutionally, to translate this analysis into actionable recommendations. We can see this, for example, in the role played by the UN's human rights teams in advance of atrocity crimes. The OHCHR focuses relatively consistently on the human rights dimensions of unfolding crises, but it often has only a limited field presence. In Sri Lanka, for example, there was only a single Human Rights Adviser, who was not consulted on major decisions, and the UN's pre-crisis engagement in Syria did not have a human rights component. Where the OHCHR did have a more significant presence, for example through BINUCA in the CAR, its work did not directly address problems associated with atrocity prevention.

The UN and other organizations have tended to lack the flexibility needed to quickly reorganize their field presence to make them better able to fulfill protection responsibilities when atrocity risks emerge. In rapidly deteriorating situations, there is a critical need for organizations to translate early warnings into decisive actions, yet in practice atrocity prevention only rarely comes to the fore amongst the contending priorities. Indeed, dating back to the Rwandan genocide, some states, including non-permanent members of the Security Council, have repeatedly complained that they were not always adequately informed about developing situations in which there was a risk of atrocity crimes and as such were unable to demand or lead decisive preventive action. Sometimes, crucial pieces of information emerge too late to be acted upon. These political problems can also create reticence about publicly identifying responsibility for civilian casualties and about confronting armed groups for their failure to comply with their legal obligations. Although in some cases, such as Syria, the UN was quick to publicly identify and attribute responsibility for atrocity crimes, in others – such as South Sudan and the CAR – it was relatively slow to do so.

Another consequence of the failure to take full account of atrocity risks in policy deliberations is that the protection of populations has tended not to be a significant factor in determining whether to withdraw staff from conflict-affected areas or keep them in place despite the heightened risk. As the UN's Internal Review Panel on Sri Lanka concluded "the relocation of international staff out of the conflict zone made it much harder for the UN to deliver humanitarian assistance to the civilian population, to monitor the situation, and to 'protect by presence.'"[19] In Sri Lanka, and more recently in the CAR, the UN was criticized for withdrawing international staff on security grounds in situations where the populations they were working with were judged to be at serious risk from atrocity crimes. Withdrawing international staff to reduce their exposure to risk effectively left their host populations to their fate and significantly reduced whatever protection could have been afforded to them, as well as limiting the UN's capacity to provide accurate and detailed information to member states.

Another issue is the coordination of preventive action within and between states and international organizations. Coordination is, of course, a long-standing issue across a whole range of UN activities and one that the Rights up Front initiative was to address. Five aspects of these larger issues relate directly to atrocity prevention.

1 There is sometimes an absence of leadership and responsibility. The UN's Internal Review Panel on Sri Lanka found that "it was unclear who had overall leadership or responsibility for the UN response to the escalating crisis."[20] This created confusion among states about who was responsible for what and what the overriding objectives of the international community's actions ought to be.

2 International engagement with developing crisis situations utilizes a number of different coordination mechanisms that are not always well cohered. These include regional early warning and response systems, humanitarian early warning, mechanisms employed by individual states, and the UN's own systems for internal coordination. Sometimes this can encourage "forum shopping" by the perpetrators, who select which international framework they think would be most favorable.

3 As crises emerge, the international community is often confronted with the challenge of having to juggle simultaneous considerations that sometimes impose contradictory demands. The UN Security Council, for example, has to balance its primary Charter-based responsibility for the maintenance of international peace and security with its more recently acquired R2P responsibilities, which may not always demand the same courses of action.[21] This places a premium on the achievement of a political consensus among the great powers and relevant regional players on the nature of the problem and the best way of addressing it, something which is often difficult to achieve owing to the different interests of states and their differing interpretations of the facts on the ground.

4 As situations evolve and escalate, the lack of a coordinated system-wide response focused on atrocity crime risk makes it more difficult for field missions to adjust themselves to reflect the new circumstances. For example, neither the mandate nor staffing of BINUCA's human rights component was altered to respond to the serious deterioration of conditions on the ground from late 2012.[22]

5 The international community rarely communicates to the parties with a single voice. Inconsistencies between the positions taken by different states

or organizations undermine the credibility and hence the effectiveness of diplomatic messages. This problem was especially pronounced in Sri Lanka, where the sending of inconsistent messages undermined demarches pointing to civilian casualties caused by government action. Mixed messages have also been a problem in Côte d'Ivoire, Darfur, South Sudan, East Timor (prior to the referendum), and Bosnia (in relation to safe areas, especially).

International action is more likely when the international community is provided with timely and accurate information about the potential for commission of atrocity crimes. Conversely, when information is sketchy, conflicted, or inaccurate, it is much more difficult to galvanize a decisive international response. This is borne out by recent experience in Sri Lanka, the CAR, and South Sudan, as well as Syria to some extent. Although significant progress has been made to improve the flow of information and analysis about atrocity risks to states, this remains a largely ad hoc process. Some aid agencies, for example, suggest that part of the reason for the world's late response to the unfolding crisis in the CAR was the slowness of the UN's humanitarian agencies and Department of Political Affairs to properly assess the situation and advise states. There was a delay of almost twelve months between the identification of credible atrocity risks by field personnel in the CAR and the launch of a concerted effort by officials in New York to bring the situation to the attention of member states. Likewise, although the threat of genocide posed by jihadist extremists in Iraq was well understood, the UN did not raise the issue publicly with states – or communicate atrocity-specific analysis and advice to them – until *after* the threat began to be realized in Iraq in mid-2014.

There are a number of reasons why the UN, in particular, sometimes finds it difficult to provide accurate and timely information about the risks of atrocity crimes. First, in some situations it may simply lack the field presence and analytical capacity to identify the warning signs. The UN's capacity for atrocity-specific analysis remains very modest. Not only do field missions not provide the Office on Genocide Prevention and R2P with regular information about emerging risks and challenges, but those agencies and departments with greater analytical capacity, such as DPA and OHCHR, do not systematically examine risks relating to atrocity crimes. Second, officials within institutions – and not just the UN – are notoriously conservative when it comes to predicting atrocities. Stemming from the "dilemma of prevention" noted earlier, there is a pervasive culture of conservatism that makes analysts and senior officials reluctant to brief on emerging threats for fear of being wrong. Perceived political imperatives dictate a degree of self-censorship. When it comes to atrocity crimes, there is not yet an embedded "precautionary principle" similar to that found in public health. Third, the corollary is that governments are often not receptive to engaging with outsiders on emerging atrocity risks. States are rarely willing to acknowledge a risk of atrocities close to home, As such, public or even private briefings on emerging risks strain relations with the state concerned, making cooperation with that state more, rather than less, difficult to manage. This is an especially acute issue where ongoing humanitarian operations depend on the cooperation of the government, but it also has an impact on the capacity of UN officials to engage constructively with the relevant government.

Prevention Through Peacekeeping

Studies have repeatedly shown that, overall, peacekeeping operations make a positive contribution to the prevention of atrocity crimes. Compared to similar cases where no peacekeepers are deployed, the deployment of peacekeepers reduces the overall number of expected civilian casualties, the duration of armed conflict, and the likelihood that violent conflict will reemerge. A 2014 study by the UN's Office of Internal Oversight Services (OIOS) found that the preventive and political work of UN peacekeeping operations has "notable and positive results" for the protection of civilian populations. Thus, "[c]ivilians invariably attach high value to missions' physical presence, which evidence suggests had a huge deterrent impact and avoided violence that otherwise would have occurred...The value of such deterrence is unquantifiable but enormous."[23] Naturally, some missions are more effective than others, but there is little doubt that collectively vulnerable populations are better served by the deployment of peacekeepers than by their non-deployment. Over the past few years, considerable progress has been made by the UN to improve implementation of civilian protection mandates, especially in relation to the provision of guidance and support to missions in the field.[24]

The challenge of atrocity prevention – and the expectations associated with it – is somewhat different in situations where multidimensional operations are deployed to countries with a high risk of atrocity crimes. Yet there are also significant points of overlap with the considerations described earlier. Effective and timely two-way communication between the field and decision makers in New York can often be a challenge; while peacekeeping operations are nowadays relatively well coordinated, they do not have a specific focus on atrocity prevention and may sometimes prioritize other goals; and while member states are typically more engaged when there is a peacekeeping mission – not least because the situation is on the Security Council's agenda – this can sometimes serve to magnify the opportunity costs associated with raising atrocity prevention concerns.

The central limitation to the prevention of atrocity crimes by UN peacekeepers is the enduring gap between the expectations attached to peacekeeping operations and the capabilities available to peacekeepers. In short, while local populations and some member states expect peacekeepers to protect populations from atrocities, UN peacekeeping missions rarely have sufficient capacity to do so.[25] This capability gap is caused by a combination of demand-side and supply-side factors. On the demand side, host states are typically reluctant to consent to the intervention of a large and well-equipped peacekeeping force unless they calculate that it is in their interests to do so, which is rare. On the supply side, the UN Security Council is reluctant to mandate, and fund, large peacekeeping operations, and troop-contributing countries are increasingly stretched.[26] As a result, most operations do not have the capabilities needed to provide comprehensive protection to civilian populations.

The problem confronted by UN peacekeeping is made more acute by the fact that peacekeepers are often deployed without necessary force enablers, such as helicopters, ground transportation, weaponry, intelligence capabilities, communication assets, and hospital support. Indeed, rarely do UN peacekeepers have access to sufficient enablers. For example, one study found a 40 percent shortfall in the number of helicopters deployed in peacekeeping operations, compared to the number judged necessary by the Security Council. Thus UNAMID in Darfur had only five of its authorized 24 helicopters and MONUSCO only 19 of the 29 authorized.[27] Even the number of helicopters authorized to these missions is well below the ratio of helicopters to soldiers found in NATO operations. Beyond helicopters, UN operations tend to lack the transportation capabilities they need to make them responsive to rapidly emerging threats and challenges, especially if these occur outside their immediate area of deployment.

The result is that even relatively large peacekeeping missions are seldom able to prevent atrocity crimes throughout their area of operations or to respond quickly and effectively to emerging situations beyond their immediate areas of deployment. Consequently, military protection efforts usually focus on specific geographic areas, be they "safe havens/areas/zones," "safe corridors" for transit, or undesignated areas close to the peacekeepers' bases. The rationale for designating safe areas is that through the concentration of force, peacekeepers can carve out secure areas.[28] The problem with this approach is that it only protects those civilians that are able to make it into the safe zone, encourages displacement as civilians flee their homes for the safety of the safe zone, and facilitates the concentration of civilian populations, making them more vulnerable to atrocities if the peacekeepers fail to defend the zone (as happened in Srebrenica in 1995). In addition, protecting civilians in one area leaves them vulnerable to violence elsewhere: by default, creating "safe zones" renders other areas as "danger zones" where atrocities might be committed with little to inhibit them.[29]

While the presence of UN peacekeepers is judged to have a significant deterrent effect on would-be perpetrators of atrocity crimes, when "civilians are actually being harmed, evidence demonstrates that performance is highly ineffective."[30] That is primarily because UN peacekeepers remain deeply reluctant to use force to protect civilians even when they have the mandate to do so. A 2014 report by OIOS found that missions with civilian protection mandates responded to attacks on civilians only 20 percent of the time, and that responses almost never involved the use of force. In the remaining 80 percent of cases, UN peacekeeping missions with protection mandates did not respond to reported attacks on civilians. During the reporting period (2010–13), UN peacekeepers suffered no casualties as a result of interposing themselves between attackers and their civilian victims, despite interposition being an option indicated by the UN's Operational Concept for peacekeeping. In none of the ten largest incidents of attacks on civilians evaluated by the report had UN peacekeepers used force during the incident. Most often, this was because they were not present at the time of the attack, but, even when they were present, peacekeepers never opted to use force despite being authorized to do so. Shows of force to deter anticipated attacks were also extremely rare, though there were some documented examples.[31] The result is that, although UN peacekeeping has an effective and inherent deterrent effect, it is ineffective at protecting civilians once an attack commences.

The OIOS identified six reasons for this reticence to use force. First were differences of view in the Security Council and among troop-contributing countries (TCCs), especially with regards to the degree of risk that should be assumed by peacekeepers, the level of violence sufficient to warrant a forcible response, and the relationship between protection and the other principles of peacekeeping (consent, impartiality, minimal use of force). Second was a de facto dual line of command through which TCCs try to minimize the risks faced by their troops by, amongst other things, issuing "national caveats" effectively ruling out the use of force. Third was confusion about the responsibility of missions to act when host governments are unable or unwilling to fulfill their responsibility to protect. Fourth was a pervasive self-image – probably driven by the material facts documented above – that UN operations are weak and outnumbered, making force an unrealistic option. Fifth was fear of incurring penalties if the use of force is subsequently judged excessive. Sixth was a frequent inadequacy in tactical-level guidance concerning the realities and complexities of operations on the ground.[32] Combined, these factors created powerful disincentives for risk taking to protect civilians, which further compounded those derived from capability limitations.

To conduct kinetic operations to prevent atrocities, military forces require access to accurate and timely intelligence in order to establish good situational awareness and a capacity to predict when and where atrocity crimes will be committed. The aforementioned point, that UN peacekeepers are hardly ever able to respond during an attack on civilians because they are seldom present, indicates that there are serious flaws in the capacity of missions to acquire, assess, and utilize information in order to predict – and prevent – atrocity crimes. It is perhaps not surprising, therefore, that several member states have pointed to the UN's limited capacity for intelligence gathering as a key limitation to the implementation of its protection of civilians mandates.[33]

The effective implementation of protection mandates imposes a heavy burden on intelligence, which is generally regarded to outstrip the capacity of most

UN peacekeeping operations to deliver. In addition to building a capacity to generate human intelligence on the emergence and direction of risks to civilian populations, UN operations also require detailed information about armed groups – their intentions, plans, supply lines, financing, locations, and equipment. All this basic information is required to enable peacekeepers to anticipate attacks and prepare adequate responses.[34] Yet, in practice, intelligence capacity falls well short of this goal.

These problems notwithstanding, there have been significant advances. The gathering of human and open source information is now done systematically and there are some examples of UN missions utilizing advanced technology to monitor situations – such as the use of CCTV by UN Force in Cyprus to monitor the Green Line in Cyprus and the employment of ground surveillance radar by the Irish Quick Reaction Force in Liberia as part of UN Mission in Liberia.[35] But this sort of equipment is embedded within the troop contributions offered by advanced developed states and is not available across UN peacekeeping operations. What is more, member states with sophisticated intelligence-gathering technology have generally proven reluctant to share that technology or the information they gather through using it with the UN.

In 2014, the UN trialed the use of unarmed, unmanned aerial vehicles (UAVs) in eastern DRC. There, subcontracted UAVs have been used to gather information on the movements of militia and arms transfers, respond to reports about potential threats to civilians, and provide the UN's humanitarian agencies with information about the accessibility of roads.[36] In other missions, western TCCs may be embedding UAV capabilities within their contributions, such as the Dutch and Swedish contingents in Mali (MINUSMA). Although a potentially important development, the use of UAVs will not by itself resolve the UN's intelligence problems for a number of reasons. On the one hand, the UAVs that the UN has at its disposal have a limited range and their use is constrained by weather and geography. On the other, UAVs can only provide certain types of information and contribute directly to protection if they are supporting a maneuverable force capable of responding quickly to emerging situations outside its immediate areas of deployment. In addition, there are a range of political and other issues that will need to be addressed, such as the extent to which information extracted from UAVs should be supplied to the relevant sanctions committee of the UN Security Council, the UN's human rights monitors, or the ICC. While there is a clear case for utilizing this information in these ways, doing so runs the risk of undermining the perceived impartiality of UN peacekeepers, making them more susceptible to attack and potentially fraying relations with host states. South Sudan, for example, has already refused to permit the UN to deploy UAVs with UNMISS, despite their obvious utility for civilian protection.

This brings us to a final point for this section, which is that, in practice, atrocity prevention is only one of a number of objectives that a UN peacekeeping operation is mandated to achieve. Not only does this reduce the singular importance of atrocity prevention, it also raises the prospect that robust action to prevent atrocities might make it more difficult for the mission to achieve its other goals. In practice, therefore, missions might make trade-offs by judging that there is more to be lost than gained by responding to threats of atrocity.

In this regard, it is worth remembering that it has proven difficult to eliminate threats to civilians entirely through the use of force, and that using force against militia groups may make it harder to secure their cooperation in the future. Cases where peacekeepers succeed in eliminating threats are rare: the British assault on the West Side Boys in Sierra Leone, NATO's strikes against the Bosnian Serbs, and the defeat of M23 militia in the DRC by the United Nations Stabilization Mission in the Democratic Republic of Congo (MONUSCO)'s Force Intervention Brigade provide the best examples, but the first involved a small and politically marginal militia group, the second came in the context of wider military reverses on the ground, and the latter succeeded in eliminating one militia but not the many others that continued to pose a threat. More often, groups are weakened by the use of force but may regroup and return to attacks on civilians. Although its earlier use of force succeeded in weakening the FDLR and restricting its freedom of movement, the UN Mission in the Democratic Republic of Congo (MONUC) neither destroyed the militia nor forced it to disarm.[37] The FDLR responded by negotiating an alliance with the DRC government, prompting the 2008 conflict with the National Congress for the Defence of the People that had devastating effects on the civilian population. The point here is that military efforts by themselves are unlikely to eliminate threats to the civilian population and might make it more difficult for the mission to secure other goals, such as a peace agreement with a particular militia group, humanitarian access to affected civilian populations, and cooperation on the implementation of sanctions, embargoes, elections, and other initiatives mandated by the Security Council.

In this context, peacekeeping missions might be encouraged to make trade-offs – setting aside protection considerations in return for cooperation on other matters on the grounds that the former would be unlikely to enhance protection and that the latter would be feasible and could make a positive difference. These trade-offs are further encouraged by the general reticence to use force described earlier.

Related concerns include the gap between those countries that champion robust protection and those that actually provide the troops to do it. Several major troop-contributing countries, including India and Pakistan, object strongly to the use of force for civilian protection, partly because they are concerned about force protection issues and partly because of their principled commitment to a traditional vision of peacekeeping. Indeed, several UN officials working in peacekeeping have expressed concern privately about the potential of a robust approach to protection to politicize and hence threaten hard-won consensus on the protection of civilians both in general and in specific situations. Another concern is that the Security Council might be encouraged to see peacekeeping primarily as a panacea for a range of atrocity prevention issues, and that the UN's member states and local actors would expect peacekeepers to provide a degree of physical protection that they are simply not able to offer. While the former might lead to more peace-keeping deployments in situations that are not suited to peacekeeping, the latter risks weakening public faith in peacekeeping by raising expectations far beyond anything that could be achieved by blue-helmeted peacekeep-ers. Whatever one thinks of the merits of individual concerns, there is little doubt that in practice the multiplicity of priorities leads to trade-offs. Given the other major challenges facing forcible responses to civilian protection threats, it is hardly surprising that it is this that is often traded for other perceived goods.

Prevention Through Deterrence: R2P and the ICC

It is sometimes said that the responsibility to protect (R2P) and international criminal justice are like cousins.[38] They are closely related but should never marry. This section seeks to explain why. We will argue that R2P and inter-national criminal justice for atrocity crimes are complementary projects that are, on the whole, mutually supportive.[39] But they are not, however, synony-mous and should not be treated as such. Nor should one agenda be instru-mentalized to serve the purposes of the other. There are two main reasons for this view. First, each has its own individual mandates and strengths. Each contributes most successfully to the overall goal of greater human protection when allowed to pursue its own agenda unfettered by the requirements of the other. Establishing a global culture of legal accountability for atrocity crimes would undoubtedly contribute to the goals of R2P. Likewise, progress on the prevention of atrocity crimes – promised by R2P – would undoubtedly help the ICC and similar institutions to achieve their goals of ensuring legal accountability for atrocity crimes and ending impunity. Making international criminal justice the handmaiden of R2P, though, risks making it selective and political without necessarily adding to the prevention of imminent atroci-ties.[40] Second, there are situations in which the demands of immediate protec-tion and the prevention of imminent crimes (R2P) may require actions that undermine principles of legal accountability. For example, negotiators may have to cut deals with the perpetrators of atrocity crimes, and peacekeepers may be dependent on cooperation with groups that have perpetrated atrocity crimes or may have to make conscious decisions not to apprehend alleged perpetrators of atrocity crimes for fear of disturbing the peace. What is more, as the political fortunes of R2P and international criminal justice ebb and flow, so does their utility to one another. In its early years, R2P was widely seen as a politically toxic concept because of its alleged association with western interventionism not always motivated by humanitarian concern, a concept best avoided by others operating in the human protection space. However, since 2011, the concept has been normalized in the work of the Security Council to the point where it is now an established norm. At the same time, the ICC has become more controversial. Where ICC advocates may have once been reluctant to utilize R2P for fear of undermining global consensus, in more recent times R2P advocates have looked to distance themselves from the ICC. In both 2014 and 2015, for example, governments and R2P advocates were prepared to drop controversial references supportive of the ICC from draft Security Council resolutions that included references to R2P.

Many advocates and scholars on both sides of the disciplinary divide between R2P and international criminal justice regard the ICC and other criminal tribunals as "tools" for implementing R2P. The ICISS report described the ICC as one potential "tool" for the prevention of atrocities and claimed that the Court's Rome Statute was one of the "sources" of R2P.[41] In his 2009 report, the UN Secretary-General noted that, "By seeking to end impunity, the International Criminal Court and the United Nations-assisted tribunals have added an essential tool for implementing the responsibility to protect, one that is already reinforcing efforts at dissuasion and deterrence."[42] Contarino and Negron-Gonzales agree, seeing the ICC as "a powerful tool for the enforcement of the R2P norm"; Weiss and Serrano situate the ICC in the UN Security Council's "toolbox" for implementing R2P; and Wallace sees the Court playing a powerful role in R2P's "operationalization."[43] But it is not only R2P scholars and advocates that have viewed the principle's relationship with the ICC in largely instrumental terms. Even the ICC's Chief Prosecutor, Fatou Bensouda, has commented that the Court is a "critical tool" for implementing R2P.[44] Her predecessor, Luis Moreno Ocampo, suggested an alternative – but no less instrumental – view of the relationship, proposing that the ICC "could add legitimacy to the Security Council's decision to apply the Responsibility to Protect concept."[45]

It is certainly true that R2P and international criminal justice can be mutually supportive. Both, for instance, rest on the principle of complementarity – the idea that the state should assume primary responsibility for protecting its populations and providing legal redress for violations should they occur and that international institutions should step in only when the state fails to fulfill its responsibility. Each state's primary responsibility to protect entails a duty to investigate and prosecute alleged atrocities, reinforcing the international criminal justice principle of complementarity. Luis Moreno Ocampo made the point emphatically when he observed that:

> the scheme envisioned by the Responsibility to Protect where each individual State has the primary responsibility to protect its populations from genocide, war crimes, ethnic cleansing and crimes against humanity, including the

prevention of such crimes, and the idea that the international community will only step in when a State is failing to do [it] is very much the scheme retained in Rome for the International Criminal Court, the same concept, including the gravity threshold retained for the Responsibility to Protect is also close to our own legal standards under the Rome Statute.[46]

Likewise, the second pillar of R2P (relating to international assistance) entails responsibilities to provide practical assistance to the ICC and other criminal tribunals and to promote capacity building to augment each state's capacity to prosecute its own perpetrators of atrocity crimes.[47]

The two projects also have much in common. They share a similar background and normative intent, both stemming from the failures to protect people from atrocity crimes in Rwanda, Bosnia, and elsewhere in the 1990s, and a commitment to improving human protection. They share a grounding in state sovereignty and an interest in promoting responsible sovereignty. They both espouse a "humanity-based defense of international authority" and, as noted above, are underpinned by the principle of complementarity. Above all, however, R2P and international criminal justice have a mutual concern with the prevention and punishment of international *crimes*. Thus the UN adopted the phrase "atrocity crimes" to explain R2P's scope and coverage, and the second Special Adviser to the UN Secretary-General, Jennifer Welsh, articulated a "crimes prevention" approach to implementing R2P, drawing from the field of criminology.[48]

But, despite the ubiquity of the claim, a marriage of this sort carries dangers for international criminal justice and R2P that could inhibit the capacity of both to deliver on their core mandates. That is because, while they share these similarities, R2P and international criminal justice are also different in important respects. Unless international society reaches a utopian condition in which all states become responsible sovereigns that protect populations from atrocities and accept the universal jurisdiction of the ICC, these differences will mean that it will not always be the case that what is required practically to achieve the goal of one (for example, the protection of a particular population) will necessarily help the cause of the other (for example, the prosecution of a particular perpetrator). Potential contradictions arise in practice, and how they play out in individual cases will need to be carefully managed to ensure that the pursuit of one objective (be it R2P or criminal accountability) does not undermine the pursuit of the other.

There are at least three key differences. First, although the overall vision of R2P and international criminal justice is arguably the same (a world without atrocity crimes), their specific *purposes* are different. R2P focuses on the prevention of atrocity crimes and their incitement and on the protection of vulnerable populations. The ICC, on the other hand, was established to prosecute the perpetrators of those crimes.[49] Thus, while – in theory at least – R2P is forward-looking and proactive, international criminal justice is by necessity backward-looking and reactive. Criminal justice is concerned with principles of accountability and judicial independence, which are at most only secondary considerations for R2P.[50] Proponents of international criminal justice complain that the appropriation of crimes language by non-judicial bodies, such as human rights monitoring missions or UN officials, has led to the uneven application of criminal-law standards and raised questions about due process (in relation to the naming of individual suspects) and investigative methodologies (i.e. witness protection).[51]

Viewed another way, we might say that R2P intends to marshal direct action to prevent atrocity crimes and protect vulnerable populations, whereas the ICC's contribution is largely indirect. Thus R2P requires that when a state manifestly fails to protect its own population from atrocity crimes, the international community should adopt measures through the UN Security Council and relevant regional organizations. In this context, states should cooperate to provide physical protection to vulnerable populations (in the form of peacekeepers, civilian monitors, humanitarian aid) while seeking to persuade and/or coerce the actual or would-be perpetrators into changing their course of action (through diplomacy and moral suasion, sanctions and embargoes, military measures), while diminishing their capacity to commit atrocities (through arms and other embargoes, etc.). International criminal justice has a much less direct effect. Proponents argue that a permanent standing court, such as the ICC, can deter future would-be perpetrators by reducing the prospects for impunity, but the initial evidence suggests that any preventive effect is indirect and applicable only under certain conditions. There is now evidence that the Court's investigations can have a strong deterrent effect on governments and non-state armed groups that seek international legitimacy, but its wider effects remain unclear.[52] Nonetheless, this can at best be an indirect and long-term cumulative effect, not the sort of direct and immediate influence required by R2P. But, in a sense, the whole debate over whether international criminal justice prevents atrocities misses the core point, namely that its purpose is the pursuit of *justice*, not the prevention of crimes or protection of populations from them.

Second, R2P and international criminal justice have different normative and institutional characteristics. Whereas R2P is a *political* commitment to implement existing legal obligations that states have under IHL through existing international institutions, the ICC is a novel and permanent legal institution designed to prosecute and punish grave violations of IHL. The latter is based on the solid foundations of international treaty law, whereas R2P's more diffuse normative status is based on a combination of hard law, soft law, and national and international practice. Whatever its long-term merits or problems, R2P's diffuse character makes the norm more flexible than hard-law institutions, such as the ICC, and thus more readily tailored to individual situations. R2P draws upon a variety of political concepts (e.g. "sovereignty as responsibility" and the "international duty of care") and legal foundations and is wedded only to the rules and institutional settings established by the UN Charter, which are themselves adaptable in the face of changing global conditions. The flexibility that derives from norm ambiguity can help build consensus amongst states with different perspectives (by allowing multiple interpretations of the norm), protect the norm from damage resulting from its application in especially controversial or difficult cases, and facilitate incremental reform aimed at securing greater compliance.[53] As a result, for example, controversy over the implementation of R2P in relation to Libya did not inhibit the norm's use by the Security Council in subsequent crises in South Sudan, Mali, the CAR, Somalia, Yemen, and even Syria.

Beyond this, the ICC is, in principle, hostile to the international use of force, preferring peaceful judicial processes. Amendments to the Rome Statute (Article 121.5) have extended the Court's jurisdiction to the crime of aggression. The 2010 Kampala agreement defined the crime of aggression as any act which constitutes by its "character, gravity, and scale" a grave violation of the UN Charter. Discussion is ongoing as to how the amendment should be activated. One potential problem is that the new clause could act to deter states from using armed intervention to save populations from atrocity crimes, including genocide, especially when the Security Council is unable to issue a mandate. States confronting a repeat of the situation in Rwanda could not know for certain whether a unilateral intervention to halt genocide would later be judged a sufficiently grave violation of the Charter to constitute aggression. Given that states are already concerned about the costs and responsibilities associated with armed intervention to end atrocities, this legal uncertainty would likely only further compound their hesitancy to act in a situation like Rwanda. By contrast, while exhibiting a strong preference for prevention and peaceful responses to atrocity crimes, R2P acknowledges that the coercive use of force may sometimes be necessary as a measure of last resort – though, by insisting that this be authorized collectively by the UN Security Council, such an intervention would not fall foul of the ICC's definition of aggression.

Third, R2P and the international criminal tribunals have different "jurisdictions." As a political commitment made by all UN member states, R2P "applies" everywhere, and all the time. As the UN Secretary-General has pointed out, there is never a situation in which states *do not* have a responsibility to protect or in which the international community does not have a responsibility to take action in response to atrocity crimes.[54] For R2P, the appropriate question is not one of *whether there is* a responsibility for protection, but how that responsibility is best *exercised*. By contrast, whereas the ICC's legal and institutional character is a source of strength, it also serves to limit the Court's jurisdiction. Only alleged crimes committed within the territory of states parties, against the citizens of states parties, or referred to the Court by the UN Security Council fall within its jurisdiction, limiting the scope of its coverage. Not surprisingly, in practice many atrocity crimes since 2005 have been committed in countries that are not states parties to the Rome Statute. In order words, in many cases where R2P is put to work, the ICC has no automatic jurisdiction. As such, given that decision making in the Security Council about whether or not to refer a situation to the Court is always highly political and three of the permanent members are not states parties, the Court's involvement in situations of ongoing atrocity crimes almost always adds political complications in practice. What is more, there are also clear signs that the selective and politicized use of the Court by the Security Council has impacted negatively on the Court's own legitimacy.

At is most fundamental, the difference between R2P and the ICC is that one is *political* and the other *legal*, yet in practice sometimes the legal is put into the service of the political and vice versa. This raises a number of obvious problems and objections. For example, diplomats and peacekeepers working under a mandate to protect populations from atrocity crimes sometimes require a degree of flexibility that the law cannot provide. In 2006, for example, the UN dispatched its Chief of Humanitarian Affairs Jan Egeland to Uganda to negotiate a peace agreement with the notorious LRA. The LRA and its leadership were, at the time, under indictment by the Prosecutor of the ICC after a self-referral from Uganda. It is possible that it was the ICC investigation that triggered the LRA's interest in negotiations but, that notwithstanding, Egeland was convinced that the group was seriously interested in peace overtures. However, the LRA insisted that the indictment against its leader be lifted as part of any agreement. This is where the clash between the political and the legal became obvious since Egeland had no authority to even request such an arrangement and, once that became clear to the LRA, the negotiations collapsed.[55] From an entirely pragmatic R2P perspective, it might be argued that the inflexibility of the ICC cost an opportunity to negotiate an end to atrocities by the LRA. From the legal perspective, however, any such compromise would have fundamentally damaged the Court's independence and its battle against impunity. The situation also illustrates why it was decided at the outset that the ICC would not be part of the UN system.

This is where we come to one of the principal critiques of R2P itself, which is that, being a norm constituted by international society, it is unable to marshal the fundamental political reforms needed to end atrocity crimes. Critics such as Heather Roff maintain that R2P is flawed precisely because it does not impose legally binding demands on states. It is easy, the critics contend, for states to commit to a nebulous international R2P since – unlike international jurisprudence – the norm places no specific demands on any particular actor.[56] Nor are its demands legal in character, limiting the extent to which they can generate state compliance. As such, some international lawyers have tended to dismiss R2P as mere political rhetoric incapable of shifting state behavior.[57] Yet they should acknowledge that legal-based approaches, dating from the 1948 genocide convention, if not earlier, have not provided the solution to the human protection challenges posed by atrocity crimes. It has been the introduction of R2P that has given new life to efforts to implement long-existing international law.

This line of critique raises fundamental questions about the drivers of change in world politics and the relationship between laws and norms in state compliance. Advocates of R2P have tended to embrace the concept's political foundations and embeddedness within the existing order, albeit while recognizing the constraints that this imposes. Part of this is to do with political pragmatism and the urgency of responding to the problem of atrocity crimes. If what is required is a legally binding set of duties to save strangers from atrocities, then we need a fundamentally different type of international society – one comprised of Kantian republics prepared to put the common good ahead of their own self-interests. States that are deeply cautious about a flexible political commitment such as R2P are hardly likely to commit themselves to binding international legislation. If possible at all, therefore, this more thoroughgoing reform is a long-term political project which leaves us with the question of what to do in the here and now.

R2P is still in its formative stages, as both a practice and field of study. There is a clear policy imperative for the careful tailoring of different measures to address the problem of preventing and responding to atrocity crimes in different contexts, yet we still do not have a sufficient evidentiary base on which to draw conclusions about the types of action most likely to support protection. This is abundantly clear, for example, in the relationship between R2P and the ICC. We have a range of case studies and anecdotes but as yet only limited systematic understanding of the relationship between prevention, protection, and prosecution. What is required is a more finely grained approach to understanding particular cases in greater depth and a more systematic approach to comparative analysis and the generation of generalizable insights about practice. Perhaps inevitably for a field so young, the study of R2P and atrocity crimes has thus far focused almost exclusively on the normative and practical value of the norm itself. What the field needs is a turn to the more careful and sober study of specific practices and cases, drawing upon a range of disciplines, so that we may get a clearer sense of causal chains.

Conclusion

Although states have repeatedly committed themselves to doing more to prevent atrocity crimes, the reality is that the record is mixed and that prevention confronts significant practical challenges. Not least, the will to prevent must compete with other priorities for attention and resources. In that context, there are many reasons why the international community too often fails to prevent atrocities. Sometimes, as in Syria, it is because one or more parties are so determined to commit atrocities that there is little besides armed intervention that would stop it. Often, states resist suggestions that they may face atrocity risks and push back against offers of assistance. Contrary to popular opinion, preventive action is no less controversial and politically sensitive than responsive action. In some ways, it is more difficult to galvanize action to prevent atrocities that have not yet occurred (and may never) than it is when the fact of atrocities is all too evident. At other times, the failure to translate early warning into decisive action stems from the inability of states to reach agreement on the nature of the threat or the most appropriate form of response. It is possible, however, to discern ways in which the UN's own practices and procedures sometimes inhibit effective atrocity prevention, some of which have been identified here. A principal issue, and recurring theme in the preceding analysis, is that in its engagement with troubled states and societies, the UN and allied organizations often have multiple concerns and, sometimes, competing priorities. This was clear in our discussion of peacekeeping and the ICC where atrocity prevention sits, not always comfortably, alongside broader peace and security issues and justice considerations respectively.

Because the international community still typically deals with atrocity risks in an ad hoc fashion, seeing them as extensions of its work on the protection of civilians, human rights, or humanitarian response, it is sometimes the case that atrocity prevention concerns are not prioritized, even when atrocities are imminent. As a result, foreign policies and international organizations are seldom configured for atrocity prevention, even when there is evident risk, and nor are they reconfigured even when the evidence of risk mounts. Although there have been enhancements to the UN system's capacity, neither the UN nor the wider international community have articulated a coherent and compelling *strategy* for atrocity prevention. Developing such a strategy ought to be a priority for the next decade.

CHAPTER SEVEN

Making a Difference: Lessons from Experience

In practice, R2P has had an uneven track record. On that, there is no question. As preceding chapters have underscored, the advent of R2P has made seminal normative, conceptual, and political contributions to thinking and policy making on the prevention of atrocity crimes and the protection of populations. Putting these insights and impulses into practice, however, has been challenging, as expected. As discussed below, there have been a number of cases in which the application of R2P principles has appeared to make a positive difference. Historical comparisons are difficult, however, because of the lack of clearly articulated international standards or strategies for preventing atrocity crimes. Neither was developed over the six decades between the adoption of the Genocide Convention in 1948 and the 2009 enunciation of Secretary-General Ban Ki-moon's R2P implementation strategy. Whatever the successes, the human cost of the failures in places like Syria, Yemen, the Sudans, and Sri Lanka has been horrendous. This chapter offers one way of identifying and weighing some of the factors that have been associated with failure or success in a series of situations. Its analysis is rough and its conclusions only suggestive, but it may raise some pertinent questions about prevailing assumptions and policy preferences, as well as point to some avenues that would benefit from more intensive and extended research.

This chapter looks at a series of factors across eight situations, four of which resulted in massive atrocities and four of which saw some initial atrocities followed by relatively successful national and international efforts to stem their escalation. Six of the factors considered in this chapter were preexisting at the time of the crisis and nine others relate to the international response. The four failed situations include Rwanda (1994), Srebrenica (1995), Sri Lanka (2009), and Syria (2011 on), while the relative successes include Kenya (2007–8), Guinea (Conakry) (2009–10), Kyrgyzstan (2010), and Côte d'Ivoire (2010–11). These cases were selected because they had identifiable critical decision-making points, as opposed to long-running armed conflicts with multiple decision points, such as the DRC, Somalia, and Sudan, and because Luck served as Special Adviser for R2P through the last six cases and was able to participate directly in the UN decision-making process. The atrocity crimes in Rwanda and Srebrenica occurred before the advent of R2P, but they were included both to provide a baseline and to get a sense of whether the lessons learned in the UN's inquiries into those failures had been absorbed in the responses to the latter crises. It would be hard to judge whether, how, and where R2P approaches to policy making have, or have not, been making a difference without looking at pre-R2P policy making.

The six preexisting factors addressed in this chapter include the following:

- a history of communal (whether ethnic, ideological, or sectarian) violence and/or the threat of such violence at the time of the crisis;
- a history of election-related violence and/or the threat of election-related violence at the time of the crisis;
- governance that was weak, repressive, and/or corrupt;
- marked economic and social decline;
- the presence of armed groups and/or militias, whether affiliated with government elites or opposition groups; and
- the perception by external actors that they had significant geopolitical stakes and/or economic stakes in the outcome of the crisis.

The nine factors related to the international crisis response considered in this chapter include the following:

- early warning;
- the active engagement of the UN Security Council;
- the presence or deployment of international peacekeepers and/or monitors;
- the active engagement of regional and/or sub-regional organizations;
- the involvement of neighbors and diaspora;
- the undertaking of distinct, purposeful, efforts at atrocity prevention;
- any efforts at conflict resolution/conflict prevention and atrocity prevention were coherent and mutually reinforcing;
- the assessment and framing of the crisis took atrocity prevention perspectives fully into account; and
- the leadership in the country in question demonstrated a reasonable degree of flexibility.

Preexisting Factors

In all eight situations, there had been a history of acute communal violence. In some places, it had been much more pronounced and more frequent than in others. In Guinea (Conakry), Kenya and Kyrgyzstan, for instance, the violence had largely been election related, sporadic, and at a much lower level than in Rwanda. In Bosnia-Herzegovina (Srebrenica), Sri Lanka, and Côte d'Ivoire, the sectarian violence was associated with ongoing armed conflict. Given the authoritarian regime in Syria, violence and dissent had both been repressed for decades, but the memory of the 1982 Hama massacre lived on three decades later. This pattern suggests two things. One, past atrocity crimes may be a likely indicator of the possibility of future atrocity crimes.

As it has long been said, the best predictor of future genocide is past genocide. Two, the history of such violence across all eight cases, whether failures or successes, suggests that historical precedents alone tell us little about
whether the prevention of a reoccurrence would be more or less likely in
such circumstances.

Election-related violence is commonly identified as a risk factor for atrocity
crimes, including in the UN's *Framework of Analysis*. Indeed, in four of the eight
situations considered here, the atrocities were associated with disputed elections. What is striking, however, is that the four cases in which some atrocities
occurred in the context of elections and/or constitutional referenda – Kenya,
Guinea, Kyrgyzstan, and Côte d'Ivoire – were also the four situations in which
it was possible to prevent an escalation through a combination of local, national,
regional, and international action. When the atrocities were not election
related, the efforts to curb their escalation were unsuccessful. It would not
be wise to draw any definitive conclusions from this small sample, as much
more extensive research is needed, but it is quite possible that these associa-
tions are more than coincidental.

It could well be, for instance, that the very fact that elections are being held
may be a sign that there are domestic groups, whether affiliated with ruling
elites or with broader civil society, that might be willing to look for political
compromise rather than following a path toward atrocity crimes. That was
certainly the case in Kenya, Guinea, and Kyrgyzstan. In these three situations,
international interlocutors were able to work with and help reinforce the
efforts of those in government or civil society who sought to stabilize the situation and avoid further violence. In Côte d'Ivoire, however, the sides could
not find room to resolve their differences over the election results peacefully,
despite extensive regional and UN engagement. This may have been due, in
part, to the identity-based politics there. The immediate crisis was finally
resolved through international enforcement action, the only relatively successful case in which that was necessary.

The overall pattern across the eight cases – with situations involving
election-related violence seeming to offer more prevention possibilities than
other situations – argues for taking a closer look at the stakes perceived by
key actors on the ground as a critical component of assessments of countries and societies under stress. It seems plausible that political solutions
are more likely to be achievable when the stakes are seen by the parties as
political rather than existential. Do the sides believe that they can find a
basis for living together once the crisis subsides, or must one of the groups
be decimated, expelled, or subjugated through mass violence first? Do leaders
see their own fates and those of their families and followers in existential
terms? As this volume has emphasized at a number of points, this individual
perspective has received too little attention from either scholars or practitioners. The concept of the individual R2P calls for more focused analysis of
how individuals respond to such situations both on the ground and in more

distant capitals, as well as in NGOs, corporate headquarters, the media, and international organizations.

As would be expected, there were governance problems in all eight situations, though the degree and nature of the difficulties varied. In all four cases in which preventive efforts failed, governance was contested and armed conflicts were underway. That was true in only one of the relative successes, Côte d'Ivoire. There were ethnic or sectarian elements to governance in all eight cases, with unresolved issues between groups related to power, resources, and trust. Confidence in governance was undermined in most of the situations by public perceptions of chronic corruption, and several of the regimes were seen as repressive from the standpoint of minority populations. Identity politics were endemic across the cases and none of the regimes had been particularly adept at handling the challenges of managing multiethnic societies. Issues of repression and human rights abuses appear to have been more prominent and more stubborn in the situations in which prevention fell short than in those where preventive engagement appeared to make a difference. Though none of the eight had anything approaching exemplary human rights records, none were near the top of worldwide lists of the worst human rights abusers for those years.

In five of the eight situations, there had been signs of marked economic and social decline prior to the crisis. These included two cases (Bosnia-Herzegovina and Syria) in which atrocity crimes escalated and three (Guinea [Conakry], Kyrgyzstan, and Côte d'Ivoire) in which prevention appeared to have worked. None of the eight societies had been thriving economically at the point of crisis, and each had pockets of the population that had been chronically doing less well than others. In these eight cases, there did not appear to be any obvious correlation between economic and social decline and the possibility of stemming the escalation of atrocity crimes once they occurred. These situations generally confirm the relationship that scholars have found between economic and social troubles and the occurrence of atrocity crimes. It may well be, however, that the direction of economic change matters more than the absolute level of poverty, and that the risks of atrocities are greater when economic differentiations within societies are associated with or perceived to be related to ethnic, tribal, or sectarian identities. These eight cases alone, however, add little to the search for definitive answers to such questions.

To one extent or another, non-state armed groups were present in all eight situations at some stage of the commission of atrocities. Many of them committed atrocities, in some cases with the tacit approval of government officials and sometimes in opposition to the government. So their presence, in and of itself, tells us little about the prospects for efforts to prevent the escalation of violence, other than that they add a complicating factor to prevention and settlement efforts. However, the role of militias, criminal elements, or armed mobs in three of the relative successes – Kenya, Guinea (Conakry), and Kyrgyzstan – was decidedly modest compared to their place in the larger-scale armed conflicts within the other five cases. That was undoubtedly a net plus in terms of preventing further atrocities.

In Syria, the political opposition was not armed in the early stages of the crisis when forces and armed militias affiliated with the government started their campaign of atrocities. That obviously changed over time as a political challenge morphed into a military one. In Côte d'Ivoire, though most reports of atrocities concerned government forces and militias, there were some reports of atrocities by opposition forces as well. Significantly, the latter subsided after a UN human rights official spoke directly with the leader of the opposition about these concerns and both UN officials and the Security Council issued condemnations of the apparent commission of atrocities. These eight experiences suggest that qualitative factors matter, that it may be productive to address the issues of atrocities by armed groups directly, and that just checking the box to indicate the existence of armed groups would be of little help to scholarship or policy making since they are likely to be present in most such situations, as well as in many others in which atrocities do not occur or are widely scattered.

Intuitively, one might well assume that preventive efforts tend to be relatively successful where external powers have strong geopolitical stakes and/or economic stakes in the outcome of the crisis. Presumably they would be more prepared to engage or intervene in such situations and this would lessen the likelihood of an escalation of violence. At least from these eight situations, this does not appear to be the case. In Bosnia-Herzegovina (Srebrenica) and Syria, the international geopolitical stakes were high but the responses decidedly inadequate. In Rwanda and Sri Lanka, the geopolitical and economic stakes were perceived in distant capitals to be low and the responses were predictably weak.

On the whole, it would be hard to argue that the international stakes were higher in the cases where prevention appeared to work than in those where it did not. Clearly, they were low in Guinea (Conakry) and arguably so in Côte d'Ivoire. Though Kyrgyzstan had been a Soviet republic, had a major US military base, and bordered on China, none of the big powers treated the crisis there as a top priority and the Security Council never addressed it. Therefore, this chapter treats this as a case in which international stakes were perceived to be low. Kenya mattered regionally for a range of economic, political, and counterterrorism reasons, but the global implications of its post-election violence were less obvious. Since Nairobi is the UN's fourth headquarters city, however, for the world body the stakes were seen as high from the onset of violence. Again, it would be premature to draw broad conclusions from such a small sample, but these eight cases do suggest the need for closer attention to whether gaining the rapt attention of major powers or – as discussed below – the Security Council is necessarily the key to the successful prevention of atrocity crimes. At times, the squabbling among major powers may instead make difficult matters worse.

Responses

The most striking finding from these eight situations relates to early warning. In all four cases of relative failure to respond effectively, there was ample early warning. In three of the four situations in which prevention seemed to work, in contrast, there was little warning of imminent atrocities. None of the civil society or UN mechanisms designed to provide early warning of such things picked up or reported the likelihood of atrocities in Kenya, Guinea (Conakry), or Kyrgyzstan. In Côte d'Ivoire, however, with its history of election violence and ongoing civil strife, there was no surprise. These patterns, though only suggestive, raise troubling questions about the assumptions behind much of the analytical and policy work underlying the effort to prevent atrocity crimes. The early warning–early action model appears to be far too simplistic. Otherwise, why should it be that in a number of situations early warning was provided but not acted upon? Why was it possible, in other situations, to exercise relatively successful prevention without much early warning? And how, based on practical experience, should the relationship between early warning and sound preventive policy making and implementation be best understood?

It should not be assumed that early warning produces the will to act in a timely or effective manner. When there is already an inclination to respond robustly, then early warning may serve as a trigger. But that is not often the case. More typically, especially when the course of response looks risky, costly, and/or uncertain to succeed, national policy makers will be looking for rationales to disengage, not engage. Given the disjuncture in most of these situations between early warning and robust response, it is evident that much more research, including comparative case studies, is needed on the relationship in practice between early warning and effective response.

Perhaps in these eight cases selection bias has distorted the picture. Yet the matter of Security Council engagement in these situations also appears counterintuitive, raising further questions about the widely held assumption that prevention works best when early warning is delivered to the Security Council in a timely and compelling manner. The Council was deeply engaged in three of the four failures (Sri Lanka being the exception). Yes, the five permanent members have been deeply divided over Syria, but there was no East–West split over Rwanda or Srebrenica, both of which had Council-authorized peace-keeping forces. Disputes and vetoes within the Council can be a problem, of course, but at other times there is a tacit agreement to look the other way or to take no more than token action. When do major powers, including but not limited to the five permanent members of the Council, decide not to react to warnings of atrocity crimes and why? Much more study, comparative and individual, is needed of their policy processes, institutional dynamics, and domestic politics in such situations. Affecting those politics and processes, of course, was (and remains) a core purpose of R2P.

Just as remarkably, there was virtually no Security Council involvement in three of the four relative successes (Kenya, Guinea [Conakry], and Kyrgyzstan). Again, Côte d'Ivoire was the exception, both in terms of Council engagement and in the use of coercive force under Chapter VII. These cases suggest the need to explore more precisely under which conditions Council engagement in preventive efforts is or is not useful, including in its relationship to regional and sub-regional initiatives. It should also be asked, given the myriad tools it has under Chapters VI, VII, and VIII of the Charter, how and when the Council should act when there is imminent danger of atrocity crimes. As noted earlier in this book, the Council has become much more concerned with atrocity prevention, genocide prevention, and R2P in recent years. In 2008, Luck, as Special Adviser, proposed to the Council that, for the purposes of the Secretary-General's authority under Article 99, the threat of the commission of atrocity crimes should be treated as a threat to international peace and security and hence be referred by the Secretary-General to the Security Council. That has since become common practice. But for the Council, like for the UN Secretariat, governments, regional arrangements, and civil society, knowing that atrocity prevention is needed and knowing how to do it consistently and effectively are two different things.

The deployment of peacekeepers, like big-power interest and Security Council engagement, is no panacea. As noted above, the UN had peacekeepers on the ground when two of the four failures to prevent occurred. In only one of the four relative successes, Côte d'Ivoire, were they either present or even contemplated when the violence broke out. Of the three cases addressed here involving international forces on the ground, this was the only one in which they were prepared and capable of taking enforcement action. In Côte d'Ivoire, as well as in other situations beyond this sample, the peacekeepers provided some protection of populations as well as prevention of further crimes. As noted in earlier chapters, UN forces in the Former Yugoslav Republic of Macedonia and African Union forces in Burundi have acted successfully as preventive deployments. But it is unlikely that governments contemplating the commissioning of atrocity crimes would consent to the deployment of international peacekeepers on their territory to prevent them. So preventive deployments are more likely to make a difference in places where governments are not yet committed to the atrocity path or where the threat comes primarily from non-state armed groups and governments need international military assistance in providing stability or in defeating them, such as in Sierra Leone from 1998 to 2005.

R2P strategy, as stressed in the 2009 and 2011 reports of the Secretary-General, has put a premium on collaboration with regional and sub-regional partners. So it was not unexpected to find that regional and sub-regional bodies and neighboring countries played significant roles in all four situations of relatively successful prevention. Indeed, their contributions were no less than instrumental in Kenya, Guinea (Conakry), and Kyrgyzstan. Their place in the endgame was more mixed in Côte d'Ivoire, the only one in which force was involved, because of policy and personality differences between the ECOWAS and African Union approaches to the conflict at critical points.

Regional actors were neither as ubiquitous, nor as helpful, in the cases of failed prevention. In Rwanda, they were active in the Arusha peace process but, like the UN, failed to comprehend the threat of genocide until it was too late. In Srebrenica, as in the Balkans more broadly, European actors spent too much time squabbling among themselves and with the United States about the best way forward. Their liabilities generally mirrored those of the UN. As the only island among these eight countries and in a region with weak institutions, Sri Lanka faced its civil strife with little regional engagement. (However, Indian forces had been deployed there at an earlier point in the long-running crisis.) In the case of Syria, its neighbors – as well as the big powers – quickly took sides, making regional unity impossible. Like South Asia, the Middle East had little history of peacemaking or atrocity prevention by regional arrangements. So these eight cases suggest that regional actors can be a critical asset in atrocity prevention, but in a number of demanding situations they failed in practice to live up to their potential. These shortcomings were often the result of political considerations, as well as of capacity gaps.

Atrocity prevention was made a policy priority by governments and international institutions in only half of these eight situations, namely the four where prevention appeared to have made a difference. In those four cases, there were distinct, purposeful, and articulated efforts to prevent atrocities as a matter of international policy. Making such a conscious choice would thus appear to make a difference. Policy choices reflected other priorities in the situations where prevention failed. This is an encouraging finding, even though the sample is small, because it suggests that trying to make a difference is the key to making a difference. In Rwanda, the international focus was on conflict prevention and peaceful settlement, not on atrocity prevention.[1] In Sri Lanka, the UN put a premium on humanitarian access over human rights and atrocity concerns.[2] In Srebrenica, the establishment of the safe areas by the Security Council was motivated, at least in part, by atrocity prevention concerns. However, the manner in which the mandate was implemented and the choices made at the time in response to the imminent threat indicated a distinct lack of will to prevent atrocities or protect populations. In Syria, the UN did make efforts to discourage the commission of atrocity crimes, but these messages were overshadowed by the dominant and divisive political struggle over the question of regime change.

Trying to make a difference may be a necessary condition, but these cases suggest that it is not always a sufficient condition for successful prevention. Atrocity prevention is rarely the only priority in international policy making and the R2P literature pays insufficient attention to how atrocity prevention and other legitimate priorities relate to each other. Policy making, after all, is all about making difficult choices among competing priorities. In the four relatively successful situations addressed here, efforts at atrocity prevention and conflict prevention were developed and implemented, at least within the UN Secretariat, in a largely coherent and mutually reinforcing manner. That was not the case, by and large, in the less successful situations, as noted above. Even information sharing within the UN Secretariat could be a problem. In his 2010 report on *Early Warning, Assessment and the Responsibility to Protect*, Secretary-General Ban Ki-moon pointed to persistent gaps in the way the world body shares and assesses information. He called for "a continuous and candid process of assessment and reassessment that utilizes the full range of information on, and analysis of, a given situation available to the United Nations system."[3] He lamented, as well, the reluctance of member states to fully share information with what they perceived to be an open and insecure world body.[4] That was certainly Luck's experience when he served as Special Adviser.

Getting accurate information to key decision makers in a timely manner is only the first step in effective decision making. The critical issue then becomes how they read and assimilate that information. There are typically several concurrent crises and, for each of them, multiple streams of information from the field to headquarters, reflecting the breadth of UN mandates. Independent sources can be valuable sources of information, though they are often advocates for specific courses of action at the same time that they are providing presumably impartial information and insights. Simultaneously, there are often interested actors promoting false and misleading information, as well as alternative theories of the meaning of developments on the ground. The most extreme case was when the government of Rwanda happened to be serving on the Security Council during the genocide in which it was complicit. So in sorting out the various information flows, it matters greatly how officials understand the nature of the situation, the motivations of key actors, and the dynamics at play. The prism through which they observe developments and assess sometimes inconsistent information in troubled situations will inevitably affect what they see and what responses they deem appropriate. It is not unusual, in that regard, for officials at the UN, in regional bodies, and in capitals to have distinct readings of the same situation.

These eight cases confirm that assessment and framing are critical to sound decision making. In the four situations where prevention went relatively well, international officials seemed to have a reasonably good understanding of what kind of a situation was developing, what the dynamics were, who the players were, what the risks of further atrocities were, and what tools were available to address the situation. In retrospect, it appears that incomplete assessment and flawed framing were serious shortcomings in each of the four situations where prevention and protection fell short. In each case, atrocity prevention concerns were either not voiced at a high enough level, squashed, or set aside in favor of other policy concerns deemed more urgent or critical. In each of these four cases, the handling of very challenging situations was made even more difficult by flawed assessment and framing in capitals, at the UN, and/or in regional and sub-regional organizations.

The Arusha peace process did matter in Rwanda. However, a devotion to the peace process should not have blinded external actors to how vehemently Hutu extremists opposed the emerging terms of the draft accords nor to the parallel need to make vigorous and targeted efforts to prevent genocide. The Independent Inquiry took the UN Secretariat, including Secretary-General Boutros Boutros-Ghali, to task for their repeated "emphasis on a cease-fire, more than moral outrage against the massacres."[5] Information that did not fit the preexisting peace narrative was downplayed or even suppressed at the UN and in key capitals.[6] Regarding Srebrenica, according to Secretary-General Annan's searing account, the temerity and insistence on impartiality that were so evident in UN deliberations was the product both of entrenched cultural preferences within the world body and of the persistent framing of the crisis in conflict-resolution terms. "We tried," he regretted, "to keep the peace and apply the rules of peacekeeping when there was no peace to keep."[7]

Despite those lessons learned – or at least voiced – and the advent of R2P, serious shortcomings in judgment persist. In Sri Lanka, the steady progression toward horrific war crimes should have been obvious for all to see, but the choice was made instead to put a premium on humanitarian access and space. This policy preference was interpreted as requiring the downplaying of human rights reporting and the exclusion of atrocity prevention perspectives from the policy-making process altogether.[8] In Syria, the dominant voices came from the major powers, whose geopolitical competition left little room for atrocity prevention perspectives. As evidence of atrocities in Syria mounted over time, in that highly charged atmosphere the horrific news tended to reinforce the dominant narrative about the imperative of regime change rather than to refocus attention on ways of trying to get the regime to change its behavior. It may well be that the latter quest never would have had much chance of success in such an authoritarian state, where the stakes were seen as existential rather than as transactional or reputational, but, from an R2P and atrocity prevention perspective, the effort to place these concerns alongside the geopolitical ones should have been made earlier and more vigorously.

These cases also underscore that the goal should not just be early action but sound, targeted, and timely action. In two ways, the 2010 R2P report of the Secretary-General emphasized the difference. First, assessments need to be revisited over time as conditions and mandates evolve. Ban "put a premium on careful, accurate and impartial assessments of conditions on the ground and of policy choices at each stage of a crisis involving the threat or commission of the four specified crimes or violations."[9] Second, he stressed that it was critical that:

> early action also be well-informed action. The United Nations needs world class early warning and assessment capacities, as called for by the 2005 World Summit Outcome, in order to ensure that it is not left with the choice between doing

nothing or taking ill-informed actions....Getting the right assessment – both of the situation on the ground and of the policy options available to the United Nations and its regional and sub-regional partners – is essential for the effective, credible and sustainable implementation of the responsibility to protect.[10]

Without sober assessment, early action can be counterproductive, untenable, and politically unsustainable. For instance, the rush in the Security Council to at least appear to be doing something to help the beleaguered populations in Bosnia-Herzegovina led to the establishment of safe areas without the international will and proximate capacity to protect them. This was fatal, not just misleading, for many who looked to the UN for protection.

The final factor to be addressed is the flexibility of the key leaders in the country in question in terms of how responsive they were to international calls for restraint. Given the general reluctance of international actors to employ coercive force in such circumstances, persuasion has emerged as a prime tool in prevention efforts. When leaders are totally committed to a course of destructive action, the room for effective international prevention narrows markedly. It may seem tautological, but national leaders demonstrated little flexibility in the four situations in which prevention failed and substantial flexibility in three of the four cases of relatively successful prevention. The one partial exception was in Côte d'Ivoire, where President Laurent Gbagbo stubbornly refused to relinquish his claims about the election results or to cede power. However, his supporters did stop marking homes by tribal affiliation when the Special Advisers objected publicly and the commission of atrocities did not escalate. More broadly, there is much debate as to whether the end to absolute impunity with the advent of the ICC has had a deterrent effect on those contemplating the commission of atrocities.[11] In Kenya and Guinea (Conakry), at least, the possibility of ICC indictments was given prominence in the messages from international leaders to the key government and opposition actors in those situations. This appeared to have some positive effect in those cases.

Some Possible Lessons

Table 7.1 provides a matrix of situations and factors considered in this chapter. It is grossly simplistic, assigning "yes/no" ratings to matters better seen as complex shadings of gray. In that regard, it does not provide any differentiation of degrees within a category or any weighting between categories of their relative importance. It shares that shortcoming with the more detailed UN *Framework of Analysis*, with its 14 risk factors and 143 indicators. Moreover, there certainly is room for debate about the labeling judgments concerning where some factors were or were not present. Through oversimplification, Table 7.1 attempts to highlight some patterns, particularly between situations in which prevention seemed to work and others in which it did not. Hopefully, this first, rough, cut will spur further research, such as a larger number of

Table 7.1 Cases and Factors

	Cases of Relative Failure				Cases of Relative Success			
EXISTING FACTORS								
Sectarian violence	Rwanda	Srebrenica	Sri Lanka	Syria	Kenya	Guinea	Kyrgyzstan	Côte d'Ivoire
Election violence	X	X	X	X	Kenya	Guinea	Kyrgyzstan	Côte d'Ivoire
Governance	Rwanda	Srebrenica	Sri Lanka	Syria	Kenya	Guinea	Kyrgyzstan	Côte d'Ivoire
Econ/soc decline	X	Srebrenica	X	Syria	X	Guinea	Kyrgyzstan	Côte d'Ivoire
Armed groups	Rwanda	Srebrenica	Sri Lanka	Syria	Kenya	Guinea	Kyrgyzstan	Côte d'Ivoire
External stakes	X	Srebrenica	X	Syria	Kenya	X	X	X
CRISIS RESPONSE								
Early warning	Rwanda	Srebrenica	Sri Lanka	Syria	X	X	X	Côte d'Ivoire
Security Council	Rwanda	Srebrenica	X	Syria	X	X	X	Côte d'Ivoire
Peacekeepers	Rwanda	Srebrenica	X	X	X	X	X	Côte d'Ivoire
Regional orgs.	Rwanda	Srebrenica	X	X	Kenya	Guinea	Kyrgyzstan	Côte d'Ivoire
Neighbors	Rwanda	Srebrenica	X	Syria	Kenya	Guinea	Kyrgyzstan	Côte d'Ivoire
Atro. prevention	X	X	X	X	Kenya	Guinea	Kyrgyzstan	Côte d'Ivoire
Coherence	X	X	X	X	Kenya	Guinea	Kyrgyzstan	Côte d'Ivoire
Framing	X	X	X	X	Kenya	Guinea	Kyrgyzstan	Côte d'Ivoire
Flexibility	X	X	X	X	Kenya	Guinea	Kyrgyzstan	X

parallel and comparative case studies that ask similar questions and can be analyzed jointly and in greater depth than was possible here.

Some degree of selection bias is probably inevitable. It might be asserted, for instance, that the four relatively successful cases were simply easier than the four that went badly. There may be something to this, but the distinction between easy and hard should not be overdrawn. As noted above, there did turn out to be actors within Kenya, Guinea (Conakry), and Kyrgyzstan who were looking for a way out of their atrocity cul-de-sacs. But there were other factors, such as a lack of early warning, of big-power interest, of Security Council engagement, and of international peacekeepers on the ground that narrowed the range of prevention and protection tools available. None of the cases seemed simple at the time. There was nothing easy about Côte d'Ivoire. Among the failures, certainly Sri Lanka and Syria were very challenging situations, not least because of the attitudes of their governing regimes at those points. Rwanda and Srebrenica, however, were arguably not as difficult as the flawed policy making at the UN and in capitals made them seem. Good policy choices tend to make things look easy, just as misjudgments may make them look daunting.

As Secretary-General Ban's R2P implementation strategy emphasized from the outset, every situation has its unique characteristics and deserves to be considered on its own merits. That cardinal rule argues for practitioners not depending too heavily on rigid templates, mathematical rankings of risk, and lengthy checklists of factors to be considered. Each of those tools has its place, but only as an adjunct to good judgment, not as its substitute. If relied on too heavily, such tools could undermine the kind of nuanced and situation-sensitive R2P implementation strategy laid out by the Secretary-General in 2008–9. There are several reasons why the misuse of such formulaic approaches could be anathema to sound decision making.

1 Crises and atrocity risks do not always emerge where the rankings and algorithms say they should. Several of the situations addressed in this chapter were not on anyone's short list of high-risk countries. Naturally, most political and analytical attention tends to be drawn to those situations highlighted in such calculations and scenarios, relegating other situations to analytical obscurity. At times, it may be wiser to expect the unexpected.

2 In that regard, the lack of early warning in several of these crises – Kenya in 2007–8, Guinea (Conakry), and Kyrgyzstan – is telling. Apparently, those situations were not perceived by most civil society monitors or policy makers as fitting the mold of the most likely candidates for atrocity crimes. That neglect sharply curtailed the amount and quality of preventive diplomacy that could be applied to them. After the scale of the violence in Kenya in 2008, of course, enormous amounts of national, regional, and global attention were focused on preventing another round of atrocities following the next election cycle five years later. If anything, the amount of effort devoted to preventing a reoccurrence in Kenya in 2012–13 seemed almost excessive, especially given the rise of communal violence in several other parts of the world at that point.

3 Viewed chronologically, each of the eight situations addressed here developed quite differently than the one preceding it. So one should be careful about applying the lessons from the last atrocity situation too strictly to the next one. Lessons, in that sense, should not be treated as predictors.

4 There is real value in listening to the actors – of all sorts – in each situation instead of concentrating on generic formulas, national statistics, or the

favored wisdom at headquarters. As noted above, more attention needs to be focused on the motivations and perceptions of the key actors on the ground. Given how subjective and non-quantifiable such assessments are likely to be, they are typically left out of estimates of the risk that certain countries or societies could spiral out of control. This human element may help to explain why two countries that appear to face quite similar challenges end up taking two distinct routes, one toward and one away from mass atrocity crimes.

5 Formulas, lists, numerical rankings, and policy templates have a way of making atrocity crimes seem like the inevitable result of circumstances and well-established patterns. This leaves out the critical matter of responsibility for the moral and political choices made by the actors on the ground, as well as those in capitals and international institutions. Mass killing is a choice, not a necessity. That is why prevention sometimes works.

6 These formulas tell us very little either about the range of policy instruments available to address atrocity threats in any particular place and time or about the domestic and international political dynamics that shape both the responses being considered and the way incoming information and warnings are read and understood.

7 Dynamic factors, including the immediate progression of events, usually matter far more than the general situation. Such rapidly unfolding events may be difficult to capture in more static models and overly cumbersome reporting systems. Agility matters when states are under stress and becoming unstable and unpredictable.

8 Templates may suggest that there is a particular way to go about preventing atrocity crimes, one that is likely to produce a positive outcome under most circumstances. Other choices, they imply, would, in all likelihood, lead to failed results. Unfortunately, experience has been a hard teacher. Preventing atrocities remains an uncertain and often elusive undertaking, where the odds of success are small and there is no assured path to get there. Mid-course corrections may be needed, no matter how thoughtful the initial approach.

9 For all these reasons, it is critical that policy makers at every level assume individual responsibility for the choices they make. They cannot claim that they acted in the way that the numbers, the formulas, or the textbooks dictated.

In other words, an overly mechanistic approach to the "science" of atrocity prevention downplays the core premise of R2P – personal and institutional responsibility. Again and again, as this chapter suggests, responsibility and judgment were the missing elements in the situations that resulted in mass atrocities and escalating violence. The first step toward prevention, as these situations underscored, is to try to prevent atrocities. When a dedicated effort was not undertaken, the results were not achieved. None of the successes resulted from inadvertence. A failure to try repeatedly led to a failure to prevent.

Two other findings are worth further study. The first is why early warning seemed to make so little difference in these eight cases. The existence of early warning did little to prevent failure, just as its absence did not inhibit success. The second finding relates to institutional culture and priorities. Clearly, as the UN's three mea culpa reports on Rwanda, Srebrenica, and Sri Lanka painfully document, institutional dysfunction has been a critical shortcoming at the United Nations. But there is no reason to assume that this is not a liability in national and regional approaches to atrocity prevention as well. Neither finding is yet well understood or sufficiently documented, even though both could have major implications for future policy and process.

Improving early warning is a major growth industry for atrocity prevention, as well as for conflict prevention. It is widely assumed that if we did a little better at early warning, then we would do that much better at undertaking timely and decisive responses. At the 2005 World Summit, the assembled heads of state and government made just such a linkage in paragraphs 138 and 139. But what if there is no clear causal relationship between warning and response? What if the preconceptions of key policy makers (and institutions or governments) are affected relatively little by the dire warnings they hear and read?

As suggested above, it may well be that early warning may trigger a timely and decisive response when policy makers are already inclined to act, but that it makes much less difference when they are already disinclined to act. This touches on one of the weak points of the original ICISS report on R2P, as too much of its attention was focused on rules for the use of force and too little on what would be required politically and strategically to convince those with the military capacity that they should employ it for these purposes. The core problem was political, not just legal. Likewise, the problem with atrocity-response decision making is not the lack of information but the lack of will. When policy makers are already convinced that the risks and costs of intervention – or even engagement – are too high, early warning may trigger more elaborate rationales for not acting rather than a rethinking of their basic assumptions about the nature of the situation and the consequences of their involvement. It may well be that some perpetrators commit particularly gruesome atrocities at the outset of their campaigns precisely to deter would-be interveners by graphically demonstrating that the costs could be higher than they or their publics would want to pay. That may be why the murder of the Belgian peacekeepers was one of the first acts in Rwanda, why peacekeepers were held hostage in Bosnia-Herzegovina and Sierra Leone, or why IS has been so public in its brutality.

When policy makers hear dissonant information, their first reaction may be denial, suppression, or an effort to repackage and reinterpret it to fit their preconceived notions, doctrines, and priorities. There was ample evidence of each of these tendencies in the four failed situations addressed in this chapter. That was true in the higher reaches of the UN Secretariat, in the Security Council, in Washington, DC, and presumably in other capitals as well. They found creative ways of handling the cognitive dissonance created by the information they received that did not fit with their preconceptions, strategies, and political priorities. Each time, they found answers other than redoubling efforts to prevent or mitigate atrocity crimes. So scholars and practitioners need to devote more attention to the policy-making processes and individual judgments in situations where preventive action is urgently required, not just to information flows. It would be particularly helpful to undertake a more extensive and deeper comparative assessment than was possible here of cases where decisions led or failed to lead to effective and timely preventive action.

The second finding with far-reaching implications – of dysfunction in institutional and governmental decision making – was more expected. For the United Nations, regional entities, and governments alike, there are competing priorities. Atrocity prevention has to take its place alongside other purposes and interests. Ironically, this may be why several of the relative successes in preventing an escalation of atrocities occurred in places where major powers and the Security Council were not heavily engaged. As noted earlier, when big powers are engaged, their interests may diverge, making a collective response harder to achieve or sustain. In Rwanda, Srebrenica, Sri Lanka, and Syria, atrocity prevention was at best a secondary priority. In none of the eight situations did atrocity prevention succeed unless it was a top priority.

Conflation between conflict prevention and atrocity prevention can be troubling because the distinction is not commonly understood or recognized, because it happens with some frequency, and because the culture of the United Nations and regional organizations favors the former over the latter. The tools for preventing atrocities usually do not fit easily with those for resolving or preventing conflict. The report by Secretary-General Annan on Srebrenica faulted the organization for its resistance to the use of force and for its insistence on impartiality and other traditional components of conflict resolution. He admitted that "we were, with hindsight, wrong to declare repeatedly and publicly that we did not want to use air power against the Serbs except as a last resort, and to accept the shelling of the safe areas as a daily occurrence."[12] He noted that "errors of judgment were made – errors rooted in a philosophy of impartiality and non-violence wholly unsuited to the conflict in Bosnia."[13] Based on "a more general tendency to assume that the parties were equally responsible for the transgressions that occurred," in his retrospective view, the "continuing negotiations with the architects of the Serb policies…amounted to appeasement."[14] Calling for reflection on "the pervasive ambivalence within the United Nations regarding the role of force in the pursuit of peace" and "an institutional ideology of impartiality even when confronted with attempted genocide," he concluded that the perpetrators "reminded the world and, in particular, the United Nations that evil exists in the world. They taught us also that the United Nations global commitment to ending conflict does not preclude moral judgments, but makes them necessary."[15]

These are powerful lessons in the ways in which policy distortions and perversities can be the result when institutional cultures cloud judgment and preclude moral choice. They reinforce, as well, two other central messages that emerge from this chapter. One is the need to treat atrocity prevention as a distinct and purposeful enterprise, not as a subset of other policy pursuits and priorities. The other is the critical importance of individual choice and responsibility. Without those attributes, the chances of preventing atrocities are likely to be small. R2P has not yet succeeded in making atrocity prevention a top priority in capitals or international institutions. Until that happens, individual responsibility, in the field, in capitals, and at headquarters, will be of paramount importance.

Conclusion

In a remarkably short space of time, the responsibility to protect (R2P) has undergone a two-staged metamorphosis. First, it was transformed from a concept proposed by an independent commission into an international norm endorsed by all the world's governments, one that shapes expectations of appropriate behavior and that has become part of the diplomatic lexicon. Second, R2P principles were then translated into a generally accepted strategy and doctrine for national and international policy makers seeking to prevent atrocity crimes and protect populations. Increasingly, R2P frames how the world thinks about the age-old challenges of prevention and protection. This book has been devoted to a third – incomplete – stage: turning these principles, strategies, and doctrines into consistent practice. This is the challenge of our times, one that has proven as difficult as it is urgent.

Efforts to implement R2P, as the preceding chapters have chronicled, have encountered a frustrating mix of successes and failures. At this point, still early in the life of R2P, we would draw the following eight lessons from this uneven experience:

1 The development of R2P needs to be understood in its historical context. In these trying times, all human rights and human protection norms are under siege from a volatile mix of cultural and geopolitical forces. This is a compelling reason to dig deeper and do better, not to retreat into despair or defeatism in the face of adversity.

2 As norms are challenged and the ranks of the vulnerable grow, there is a renewed urgency to make R2P principles a living reality. It is time to accelerate the transition to stage three of the R2P metamorphosis, so as to ensure that the progress that has been made both in norm development and in the realm of policy and practice becomes fully sustainable.

3 This transition to implementation demands a broader understanding of the core concept of responsibility, so that it encompasses individual and group responsibility as well as institutional, national, and international responsibility. None of the latter will assume their responsibilities unless individuals – inside and outside – make them.

4 A decade of applying R2P to crisis situations has underscored that the key to curbing atrocities is to make it a policy priority. When it comes to atroc-

ity prevention and response, trying to make a difference usually does make a difference.

5 Practice has also made it abundantly clear that R2P is not – and should not be – the only priority. It must find its place at the table and in the mix of other legitimate concerns of public policy. Efforts to understand how atrocity prevention and protection concerns should interact with other policy priorities, which may at times and in places be mutually supportive and at others competitive, have only just begun.

6 Though the toughest normative battles have been fought and won, R2P's development as an international standard has not reached a fully mature stage. Its acceptance could be both broader and deeper. Its normative and conceptual development needs to continue to be informed by practice, case by case, year by year.

7 The strategic and doctrinal development of R2P has been asymmetrical, with conceptual advances made within the United Nations unevenly reflected in national capitals and regional and sub-regional organizations. The critical contributions that could come from civil society and the private sector, particularly from local experience, have still not been sufficiently taken into account.

8 Experience has demonstrated that the most persistent obstacle to R2P implementation has come from concerns about decision-making sovereignty, not territorial sovereignty. The former has proven more difficult to overcome than the latter, suggesting that the locus of future debates should be less between countries from the North and South in global fora and more between competing conceptions of national interest and international responsibilities both within countries under stress and within other countries with the capacity to do more to make a difference when it comes to prevention and protection. This is the essence of turning norms into practice, and this is where the promise of R2P has most dramatically fallen short.

The remainder of this chapter addresses each of these eight lessons in greater depth.

Lesson One: Historical Context

R2P cannot, and has not, changed everything. It is unfolding in a larger historical context in which international norms and institutions are being challenged from many sides. Its advocates must help it take root in marginal, even barren, soil. In seeking to translate R2P principles into lived reality, it is essential not to confuse the mixed results achieved thus far with a sense of almost perpetual crisis. Michael Ignatieff, one of the more prominent members of the ICISS commission, warned recently of a "new world disorder" characterized by a rise of "violence and hate," while Louise Arbour has argued that the increase in global violence since 2011 shows that the international community's approach to the problem, typified by R2P, "just doesn't work."[1] Jennifer Welsh, the UN's second Special Adviser on R2P, has written eloquently of the "return of history" to world politics, as barbarism (warfare unregulated by IHL), mass migration, a renewed Cold War, and increasing inequality challenge the liberal order from within and without.[2] Practitioners must learn how to make atrocity prevention both more effective and more sustainable against such political and cultural headwinds.

In terms of sustainability, it should be recognized that R2P has yet to give rise to deep institutional reform or to complete the transition from ad hoc practices to a more systematic and strategic approach. In terms of effectiveness, the picture has been decidedly mixed over the short term (the last five or six years). Over the past few decades, however, there is reason to believe that the commission of atrocity crimes has become less accepted as an inevitable part of human interaction. Over the longer term, the actual levels of violence – and their acceptability – have declined markedly. Confronted by the crises and atrocities that plague the present, it is easy to forget the outrages of the past. As Steven Pinker recalled, "customs such as slavery, serfdom, breaking on the wheel, disemboweling, bear-baiting, cat-burning, heretic-burning, witch-drowning, thief-hanging, public executions, the display of rotting corpses on gibbets, dueling, debtors prisons, flogging, keelhauling and other practices [have] passed from unexceptionable to controversial to immoral to unthinkable."[3] R2P aims to help make atrocity crimes go the same way.

Lesson Two: Growing Urgency

From its initial inception, R2P has reframed the way we understand the politics and practice of responding to genocide and other atrocity crimes. It has demanded that our starting point be the protection of vulnerable populations from atrocities, not the rights of interveners. This requires an unflinching recognition of the evil of genocide and atrocities, and their threat, when we are confronted by it.

Never has the need for R2P to work as intended been so pressing. Never, since the conception of R2P, have so many vulnerable people needed protection so urgently. The ranks of forcibly displaced populations are at the highest level since the end of World War II. After declining some 72 percent from 1990s, the number of major civil wars grew from four to eleven after 2011, with the cumulative battle deaths reaching levels in 2014 and 2015 not seen since the end of the Cold War.[4] More ominously, global trends also show a sharp increase in "one-sided" violence against civilians, beginning in 2013.[5] Minor civil wars also increased, reaching a level not seen since the mid-1990s.[6]

These trends underscore the urgency both of speeding the transition from promise to practice and of engaging in sober reflection of how to make R2P principles relevant in the most demanding and unpromising situations. Progress toward implementing R2P has varied markedly by region and by type of conflict. The increases in worldwide violence can be largely attributed to two sources: (1) armed conflicts in the Middle East, particularly in Syria, but also in Iraq and Yemen; and (2) violent extremism by radical Islamist non-state armed groups, such as IS, al-Qaeda, and its affiliates, Boko Haram, and al-Shabaab.[7] These groups overtly challenge established international norms and advocate what Hugo Slim described as "anti-civilian norms" – positions that contest the very legal and normative foundations of R2P.[8] Although the upward trend in violence after 2011 eased slightly in 2015–16, atrocities remain at levels not witnessed since 2001, though still significantly lower than the levels experienced in the decades before that.

In the face of such enormous and pressing needs, R2P principles and strategies emphasize the value of early and comprehensive engagement by multiple actors. Thinking in terms of R2P and its three pillars, rather than in terms of humanitarian intervention, also entails recognition that prevention and response are interrelated – and that conceptual, political, and practical divisions between them are unhelpful. As we have stressed throughout, R2P requires that we should start not with the "toolbox" of prescribed measures but with bottom-up as well as top-down policy making, with clear-eyed understandings of situations on the ground, including the motivations of key actors, of points of leverage, of critical dangers and opportunities, and of honest assessments of capacities to make a difference and the will to employ them. Crafting strategies should follow early, dynamic, and keen assessment, not vice versa. Tools are precisely that: tools. They are employed to fulfill strategies. Yet all too often the application of a tool is taken to be a strategy.

Lesson Three: Individual Responsibility

The initial conception of R2P was all about states and, secondarily, interstate organizations. In practice, however, the choices of individuals – at all levels – is often determinative. If key individuals do not assume responsibility, it is unlikely that either international institutions or national governments will undertake their collective responsibilities. In this volume, therefore, we have adopted an individual responsibility to protect (IR2P) perspective across much of our analysis.[9] Both conceptually and practically, individual responsibility provides an essential connective tissue. It recognizes that many different sorts of actors have come together in an informal and transnational epistemic community to collaborate on and compare lessons learned in the hard work of atrocity prevention. Highlighting the place of individuals enriches, rather than distracts from, our understanding of how governments and institutions work. An IR2P perspective also allows a fuller appreciation of the unique contributions of players on the ground, whether in governments, civil society groups, the private sector, or the media. For international decision makers, however, an intimate, nuanced, and dynamic understanding of the motivations and perceptions of local actors is as critical as it is rare.

When atrocity crimes are imminently apprehended, the degree to which global actors can make a difference depends on whether local, group, and national leaders are willing to listen to international appeals and whether international warnings are deemed by them to be credible. Do they believe, for instance, that their reputations and futures could be adversely affected by escalating violence? When they do not care what others think, have very different value systems, see their choices in existential terms, and/or are highly resentful of external interference, the range of options for international action narrows markedly. Under such circumstances, the value of building bridges to local and national civil society may well rise.

Very often, decisions about whether to perpetrate atrocities are driven by domestic politics and personal ambitions. Opposition, for example, to such preventive measures as international reporting and monitoring can be driven more out of concern that it will empower domestic opposition groups and embarrass the ruling regime than out of worry about what, precisely, will be reported. Likewise, political leaders tend to be swayed more by what their political allies and financial backers are telling them than by the protests of outsiders. If major trading, economic, political, or security partners are capable of making and are prepared to make perpetrators pay a significant price for bad behavior, they will weigh their options differently. Such partners can, of course, act as spoilers instead.

Practitioners need to cast the net of engagement in atrocity prevention much more widely than they hitherto have, for actors outside the international system can be not only important sources of preventive action themselves, they can also wield significant influence over those within the system. Likewise, prospects of making a difference rise if there are neutral or sympathetic elements of civil society, government, and the private sector with which to work. In countries and societies under stress, the influence of such groups is likely to ebb as tensions rise and politics become more polarized over time. This argues for earlier and wider engagement, especially in places where leaders and groups are not fully and irrevocably committed to mass violence as a political choice. We have seen a number of such cases in recent years, along with those in which leaders and groups have been irrevocably committed to mass violence.

Experience also tells us to think in less rigid and more creative ways about the roles of foreign governments and individual leaders. Countries with leverage can make the jobs of international officials mandated to curb atrocities either relatively easy or completely impossible. It matters whether the leaders of neighboring countries and regional organizations are ready to reinforce international standards and messages and to take steps to discourage further atrocities. Two-way global–regional/regional–global cooperation and communication can be very helpful in fostering actions that are, and appear to be, coordinated. Early and quiet international engagement is more likely to be persuasive than are appeals or demands that come only after local perpetrators have already started down a violent path from which retreat would be difficult.

Lesson Four: Responsibility to Try

The record of practice thus far suggests that a deliberate, conscious, and concerted focus on atrocity prevention does tend to produce the best effects. When it comes to atrocity prevention and response, trying to make a difference often does make a difference. Key successes since 2005 – in Kenya (twice), Guinea (Conakry), Kyrgyzstan, Côte d'Ivoire, and initially in Libya – were achieved because concerted national, regional, and international efforts focused on the prevention of atrocity crimes. Atrocity prevention was more than a priority. It was the lens through which policy makers framed their individual and collective responses to the crises. Atrocity prevention and protection also figured large, albeit among other priorities, in several cases where the outcomes were more mixed but where the Security Council authorized specific steps to try to protect vulnerable populations. These included the Democratic Republic of the Congo (DRC), the Central African Republic (CAR), Mali, and South Sudan.

Where no dedicated approach is taken and other concerns are accorded a higher priority, results tend to be worse. The most significant failures have come in those cases where atrocity prevention was considered, if at all, as subsidiary to other goals. In Rwanda and Bosnia, for example, the international community prioritized peace processes – such as they were – above atrocity prevention. It was sometimes quite staggering just how far UN officials were prepared to go to preserve peace processes and to downplay the threat of atrocity crimes. When, for example, the Bosnian Serb Army launched five shells into Sarajevo's market in August 1995, the UN Protection Force's Head of Communications, David Harland, advised officials to report that it was unclear who had fired the shells, so as not to destabilize the peace process. The UN force commander Rupert Smith repeated this line several times, even though all indications at the time pointed to the Bosnian Serbs.

In Sri Lanka, the highest echelons of the UN Secretariat deliberately assigned atrocity prevention a lower priority than humanitarian access. For many members of the Security Council, it was considered less important than the elimination of a proscribed terrorist organization – the Tamil Tigers (LTTE). More recently, the protection of Syrians has not counted among the priorities of any of that country's neighbors or of the great powers. For them, the pursuit of localized rivalries, geopolitical and security objectives, and the question of regime change have proven more important than questions about whether – and how – to protect the country's population from atrocity crimes. Not trying to protect is the equivalent of failing to protect.

Lesson Five: Interacting with Other Priorities

R2P does not exist in a social or political vacuum. In practice, the pursuit of R2P purposes necessarily interacts with policies and practices intended to further other legitimate norms and objectives. At some times and places, these various pursuits are mutually reinforcing. At others, they are subject to political contestation. For example, even if actors agree on the substance of R2P as a principle, they may still disagree radically on the best way of forwarding it in specific circumstances given limited capacity and competing priorities, such as stability and order. Justin Morris coined the apt phrase "dual responsibility" to point to the fact that the world's great powers have not just a responsibility to protect but also a responsibility to maintain international peace and security, imperatives that may not always correspond with each other.[10] The pursuit of long-term principles may be postponed or set aside in the face of short-term exigencies.

So it follows that atrocity prevention tends to be more successful when there are fewer competing priorities. The situations we addressed in chapter 7 would seem to confirm this. This may be one of the reasons that efforts to implement R2P have tended to be more successful in low-profile situations than in high-profile ones. It may also be that the natural urge among activists to want to escalate responses by engaging major powers and the Security Council may at times be misplaced. With the injection of the major powers into a situation come their larger geopolitical agendas and the potential of displacing atrocity prevention as the principal concern.

Experience suggests that Security Council engagement is no panacea. Indeed, taken by itself, the Council's record is no better – nor worse, for that matter – than that of any other institution. In some situations, other actors have greater freedom of maneuver when the Council is not seized of the matter. Here, we are thinking of the roles played by the OSCE in Kyrgyzstan, by Annan's mediation team in Kenya, and by ECOWAS in Guinea. In all of these cases, the Security Council took a back seat. There are, nonetheless, situations where the Council's unique authority and legitimacy are indispensable. It played a crucial role, for example, in Côte d'Ivoire in 2011. Significantly, in that case the Council was focused on the prevention both of atrocity crimes and of a resumption of civil war, goals that were, at that point, mutually reinforcing.

Two conclusions follow. First, given the central importance of a conscious and deliberate focus on the prevention of atrocity crimes, more work – analytical, political, and institutional – is needed on the further development of a distinctive atrocity prevention approach. Second, at the same time, more thought is needed on how to promote atrocity prevention strategies alongside the pursuit of other critical policy objectives. Our approach to atrocity prevention can be both distinctive and complementary, both determined and collegial. We need a keener analysis of decision-making patterns in those situations in which R2P and other policy tracks proved to be mutually reinforc-ing, resulting in outcomes that were more than a sum of the parts. Although each case is unique, insights from past practice can inform future practice about ways to enhance complementarity while ensuring that atrocity pre-vention and human protection receive the timely and high-level attention they deserve.

Lesson Six: Further Normative Development

R2P has been at its most effective in establishing a shared normative standard for how we think about and respond to atrocity crimes. But it is equally evident that the normative quest is not complete, in part because practice keeps revealing areas in which further refinements are needed. On the plus side, R2P has emerged as an accepted normative standard against which behav-ior can be judged. It has served, as well, to link existing legal standards on different dimensions of atrocity prevention to a relatively coherent strategic framework for advancing compliance across all of these distinct legal instru-ments. R2P has focused on compliance, not on creating new law, for a simple but compelling reason. Historically, despite well-established norms against such crimes, states have repeatedly failed to protect their populations and the international community has done little about it. R2P was intended to highlight and, if possible, to begin to narrow this compliance gap and thus to start to ease the vast human suffering it has produced.

In that sense, R2P is composed of highly aspirational principles. It aims not to confirm current national and international practice but to challenge states, international institutions, groups, and individuals to do much better in the future. It seeks to raise expectations while underscoring the unacceptability of the long-accepted status quo. It offers a journey, not a map, a direction, not an assured destination or schedule. R2P sought to create expectations that it could not meet, at least in the short run. The core of those expecta-tions, of course, is that practice must improve. As this volume has asserted in many ways, there has been significant progress in framing and implement-ing more effective strategies, doctrines, and policies for prevention and pro-tection, but these efforts are still at an early and fragile stage. Much more thought and work are needed.

Inevitably, its aspirational quality exposed R2P to criticism from the outset, with critics pointing out that the half-hearted responses to crises in Darfur, Sri Lanka, and elsewhere fell well short of the mark demanded by R2P. The same could be said, of course, about any number of human rights and humanitarian norms, including anti-slavery norms codified centuries ago. In our view, some advocates responded too defensively to these critiques. In trying to make R2P invulnerable to criticism, there has been a tendency to overemphasize R2P's preventive side and to underemphasize its responsive side. Artificial lines have been drawn between prevention and response and between Pillars One and

Two and Pillar Three of the Secretary-General's 2009 implementation strategy. In practice, these distinctions tend to become blurred as one grapples with a small range of feasible tools to address specific situations.

The goal should not be to tame R2P principles to such an extent that all states are comfortable with them all of the time. Without some level of discomfort and dissatisfaction with current practice, the world would never get better at prevention and protection. We should not forget that R2P was created because the status quo was not acceptable: horrific crimes, with hundreds of thousands of casualties, had unfolded with no one taking responsibility or acting effectively to prevent or curb them. R2P was to embody a new political dynamic for change, one that would affect attitudes, priorities, policies, and practices. That edge should not be dulled or lost.

There are obvious signs that R2P has, indeed, helped change popular perceptions and public standards about acceptable and unacceptable behavior. It has reshaped our expectations about how the world ought to respond to atrocity crimes. It bears remembering that in the wake of the Nuremberg trials, Rafael Lemkin lamented that had Nazi Germany exterminated only German Jews, and not committed aggression against its neighbors, it would have committed no international crime.[11] Today, however, genocide, war crimes, and crimes against humanity are recognized as international crimes; states have positive legal, political, and moral duties to prevent them and offer assistance across borders; the UN Security Council understands these to be matters of international peace and security falling within its purview; and a range of national, regional, and international institutions has been established to assist states and to hold them to account. In that regard, it is significant that the General Assembly has adopted a series of resolutions criticizing the Security Council for not doing more to stop the carnage in Syria. By consolidating norms, raising expectations, and spurring better practice, R2P is beginning to demonstrate its potential as a catalyst for action.

Lesson Seven: Getting Beyond the United Nations

For all of the ongoing efforts at the national and regional levels, the R2P project remains overly UN-centric and, within the UN, too New York-centric. As practice has repeatedly documented, the United Nations has accomplished relatively little in the way of prevention or protection without regional and national partners. Yet still relatively few national and local policy makers, religious and opinion leaders, parliamentarians, entrepreneurs, or educators are aware of R2P and of its implications for their societies. As a result, support for R2P is as shallow as it is broad. Going forward, implementation will require deeper and more sustained political commitments at all levels. UN leadership may be a necessary condition for advancing the practice of R2P, but it certainly is not a sufficient one. In that regard, scholars and commentators should be careful not to exaggerate the international community's capacity to influence domestic politics either in states under stress or in countries with the capacity to respond, as interventions are costly and risky undertakings.

The world body serves best when it acts as a catalyst for practical steps by governments, civil society, and regional/sub-regional institutions. Global rhetoric and standard setting rings hollow without local, national, and regional follow-up. Unfortunately, there is evidence of declining compliance with fundamental tenets of international humanitarian, human rights and refugee law, not just by the violent extremists and authoritarian states that perpetrate atrocity crimes but by states of good standing and even some past champions of human protection. The US government, for example, has eased targeting restrictions aimed at protecting civilians from indiscriminate or disproportionate attacks.[12] Several others, including Hungary and Australia, have adopted refugee policies that, the UNHCR believes, contradict their legal obligations under the Refugee Convention and associated protocol. Burundi has withdrawn from the International Criminal Court, and South Africa and the Gambia threatened to do likewise, placing this young institution under immense political pressure. Others, such as the Philippines, could follow suit largely because the Court has become an inconvenience to states that may be responsible for committing crimes against humanity.

There has also been a significant increase in the involvement of external states in civil wars. According to well-established data collectors, in 1990, only 4 percent of civil wars were "internationalized" through the direct involvement of other states. By 2015, that figure had increased to 40 percent, and many of these, including Syria and Yemen, experienced interventions by multiple external states.[13] Some of these external actors, such as Russia in Syria and Saudi Arabia in Yemen, have used force in support of actors responsible for widespread and systematic atrocity crimes, have supported such uses of force, and have themselves directed attacks that have resulted in large-scale civilian casualties. External supporters enable violence and prolong the killing. Research shows that in cases where external interventions fail to deliver a rapid and decisive outcome, they tend to make civil wars longer and deadlier.[14] Syria provides an apt example, since the involvement of external actors, such as Russia, Turkey, Iran, Saudi Arabia, Qatar, and Hezbollah, has served primarily to extend the violence and further complicate peace efforts.

States and state leaders have also used their political influence to shield the perpetrators of atrocities. For example, in 2016 South Africa's Constitutional Court ruled that the South African government breached its legal obligations by not arresting Sudanese President Omar al-Bashir and transferring him to the ICC as required by the Rome Statute, to which South Africa is a states party. Meanwhile, Russia and China have repeatedly blocked efforts to hold those responsible for atrocity crimes in Syria accountable, vetoing draft Security Council resolutions referring the situation to the ICC.

This resistance to legal accountability prompted the UN General Assembly to take the unprecedented step of establishing its own mechanism to support the future criminal prosecution of those responsible for atrocity crimes in Syria.[15] Decades earlier, the Security Council, which had done too little to stop the atrocities in Rwanda and the Balkans, established ad hoc tribunals to try to hold some perpetrators accountable, just as the International Court of Justice did in the case of the massacre in Srebrenica. Moreover, through the principle of complementarity, the ICC is helping to narrow the gap between global legal standards and accountability mechanisms at the national level. R2P needs to encourage the further development of such global–regional–national connections as a way of shaping the politics of atrocity prevention and human protection.

Lesson Eight: Decision-Making Sovereignty

Contrary to the assumptions that framed the initial conception of R2P in 2001, in practice decision-making sovereignty, not territorial sovereignty, has proven to be the key inhibitor to the consistent implementation of R2P principles. Norms are intended to condition the choices people and leaders make at every level. When government and civil society leaders in states under stress observe R2P principles, the question of territorial sovereignty never arises. Only when they fail to do so would the responsibility of others to respond to atrocities in a timely and decisive manner come into play. On both sides of the equation, leaders jealously guard their right to decide for themselves, on a case-by-case basis, which legal and political responsibilities they will fulfill and the manner in which they will do so. Changing choices, and with it behavior, is the ultimate test of whether R2P is making a difference. This will take time and, so far, the results are both uneven and uncertain.

This enduring attachment to decision-making sovereignty has not only inhibited the institutionalization of R2P, it has ensured that responses to atrocity crimes have remained ad hoc rather than consistent or systematic. This helps explain why early warning has tended to make more of a difference when there already exists a predisposition to act than when the will has to be created. The resulting inconsistencies have undermined the credibility and legitimacy of R2P as a normative standard.

Despite their surface commitment to R2P, states are still too often reluctant to act until they see the casualties mounting. Commitment to act has sometimes been lacking even when atrocities occur. For example, the risk of atrocity crimes in Syria was identified almost at the outset of the crisis there in 2011, including by the UN Special Advisers, yet the world could not find sufficient will or consensus to prevent it. The United States, for example, responded initially by ruling out strong action in Syria before switching emphasis to demands for an immediate end to the violence and for Assad to "step aside." But at no stage has either the United States or its western allies shown a willingness to take the steps necessary to achieve their often-stated goals. Russia and China have actively opposed attempts to get the Security Council more engaged in trying to curb atrocity crimes in Syria. Regional arrangements are weakest where they are most urgently needed.

In Yemen, warnings about the dangers confronting the civilian population have not been translated into much more than humanitarian aid and plans for an investigation of abuses by the UN High Commissioner for Human Rights. Humanitarian support for Yemen has been so inadequate that by 2017 the UN was moved to argue that Yemen was the world's gravest humanitarian emergency and that significant populations confronted the risk of famine and severe malnutrition.[16] A year earlier, the ICRC had observed that the humanitarian situation in Yemen was at a "tipping point."[17] Despite the massive flows of forcibly displaced populations from Syria and Yemen that have placed a substantial burden on some neighboring countries, the region remains bitterly divided on how to proceed.

Elsewhere, early warnings of atrocity crimes have translated into preventive actions only incrementally, as in the CAR and Burundi. Another example comes from the treatment of those fleeing atrocities. The granting of safe passage and asylum to populations threatened by atrocity crimes remains one of the most direct ways in which states can support human protection but – with only a few notable exceptions, such as Germany and Canada – domestic politics have moved their national policies in the opposite direction, adopting a less hospitable and more punitive approach to asylum seekers largely inconsistent with the 1951 Convention Relating to the Status of Refugees and subsequent 1967 Protocol and certainly inconsistent with the spirit and intention of human protection.

As R2P transitions through the third stage of its metamorphosis – from norm development to policy and practice – it is confronting ever steeper tests, whether from non-state armed groups, authoritarian leaders unwilling to cede power, weak regional and global institutions, or great powers unprepared to uphold human rights and humanitarian norms. Where R2P calls for the exercise of responsible sovereignty, we are instead seeing the return of what Hedley Bull described, in a different context, as the "great irresponsibles." By pursuing an increasingly narrow interpretation of their national interests at the expense of their global responsibilities, the great powers are in danger of "forfeiting the claims they had begun to build up…to be regarded by others as responsible managers of international society as a whole."[18] The five permanent members of the UN Security Council, in particular, should heed Bull's caution that "great powers cannot expect to be conceded special rights if they do not perform special duties."[19] The alternative is a more disorderly and violent world in which other states and societies look outside established norms and institutions for answers to the problems they face, including the threat of genocide and atrocity crimes.

Those concerned about ceding decision-making sovereignty should be reminded that R2P does not seek to dictate the precise path that prevention and protection efforts should take. It emphasizes, instead, the need for early and flexible response tailored to the special circumstances of each situation. Practice has demonstrated the wisdom of such flexibility. In place after place, practice has shown the benefits of early engagement, well before policy options are narrowed to a binary choice between coercive military intervention and looking the other way. But, as underscored above, R2P principles do impose an abiding obligation to try.

R2P principles demand that we not neglect the enormity of the human stakes involved in getting this right. In all of the debates over fine-tuning R2P and its implementation, we should never forget the tens of millions of lives lost to mass atrocity crimes over the past century. The horrors of the Holocaust, the killing fields of Cambodia, the genocide in Rwanda, the summary executions of Srebrenica, the mass rapes in the DRC, and the millions forcibly displaced from Darfur, Syria, and Yemen speak to the centrality, as well as the urgency, of the task. Claims of sovereignty, whether of the territorial or decision-making variety, cannot supersede the moral and legal claims imposed by the responsibility to protect.

History tells us that the journey from principle to practice is never quick or sure. It demands persistence as much as intellect, learning from mistakes as well as from successes, and never forgetting where we are going or why we undertook the journey in the first place. Stepping aside, giving up, looking for easier paths is not an option. Curbing atrocities is as difficult as it is compelling. But experience also shows that it can be done. Those are the core lessons from R2P's early years. They offer the promise of stronger institutions, deeper commitments, and better policy in the years ahead. R2P is just getting started.

Notes

Introduction

1 Throughout the book, we use "atrocity crimes" as shorthand for genocide, war crimes, ethnic cleansing, and crimes against humanity.

2 We use the acronym "R2P" because it has become standard usage globally. We recognize, though, that R2P is problematic in non-English languages (the number 2 translates as *dos* in Spanish, for instance, rendering the acronym meaningless), which is why the UN adopted the form "RtoP." We note, though, that "R2P" has caught on even in the non-English-speaking world.

3 Introduced in Secretary-General Ban's first R2P report, *Implementing the Responsibility to Protect*, A/63/677 of January 12, 2009, the IR2P approach is developed in Edward C. Luck and Dana Zaret Luck, "The Individual Responsibility to Protect," in Sheri P. Rosenberg, Tibi Galis, and Alex Zucker (eds), *Reconstructing Atrocity Prevention* (Cambridge, UK: Cambridge University Press, 2016), pp. 207–48.

4 Foreshadowed by Simon Chesterman, *Just War or Just Peace? Humanitarian Intervention and International Law* (Oxford: Oxford University Press, 2001).

Chapter 1 R2P as Principle and Policy

1 At the United Nations, and in many governments, a norm is expected to have a binding legal character. The authors neither assert that that is the case with R2P nor believe that R2P needs to have that status to be effective in a public policy context.

2 United Nations, *Report of the Secretary-General on the Work of the Organization*, A/46/1, September 13, 1991, pp. 1–2.

3 Edward C. Luck, *UN Security Council: Practice and Promise* (London: Routledge, 2006), Figure 1.1, p. 8.

4 United Nations, Security Council, Statement by the President, S/23500, January 31, 1992.

5 United Nations, Report of the Secretary-General, *An Agenda for Peace: Preventive Diplomacy, Peacemaking, and Peacekeeping*, A/47/277, June 17, 1992, p. 8, para. 29.

6 Ibid., p. 4, para. 17.

7 United Nations Development Program (UNDP), *Human Development Report 1994* (Oxford: Oxford University Press, 1994), p. 22.

8 Commission on Global Governance, *Our Global Neighborhood* (Oxford: Oxford University Press, 1995), p. 81.

9 Ibid., p. 84.

10 S/PV.3977, February 12, 1999, p. 31.

11 United Nations Development Programme (UNDP), *Human Development Report 1994* (Oxford: Oxford University Press, 1994), p. 22.

12 Ibid., Box 3.1, p. 47.

13 A/51/306, August 26, 1996, p. 1, para. 2.

14 Lotta Harborn and Peter Wallensteen, "Armed Conflict and Its International Dimensions, 1946–2004," *Journal of Peace Research* 42(5) (September 2005), Table II: 624.

15 United Nations, Report of the Secretary-General, *Supplement to An Agenda for Peace*, A/50/60–S/1995/1, January 3, 1995, para. 18, p. 6.

16 See United Nations, Report of the Secretary-General, *The Fall of Srebrenica*, A/54/549, November 15, 1999, p. 106, para. 493.

17 United Nations, General Assembly, A/RES/46/182, December 19, 1991, preambular language.

18 *Human Development Report 1994*, op. cit., p. 47.

19 Graça Machel, *Impact of Armed Conflict on Children*, report for the United Nations and UNICEF, 1996, p. 9, para. 24.

20 United Nations, *Supplement*, op. cit., para. 12, p. 5.

21 United Nations, Security Council, S/PV.3977, February 12, 1999, p. 31.

22 United Nations, Economic and Social Council, E/CN.4/1993/35, Annex, January 21, 1993, p. 3. Deng produced a lengthy two-volume report on internal displacement in 1996 and 1998. E/CN.4/1996/52/Add.2 and E/CN.4/1998/53/Add.1.

23 United Nations, Economic and Social Council, E/CN.4/1998/53/Add.2, February 1998.

24 United Nations, General Assembly, A/RES/44/25, November 20, 1989.

25 United Nations, General Assembly, A/RES/48/157, December 20, 1993.

26 Ibid., preambular paragraphs.

27 Ibid., para. 7.

28 *Impact on Children*, op. cit., p. 5, paras. 2 and 1, respectively.

29 United Nations, Security Council, resolution 827 (1993), May 25, 1993.

30 United Nations, Security Council, resolution 955 (1994), November 8, 1994, operative para. 1.

31 Ibid, Annex, Article 3(g).

32 United Nations, Security Council, Resolution 1325 (2000), October 31, 2000, operative para. 11.

33 S/PV.3977, February 12, 1999, p. 15.

34 Ibid.

35 Ibid., p. 30.

36 Ibid., p. 31.

37 United Nations, Security Council, Resolution 1265 (1999), September 17, 1999.

38 United Nations, Report of the Secretary-General, *An Agenda for Peace: Preventive Diplomacy, Peacemaking and Peacekeeping*, A/47/277, S/7411, June 17, 1992, p. 6, para. 21.

39 Adekeye Adebajo, *Building Peace in West Africa: Liberia, Sierra Leone, and Guinea-Bissau* (Boulder, CO: Lynne Rienner, 2002) and John Hirsch, "Sierra Leone," in

David M. Malone (ed.), *The UN Security Council: From the Cold War to the 21st Century* (Boulder, CO: Lynne Rienner, 2004), pp. 521–35.

40 Francis M. Deng, Sadikiel Kimaro, Terrence Lyons, Donald Rothchild, and I. William Zartman, *Sovereignty as Responsibility: Conflict Management in Africa* (Washington, DC: The Brookings Institution, 1996), p. 27.

41 Ibid., p. 33.

42 Kwesi Aning and Frank Okyere, "The African Union," in Alex Bellamy and Tim Dunne (eds), *The Oxford Handbook of the Responsibility to Protect* (Oxford: Oxford University Press, 2016), pp. 355–72 (especially pp. 356–8).

43 United Nations, Security Council, Letter Dated 8 March 1999 from the Secretary-General Addressed to the President of the Security Council, S/1999/339, March 26, 1999.

44 United Nations, Security Council, Letter Dated 15 December 1999 from the Secretary-General Addressed to the President of the Security Council, S/1999/1257, December 16, 1999, p. 54.

45 Ibid., p. 55.

46 Ibid., p. 57.

47 Ibid., p. 58, Recommendation 12.

48 Colin Keating, "Rwanda: An Insider's Account," in Malone, *The UN Security Council*, op. cit., pp. 502–5.

49 On US decision making, see Samantha Power, *"A Problem from Hell": America and the Age of Genocide* (New York: Harper Collins, 2002), pp. 337–69.

50 Edward C. Luck, "Sovereignty, Choice, and the Responsibility to Protect," *Global Responsibility to Protect* 1(1) (2009): 10–21.

51 United Nations, *Fall of Srebrenica*, op. cit., p. 106, para. 496 and p. 108, para. 503, respectively.

52 Ibid., p. 108, para. 506.

53 Ibid., p. 106, para. 495.

54 Ibid., p. 107, paras. 500, 497, and 499, respectively.

55 Paul Lewis, "U.N. Agrees to Declare Bosnian Town a Safe Haven," *New York Times*, April 17, 1993.

56 United Nations, *Fall of Srebenica*, op. cit., p. 108, para. 505.

57 Ibid., p. 108, paras. 502 and 504.

58 These can be found in United Nations, *The Question of Intervention: Statements of the Secretary-General* (New York: United Nations Department of Public Information, DPI/2080, December 1999).

59 Ibid., p. 7.

60 Ibid., p. 6.

61 Ibid.

62 Ibid., p. 13.

63 Ibid., pp. 37–44.

64 Kofi A. Annan, Report of the Secretary-General, *We the Peoples: The Role of the United Nations in the 21st Century* (New York: United Nations Department of Public Information, 2000), pp. 47–8.

65 Ramesh Thakur, "The Responsibility to Protect at 15," *International Affairs* 92(2) (2016): 417.

66 International Commission on Intervention and State Sovereignty (ICISS), *The Responsibility to Protect* (Ottawa: International Development Research Centre, 2001), p. 2, para. 1.7.

67 Ibid., p. 73, para. 8.24.
68 Thakur, "R2P at 15," op. cit., p. 416.
69 Ibid., p. 417.
70 Thomas G. Weiss, *Humanitarian Intervention: Ideas in Action*, 2nd edn (Cambridge, UK: Polity Press, 2012), p. 111.
71 ICISS, op. cit., p. VII.
72 Ibid. Also see pp. 1–3 on "the intervention dilemma."
73 Ibid., p. 8, para. 1.38.
74 Ibid., p. 9, paras. 1.39–1.41.
75 Ibid., p. 11, para. 2.2.
76 Ibid., p. 17, para. 2.29.
77 Ibid., p. 16, para. 2.26.
78 Ibid., p. 15, para. 2.24.
79 Ibid., p. 13, paras. 2.14–2.15, emphasis in original.
80 Ibid., p. 17, para. 2.32 and p. 75, para. 8.32; p. 13, para. 2.15, p. 16, para. 2.27 and p. 75, para. 8.31; p. 75, paras. 8.31–8.32; and p. 16, para. 2.25, respectively.
81 Ibid., p. 15, para. 2.21.
82 Ibid., p. 15, para. 2.22 (emphasis in the original).
83 Ibid., p. 15, para. 2.23.
84 See, for instance, p. 31, para. 4.13, p. 74, para. 8.25, and p. 75, para. 8.34.
85 Ibid., p. 31, para. 4.13 and p. 75, para. 8.34.
86 Ibid., p. 74, para. 8.25.
87 Ibid., p. 69, para. 8.1 and p. VIII.
88 Ibid., p. XI, point (1) B.
89 Ibid., p. XII, point (1) A. and B.
90 Ibid., p. 29, para. 4.2.
91 Ibid., pp. XII and 32–7.
92 Ibid., p. XIII, points (3) E. and F.
93 Ibid., Section 3, "The Responsibility to Prevent," pp. 19–27, quote from p. 19, para. 3.2.
94 Ibid., p. 19, paras. 3.2 and 3.3, respectively.
95 ICISS, op. cit., p. 22, paras. 3.15–3.16.
96 Ibid., p. 25, paras. 3.34–3.35.
97 Ibid., p. 23, para. 3.25.
98 Ibid., p. 24, para. 3.30.
99 Ibid., p. XI, point (4) A.
100 Ibid., p. 39, para. 5.1.
101 United Nations, Report of the Secretary-General, *The Causes of Conflict and the Promotion of Durable Peace and Sustainable Development in Africa*, A/52/871–S/1998/318, April 13, 1998.
102 ICISS, op. cit., p. 45, para. 5.31.
103 United Nations, Report of the Secretary-General's High-Level Panel on Threats, Challenges and Change, *A More Secure World: Our Shared Responsibility* (New York: UN Department of Public Information, 2004), pp. 65–6, paras 199–203.
104 Ibid., p. 66, para. 203.
105 United Nations, Report of the Secretary-General, *In Larger Freedom: Towards Development, Security and Human Rights for All*, A/59/2005, March 21, 2005, p. 35, para. 135.

106 Ibid., p. 33, para. 122 and p. 35, para. 135; and p. 35, para.135, respectively.
107 Ibid., p. 35, para. 135.
108 Ibid.
109 Ibid., p. 33, para. 122, p. 33, para. 125, p. 34, para. 129, and p. 35, para. 132, respectively.
110 Alex J. Bellamy, *Responsibility to Protect: The Global Effort to End Mass Atrocities* (Cambridge: Polity, 2010) p. 68; and Luck, "Sovereignty," op. cit., pp. 17–18.
111 Bellamy, ibid., p. 67.
112 Luck, "Sovereignty," op. cit., pp. 18–20.
113 International Peace Institute, the Office of the UN Special Adviser on the Prevention of Genocide, and the InterAfrica Group, *The Responsibility to Protect (R2P) and Genocide Prevention in Africa* (International Peace Institute, June 2009), Annex II, p. 11.
114 Edward C. Luck, "From Promise to Practice: Implementing the Responsibility to Protect," in Jared Genser and Irwin Cotler (eds), *The Responsibility to Protect: The Promise of Stopping Mass Atrocities in Our Time* (Oxford: Oxford University Press, 2012), pp. 89–90.
115 United Nations, Report of the Secretary-General, *Implementing the Responsibility to Protect*, A/63/677, January 12, 2009, p. 8, para. 10(a).
116 United Nations, Press Release, "Secretary-General Defends, Clarifies 'Responsibility to Protect," at Berlin Event on "Responsible Sovereignty: International Cooperation for a Better World," SG/SM/11701, July 15, 2008.
117 *Implementing R2P*, op. cit.
118 Ibid., pp. 18–19, para. 41.
119 Ibid., pp. 18–19, paras. 40-2.
120 Ibid., p. 18, para. 40.
121 Ibid., pp. 22–3, para. 50.
122 *Implementing R2P*, op. cit., p. 14, para. 27.
123 Edward C. Luck and Dana Zaret Luck, "The Individual Responsibility to Protect," in Sheri P. Rosenberg, Tibi Galis, and Alex Zucker (eds), *Reconstructing Atrocity Prevention* (Cambridge, UK: Cambridge University Press, 2016), pp. 207–48.

Chapter 2 R2P in World Politics

1 UN, "Effective Prevention Requires Early, Active, Sustained Engagement Stresses Secretary-General at Ministerial Roundtable on the Responsibility to Protect," SG/SM/13838, September 23, 2011.
2 Liu Tiewa and Zhang Haibin, "Debates in China about the Responsibility to Protect as a Developing International Norm: A General Assessment," *Conflict, Security and Development* 14(4) (2014): 408.
3 Peter Katzenstein, "Introduction," in Peter Katzenstein (ed.), *The Culture of National Security: Norms and Identity in World Politics* (New York: Columbia University Press, 1996), p. 5.
4 *Implementing the Responsibility to Protect: Report of the Secretary-General*, A/63/677, January 12, 2009, para. 13.
5 International Commission on Intervention and State Sovereignty, *The Responsibility to Protect* (Ottawa: IDRC, 2001).

6 See Michael W. Doyle, "International Ethics and the Responsibility to Protect," *International Studies Review* 13(1) (2011): 82.

7 Ekkehard Strauss (ed.), *The Emperor's New Clothes? The United Nations and the Implementation of the Responsibility to Protect* (Berlin: Nomos, 2009), pp. 57–8.

8 Ibid., p. 58.

9 *Report of the Commission of Inquiry on Human Rights in the Democratic People's Republic of North Korea*, UN General Assembly, A/HRC/25/63, February 7, 2014.

10 Alex J. Bellamy, "A Chronic Protection Problem: The DPRK and the Responsibility to Protect," *International Affairs* 91(2) (2015): 225–44.

11 For summaries of these debates and full publication of the statements by member states, see the Global Centre for the Responsibility to Protect: www.globalr2p.org

12 S/PRST/2011/16, August 3, 2011.

13 S/PV.6627, October 4, 2011, pp. 3 and 5.

14 Statement by Abhishek Singh, First Secretary, Permanent Mission of India to the United Nations at the Informal Interactive Dialogue of the General Assembly on the Responsibility of States to protect their populations by preventing genocide, war crimes, ethnic cleansing and crimes against humanity through appropriate and necessary means, September 8, 2014.

15 Andrew Gilmour, "The Future of Human Rights: A View from the United Nations," *Ethics and International Affairs* 28(2) (2014): 239–50.

16 Simon Chesterman, "Leading from Behind: The Responsibility to Protect, the Obama Doctrine, and Humanitarian Intervention After Libya," *Ethics and International Affairs* 25(2) (2011): 279.

17 Justin Morris, "The Responsibility to Protect and the Great Powers: The Tensions of Dual Responsibility," *Global Responsibility to Protect* 7(3–4) (2015): 398–421.

18 Resolutions 2171 (2014), 2150 (2014), 2117 (2013), 1894 (2009), 1706 (2006), and 1674 (2006).

19 Arthur Boutellis and Paul D. Williams, "Peace Operations, the African Union and the United Nations: Toward More Effective Partnership" (New York, International Peace Institute, 2013).

20 Peter Wallensteen and Isak Svensson, "Talking Peace: International Mediation in Armed Conflicts," *Journal of Peace Research* 51(2) (2014): 315–27.

21 Sara E. Davies, Kimberly Nackers, and Sarah Teitt, "Women, Peace and Security as an ASEAN Priority," *Australian Journal of International Affairs* 68(3) (2014): 333–55.

22 Vaughn P. Shannon, "Norms Are What States Make of Them: The Political Psychology of Norm Violation," *International Studies Quarterly* 44(2) (2000): 297.

23 A.66/L.36, February 16, 2012.

24 GA/11266, August 3, 2012.

25 "UN Report: Security Council Bears Responsibility for War Crimes in Syria," *Al Jazeera*, March 5, 2014.

26 Jennifer M. Welsh, "Implementing the Responsibility to Protect: Catalyzing Debate and Building Capacity," in Alexander Betts and Phil Orchard (eds), *Implementation and World Politics: How International Norms Change Practice* (Oxford: Oxford University Press, 2014), p. 126.

27 Thomas Franck, *The Power of Legitimacy Among Nations* (New York, Oxford University Press, 1990), p. 52.

28 Edward C. Luck, *The UN Security Council: Practice and Promise* (London: Routledge, 2006), p. 8.

29 Scott Straus, *Making and Unmaking Nations: War, Leadership and Genocide in Modern Africa* (Ithaca: Cornell University Press, 2015), p. 326.

30 Stephen McLoughlin and Deborah Mayersen, "Reconsidering Root Causes: A New Framework for the Structural Prevention of Genocide and Mass Atrocities," in Bert Ingelaere, Stephan Parmentier, Jacques Haers and Barbara Segaert (eds), *Genocide, Risk and Resilience: An Interdisciplinary Approach* (Basingstoke: Palgrave, 2013).

31 Donald C. F. Daniel, "Contemporary Patterns in Peace Operations: 2000–2010," in Alex J. Bellamy and Paul D. Williams (eds), *Providing Peacekeepers: The Politics, Challenges and Future of United Nations Peacekeeping Contributions* (Oxford: Oxford University Press, 2013).

32 Carnegie Commission on Preventing Deadly Conflict, *Preventing Deadly Conflict* (New York: Carnegie Commission, 1998).

33 See Benjamin A. Valentino, "The True Costs of Humanitarian Intervention," *Foreign Affairs*, November/December 2011.

34 Ban Ki-moon, *Responsibility to Protect: Timely and Decisive Response. Report of the Secretary-General*, A/66/874–S/2012/578, July 25, 2012.

35 Ruben Reike, "The Responsibility to Prevent: An International Crimes Approach to the Prevention of Mass Atrocities," *Ethics & International Affairs* 28(4) (2014): 451–76.

36 Edward C. Luck, "Sovereignty, Choice and the Responsibility to Protect," *Global Responsibility to Protect* 1(1) (2009): 20–1.

37 Reike, "The Responsibility to Prevent."

38 Colin Keating, "The Role of the UN Security Council," in Adam Lupel and Ernesto Verdeja (eds), *Responding to Genocide: The Politics of International Action* (Boulder, CO: Lynne Rienner, 2013), p. 182.

39 Luck, *The UN Security Council*, p. 8.

40 See Historical Clarification Commission, *Memory of Silence: Report of the Commission for Historical Clarification: Conclusions and Recommendations*; Tom Fawthorp and Helen Jarvis, *Getting Away with Genocide: Elusive Justice and the Khmer Rouge Tribunal* (Sydney: University of New South Wales Press, 2005); and Daniela Kroslak, *The French Betrayal of Rwanda* (London: Hurst and Co., 2007).

41 Paul D. Williams and Alex J. Bellamy, "The Responsibility to Protect and the Crisis in Darfur," *Security Dialogue* 36(1) (2005): 27–47.

42 Vaughan Lowe, Adam Roberts, Jennifer Welsh, and Dominik Zaum, "Introduction," in Vaughan Lowe, Adam Roberts, Jennifer Welsh and Dominik Zaum (eds), *The United Nations Security Council and War: The Evolution of Thought and Practice since 1945* (Oxford: Oxford University Press, 2008), p. 30.

43 See Nayan Chanda's interview with Gareth Evans, *Yale Global Online*, April 15, 2011.

44 Justin Morris, "Libya and Syria: R2P and the Spectre of the Swinging Pendulum," *International Affairs* 89(5) (2013): 1265–83.

45 E.g. Alex de Waal, "Darfur and the Failure of the Responsibility to Protect," *International Affairs* 83(6) (2007): 1039–54.

46 See John Forrer and Conor Seyle (eds), *The Role of Business in the Responsibility to Protect* (Cambridge: Cambridge University Press, 2016).

47 De Waal, "Darfur and the Failure of R2P."

48 Morris, "Dual Responsibilities."

49 Wil Verwey, "The Legality of Humanitarian Intervention after the Cold War," in Elizabeth Ferris (ed.), *A Challenge to Intervene: A New Role for the United Nations?* (Uppsala: Life and Peace Institute, 1992), p. 114.

50 Michael Walzer, *Just and Unjust Wars: A Moral Argument with Historical Illustrations* (New York: Basic Books, 1977), pp. 155–6.

51 Nicholas J. Wheeler, *Saving Strangers: Humanitarian Intervention in International Society* (Oxford: Oxford University Press, 2000), pp. 38–9.

52 Welsh, "Implementing the Responsibility to Protect," p. 126.

53 Welsh, "Implementing the Responsibility to Protect," p. 136.

Chapter 3 Unexpected Challenges and Opportunities

1 Stephen Mcloughlin, *The Structural Prevention of Mass Atrocities: Understanding Risk and Resilience* (London: Routledge, 2014).

2 Stephen Krasner, *Sovereignty: Organized Hypocrisy* (Princeton, NJ: Princeton University Press, 1999).

3 *A Vital and Enduring Commitment: Implementing the Responsibility to Protect*, Report of the Secretary-General, A/69/981–S/2015/500, July 13, 2015, para. 46.

4 Luke Glanville, *Sovereignty and the Responsibility to Protect: A New History* (Chicago: Chicago University Press, 2011).

5 Edward C. Luck, "Briefing to the UN Security Council Arria Formula Meeting on the Responsibility to Protect and Non-State Actors," New York, December 14, 2015.

6 Luck, "Briefing to the UN Security Council."

7 *Implementing the Responsibility to Protect.* Report of the Secretary-General, A/63/677, January 12, 2009, para. 29. Also see para. 40.

8 Statement by the Permanent Representative of the Netherlands on Behalf of the Group of Friends of R2P at the "Arria formula" meeting of the UN Security Council on the Responsibility to Protect and Non-State Armed Groups, December 14, 2015.

9 Marco Sassoli, "Taking Armed Groups Seriously: Ways to Improve their Compliance with International Humanitarian Law," *International Humanitarian Legal Studies* 1 (2010): 5–51.

10 Edward C. Luck, "Foreword," in Kurt Mills and David Jason Karp (eds), *Human Rights Protection in Global Politics: Responsibilities of States and Non-State Actors* (Basingstoke: Palgrave, 2015), p. ix.

11 "Violent Non-State Actors as Perpetrators and Enablers of Atrocity Crimes," Stanley Foundation Policy Dialogue Brief, 2015, p. 2.

12 Raphael van Steenberghe, "Non-State Actors," in Gentian Zyberi (ed.), *An Institutional Approach to the Responsibility to Protect* (Cambridge: Cambridge University Press, 2013), p. 55.

13 *Plan of Action to Prevent Violent Extremism.* Report of the Secretary-General, A/70/674, December 24, 2015, para. 1.

14 Plan of Action to Prevent Violent Extremism, para. 6.

15 Plan of Action to Prevent Violent Extremism, para. 44.

16 Edward C. Luck and Dana Zaret Luck, "The Individual Responsibility to Protect," in Sheri P. Rosenberg, Tibi Galis, and Alex Zucker (eds), *Reconstructing Atrocity Prevention* (Cambridge: Cambridge University Press, 2016), p. 233.

17 Plan of Action to Prevent Violent Extremism, para. 11(c).

18 Luck and Luck, "The Individual Responsibility to Protect," p. 223.

19 Naomi Kikoler, "Guinea: An Overlooked Case," in Serena K. Sharma and Jennifer M. Welsh (eds), *The Responsibility to Prevent: Overcoming the Challenges to Atrocity Prevention* (Oxford: Oxford University Press, 2015), pp. 304–23.

20 Compare James Pattison, *Humanitarian Intervention and the Responsibility to Protect: Who Should Intervene?* (Oxford: Oxford University Press, 2010) and Heather M. Roff, *Global Justice, Kant and the Responsibility to Protect* (London: Routledge, 2014).

21 Independent Commission, *Report of the Independent Inquiry into the Actions of the United Nations During the 1994 Genocide in Rwanda*, December 12, 1999, p. 1.

22 Independent Commission, *Report*, p. 2.

23 Independent Commission, *Report*, p. 2.

24 Luck and Luck, "The Individual Responsibility to Protect," p. 224.

25 Alex J. Bellamy and Paul D. Williams, "Libya," in Sebastian von Einsiedel, David M. Malone and Bruno Stagno Ugarte (eds), *The UN Security Council in the 21st Century* (Boulder: Lynne Rienner, 2016), p. 703.

26 Ban, *Implementing the Responsibility*, para. 68.

27 See Andrew Gilmour, "The Future of Human Rights: A View from the United Nations," *Ethics and International Affairs* 28(2) (2014).

28 Gerrit Kurtz, 'With Courage and Coherence: The Human Rights Up Front Initiative of the United Nations," Global Public Policy Institute Policy Paper, Berlin, July 2015, p. 27.

29 UN Office on Genocide Prevention and R2P, *Framework of Analysis for Atrocity Crimes: A Tool for Prevention* (New York: UN, 2014). Referred to hereafter as simply "the UN's *Framework of Analysis*."

30 Julie Flint and Alex de Waal, *Darfur: A New History of a Long War* (London: Zed Books, 2008), pp. 172–3.

31 Alex J. Bellamy and Charles T. Hunt, "Twenty-First Century UN Peace Operations: Protection, Force and the Changing Security Environment," *International Affairs* 91(6) (2015): 1277–98.

32 High-Level Advisory Panel on the Responsibility to Protect in Southeast Asia, *Mainstreaming the Responsibility to Protect in Southeast Asia, Pathway towards a Caring ASEAN Community*, presented to the UN in New York, September 2014.

33 S. Neil MacFarlane and Yuen Foong, *Human Security and the UN* (Bloomington: Indiana University Press, 2006), p. 174.

34 Ban Ki-moon, *The Role of Regional and Sub-Regional Arrangements in Implementing the Responsibility to Protect. Report of the Secretary-General*, A/65/877–S/2011/393, June 28, 2011.

35 Alex de Waal, "African Roles in the Libyan Conflict of 2011," *International Affairs* 89(2) (2013): 365–79.

36 See Kurt Mills, *International Responses to Mass Atrocities in Africa: Responsibility to Protect, Prosecute and Palliate* (Philadelphia: University of Pennsylvania Press, 2015); and Mark Kersten, *Justice in Conflict: The Effects of the International Criminal*

Court's Interventions on Ending War and Building Peace (Oxford: Oxford University Press, 2016).

37 Luck and Luck, "Individual Responsibility to Protect."

Chapter 4 In Search of the International Community

1 United Nations, General Assembly, Resolution 60/1, October 24, 2005, World Summit Outcome Document, paras. 138, 139, and 140.

2 Ibid., para. 139.

3 Ibid., para. 139.

4 David Mitrany, "The Functional Approach to International Organization," *International Affairs* 24 (July 1948), pp. 350–63, and *The Progress of International Government* (New Haven: Yale University Press, 1933).

5 See, in particular, Articles 33(1), 37(1), 52(2).and 52(3) of the UN Charter.

6 Lise Morjé Howard, *UN Peacekeeping in Civil Wars* (Cambridge, UK: Cambridge University Press, 2008), pp. 333–4.

7 United Nations, Report of the Secretary-General, *Implementing the Responsibility to Protect*, A/63/677, January 12, 2009.

8 General Assembly Resolution A/RES/60/1180 and Security Council Resolution 1645 (2005).

9 See United Nations, Letter Dated 29 June 2015 from the Chair of the Advisory Group of Experts for the 2015 Review of the United Nations Peacebuilding Architecture Addressed to the Presidents of the Security Council and the General Assembly, Report of the Advisory Group, *The Challenge of Sustaining Peace*, A/69/968–S/2015/490, June 29, 2015.

10 Edward C. Luck, "Why the United Nations Underperforms at Preventing Mass Atrocities," *Genocide Studies and Prevention* 11(3), 2018, pp. 32–47.

11 Edward C. Luck, "Getting There and Being There: The Dual Roles of the Special Adviser," in Alex J. Bellamy and Tim Dunne (eds), *The Oxford Handbook on the Responsibility to Protect* (Oxford: Oxford University Press, 2016).

12 The report of the Internal Review Panel of November 2012 was not published by the UN, but it can be found online, with some passages redacted.

13 United Nations, Report of the Secretary-General, *Early Warning, Assessment and the Responsibility to Protect*, A/64/864, July 14, 2010.

14 United Nations, Report of the Secretary-General, *Mobilizing Collective Action: The Next Decade of the Responsibility to Protect*, A/70/999–S/2016/620, July 22, 2016, p. 17, para. 60.

15 Simon Adams, *Failure to Protect: Syria and the UN Security Council*, Occasional Paper, Global Centre for the Responsibility to Protect, 2015.

16 An exception was the quick and non-controversial air intervention by the United States in Iraq to protect Yazidi populations threatened with genocide by the Islamic State (IS). See White House, Statement by the President on the Humanitarian Operation in Iraq, August 7, 2014.

17 See Security Council Resolutions 1933 (2010), 1962 (2010), 1967 (2011), and 1975 (2011) on Côte d'Ivoire, 1970 (2011) and 1973 (2011) on Libya, 2100 (2013) on Mali, 2127 (2013) on CAR, 2098 (2013) and 2147 (2014) on DRC, and 2206 (2015) and 2304 (2016) on South Sudan.

18 United Nations Security Council, "Letter Dated 30 December 2008 from the Permanent Representative of South Africa Addressed to the President of the Security Council," S/2008/836, December 31, 2008, p. 13.
19 United Nations, Human Rights Council, Report of the Commission of Inquiry on Human Rights in the Democratic People's Republic of Korea, A/HRC/25/63 and Detailed Findings, A/HRC/25/CRP.1, February 7, 2014.
20 United Nations, General Assembly, A/RES/71/248 of December 21, 2016.
21 Julian Borger, "Russia Denied Membership of UN Human rights Council," *The Guardian*, October 28, 2016.
22 United Nations, *The Question of Intervention: Statements of the Secretary-General* (New York: United Nations Department of Public Information, DPI/2080, December 1999).
23 Jean-Marie Guéhenno, *The Fog of Peace: A Memoir of International Peacekeeping in the 21st Century* (Washington, DC: Brookings Institution Press, 2015), pp. 186, 286, 305, and 310.
24 Lisa Hultman, Jacob Kathman, and Megan Shannon, "United Nations Peacekeeping and Civilian Protection in Civil Wars," *American Journal of Political Science* 57(4) (October 2013): 875–91.
25 United Nations, Security Council, S/RES/1996, July 8, 2011.
26 For the Brazilian concept paper, see United Nations, A/66/551–S/2011/701, November 11, 2011.
27 Edward C. Luck, *UN Security Council: Practice and Promise* (London: Routledge, 2006), pp. 24–5 and 136.

Chapter 5 The Domestic Dimensions

1 Quoted by Stanley Meisler, *Kofi Annan: A Man of Peace in a World of War* (New York: John Wiley & Sons, 1997), p. 172.
2 Straus, *Making and Unmaking Nations*, p. 326.
3 Christopher Clark, *The Sleepwalkers: How Europe Went to War in 1914* (London: Penguin, 2013), p. xxvii.
4 Ibid, p. xxvii.
5 Ban Ki-moon, *Responsibility to Protect: State Responsibility and Prevention. Report of the Secretary-General*, A/67/929–S/2013/399, July 9, 2013.
6 Ban, *State Responsibility*, para. 16.
7 UN, *Framework of Analysis*.
8 Alex J. Bellamy, "Mass Atrocities and Armed Conflict: Links, Distinctions and Implications for the Responsibility to Protect," Policy Analysis Brief for the Stanley Foundation, February 2011.
9 Ban, *State Responsibility*, para. 18.
10 Ban, *State Responsibility*, para. 19.
11 Ban, *State Responsibility*, para. 20.
12 Ban, *State Responsibility*, para. 20.
13 Ban, *State Responsibility*, para. 21.
14 See Frances Stewart (ed.), *Horizontal Inequalities and Conflict: Understanding Group Violence in Multiethnic Societies* (London: Palgrave, 2008).

15 Raymond Gilpin, "Economic Drivers of Mass Atrocities: Implications for Policy and Practice," Policy Analysis Brief for the Stanley Foundation, August 2015.

16 Straus, *Making and Unmaking Nations*, p. 334.

17 Barbara Harff, "No Lessons Learned From the Holocaust? Assessing Risks of Genocide and Political Mass Murder since 1955," *American Political Science Review* 97(1) (2003): 57–73, 63.

18 Hugo Slim, *Killing Civilians: Method, Madness and Morality in War* (London: Hurst and Co., 2007); and Jonathan Maynard Leader, "Rethinking the Role of Ideology in Mass Atrocities," *Terrorism and Political Violence* 26(5) (2014): 821–41.

19 Harff, "No Lessons Learned", p. 66.

20 Matthew Krain, "Democracy, Internal War, and State-Sponsored Mass Murder", *Human Rights Review* 1(3) (2000): 40–8.

21 Benjamin A. Valentino, *Final Solutions: Mass Killing and Genocide in the Twentieth Century* (Ithaca: Cornell University Press, 2004).

22 Frederic Megret, "Beyond the 'Salvation' Paradigm: Responsibility to Protect (Others) vs. the Power of Protecting Oneself," *Security Dialogue* 40(6) (2009): 575–95.

23 Stanley Foundation, "Preventing Mass Atrocities: Resilient Societies, State Capacity and Structural Reform," Policy Memo, October 30, 2013, p. 3.

24 This term was introduced by the then Special Adviser for the Prevention of Genocide, Francis Deng.

25 "Strategies and Next Steps for the Responsibility to Protect: A Conversation with UN Member States", Stanley Foundation, Tarrytown, February 12–14, 2014, p. 4.

26 Straus, *Making and Unmaking Nations*, p. 323.

27 Ibid.

28 Kwesi Aning and Frank Okyere, *Responsibility to Prevent in Africa: Leveraging Institutional Capacity to Mitigate Atrocity Risk*, Policy Analysis Brief for the Stanley Foundation, January 2015, p. 4.

29 Straus, *Making and Unmaking Nations*, p. 323.

30 See Aning and Okyere, *Responsibility to Prevent in Africa*, p. 6.

31 See Serena K. Sharma, "The 2007–08 Post Election Crisis in Kenya: A Success Story for the Responsibility to Protect," in Julia Hoffmann and Andre Nollkaemper (eds), *Responsibility to Protect: From Principle to Practice* (Amsterdam: Pallas Publications, 2012).

32 UN, *Framework of Analysis*, p. 3.

33 *Report of the Secretary-General on the Rule of Law and Transitional Justice in Conflict and Post-Conflict Societies*, S/2004/616.

34 Cecilia Jacob, "Evaluating the United Nations' Agenda for Atrocity Prevention: Prospects for the International Regulation of Internal Security," *Politics and Government* 3(3) (2015): 16–26.

35 Paul Collier and Nicholas Sambanis, *Understanding Civil War: Volume 1: Africa* (Washington, DC: The World Bank, 2005), p. 309.

36 Ukoha Ukiwo, "Horizontal Inequalities and Ethnic Violence: Evidence from Calabar and Warri, Nigeria," in Frances Stewart (ed.), *Horizontal Inequalities and Conflict: Understanding Group Violence in Multiethnic Societies* (London: Palgrave, 2008), pp. 205–36.

37 Frances Stewart, "The Causes of Civil War and Genocide: A Comparison," in Adam Lupel and Ernesto Verdeja (eds), *Responding to Genocide: The Politics of International Action* (Boulder, CO: Lynne Rienner, 2013), p. 73.
38 *Civil Society Perspectives: Building State Capacity to Prevent Atrocity Crimes*, Stanley Foundation event summary, September 9, 2013, p. 6.
39 Ban Ki-moon, *Implementing the Responsibility to Protect: Report of the Secretary-General*, A/63/677, January 12, 2009, paras. 17, 27, 37, 43, 44, 45, 47, 59.
40 Aning and Okyere, *Responsibility to Prevent in Africa*, p. 6.
41 A/HRC/RES/27/3, October 3, 2014.
42 All drawn from *Report of the Special Rapporteur on the promotion of truth, justice, reparation and guarantees of non-recurrence, Pablo de Grieff*, A/HRC/30/42, September 7, 2015.
43 The White House, *National Security Strategy*, May 2010, p. 48.
44 Genocide Prevention Task Force, *Preventing Genocide: A Blueprint for US Policymakers* (Washington, DC: US Holocaust Memorial Museum, American Academy of Diplomacy and US Institute of Peace, 2008).
45 The White House, *Fact Sheet: A Comprehensive Strategy and New Tools to Prevent and Respond to Atrocities*, Office of the Press Secretary, April 23, 2012.
46 Stephen M. Walt, "Is the Atrocity Prevention Board a Good Idea?," *Foreign Policy*, April 24, 2012.
47 James P. Finkel, "Moving Beyond the Crossroads: Strengthening the Atrocity Prevention Board," *Genocide Studies and Prevention* 9(2) (2015): 138–47.
48 Jason Ralph, "Mainstreaming the Responsibility to Protect in UK Strategy," Report for the UN Association of the UK, 2014.
49 Global Centre for the Responsibility to Protect, *National Focal Points: Recommendations*, p. 1.
50 Ibid., p. 1.
51 Argentina, Bolivia, Brazil, Chile, Colombia, Costa Rica, the Dominican Republic, Ecuador, El Salvador, Guatemala, Honduras, Mexico, Nicaragua, Panama, Paraguay, Peru, Uruguay, and Venezuela.
52 Information and quotes from "Auschwitz Institute Launches Network for Genocide Prevention," Auschwitz Institute for Peace and Reconciliation press release, April 3, 2012.
53 Statement by the Group of Friends on Responsibility to Protect on the Situation in the Libyan Arab Jamahiriya, February 25, 2010.
54 I. William Zartman and Mark Anstey, "The Problem: Preventing Identity Conflicts and Genocide," in I. William Zartman, Mark Anstey, and Paul Meerts (eds), *The Slippery Slope to Genocide: Reducing Identity Conflicts and Preventing Mass Murder* (Oxford: Oxford University Press, 2012), p. 16.
55 *Responsibility to Protect: Timely and Decisive Response. Report of the Secretary-General*, A/66/874–S/2012/578, July 25, 2012, para. 13.
56 Christian Gerlach, *Extremely Violent Societies: Mass Violence in the Twentieth Century World* (Cambridge: Cambridge University Press, 2010).
57 Greg Fealy, "Killing for God," *Inside Indonesia* 99, January–March 2010.
58 See Michael J. Kelly, "Prosecuting Corporations for Genocide Under International Law," *Harvard Law and Policy Review* 6(2) (2012): 340.
59 See MONUC, *Report on the Conclusions of the Special Investigation Concerning Allegations of Summary Executions and other Human Rights Violations Perpetrated by the*

Armed Forces of the Democratic Republic of the Congo (FARDC) in Kilwa (Katanga Province) on 15 October 2004, unauthorized translation, 2005.

60 Vesselin Popovski, "Corporate Responsibility to Protect Populations from Mass Atrocities," in Forrer and Seyle (eds), *Role of Business in R2P*.

61 Kelly, "Prosecuting Corporations," p. 340.

62 Steven K. Baum, *The Psychology of Genocide: Perpetrators, Bystanders and Rescuers* (Cambridge: Cambridge University Press, 2008), p. 153.

63 Laurel E. Fletcher, "From Indifference to Engagement: Bystanders and International Criminal Justice," *Michigan Journal of International Law* 26 (2004): 1026–7.

64 Samantha Power, *A Problem from Hell: America and the Age of Genocide* (New York: Basic Books, 2002), p. 113.

65 Steven Pinker, *The Better Angels of our Nature: The Decline of Violence in History and its Causes* (New York: Allen Lane, 2011), pp. 284–8.

66 International Coalition for R2P, "Civil Society and RtoP," undated, p. 4.

67 Bruce E. Barnes and Fatahilla Abdul Syukur, "Mediating Conflicts: Southeast Asia," in Dale Bagshaw and Elizabeth Porter (eds), *Mediation in the Asia-Pacific Region: Transforming Conflicts and Building Peace* (London: Routledge, 2009), p. 201.

68 Patrick Kingsley, "The White Helmet Leader: We Can Anticipate the Scale of Destruction Based on the Sound of the Plane," *The Guardian*, October 4, 2016.

69 David Keen, *Complex Emergencies* (Cambridge: Polity, 2008), p. 146.

70 See International Committee of the Red Cross (2012), *Enhancing Protection for Civilians in Armed Conflict and Other Situations of Violence* (Geneva: ICRC, 2012), p. 27.

71 Philip Zimbardo, *The Lucifer Effect: Understanding How Good People Turn Evil* (New York: Random House, 2008).

Chapter 6 The Challenge of Prevention

1 Ban Ki-moon, "Renewing our Commitment to the Peoples and Purposes of the United Nations," speech given at UN Headquarters, November 22, 2013.

2 "Report of the Secretary-General's Internal Review Panel on United Nations Action in Sri Lanka," November 2012 (hereafter "Internal Review Panel").

3 Ban, "Renewing our Commitment."

4 Carnegie Commission on Preventing Deadly Conflict, *Preventing Deadly Conflict* (New York: Carnegie Commission, 1997).

5 Roland Paris, "Peacebuilding," in Alex J. Bellamy and Tim Dunne (eds), *The Oxford Handbook on the Responsibility to Protect* (Oxford: Oxford University Press, 2016).

6 Straus, *Making and Unmaking Nations*, p. 326.

7 Alex J. Bellamy, "Mass Atrocities and Armed Conflict: Links, Distinctions and Implications for the Responsibility to Protect," Policy Brief for the Stanley Foundation, February 2011.

8 Lawrence Woocher, "The Responsibility to Prevent: Towards a Strategy," in Andy Knight and Frazer Egerton (eds), *Routledge Handbook on the Responsibility to Protect* (London: Routledge, 2012).

9 Lisa Hultman, "Keeping Peace or Spurring Violence? Unintended Effects of Peace Operations on Violence Against Civilians," *Civil Wars* 12(1–2) (2010).

10 Straus, *Making and Unmaking Nations*, pp. 328–9.

11 Scott Straus, "Triggers of Mass Atrocities," *Politics and Governance* 3(3) (2015): 5–15.

12 Jennifer Welsh, "Civilian Protection in Libya: Putting Coercion and Controversy Back into RtoP," *Ethics and International Affairs* (2011): 6–7.

13 Internal Review Panel, para. 80.

14 Colin Keating, "The Role of the UN Security Council," in Lupel and Verdeja (eds), *Responding to Genocide*, p. 182.

15 Internal Review Panel, para. 59.

16 Serena K. Sharma, "The 2007–08 Post-Election Crisis in Kenya: A Success Story for the Responsibility to Protect?," in Julia Hoffmann and Andre Nollkaemper (eds), *Responsibility to Protect: From Principle to Practice* (Amsterdam: Pallas, 2012), pp. 27–38.

17 Internal Review Panel, para. 77.

18 John Holmes, *The Politics of Humanity: The Reality of Relief Aid* (London: The Bodley Head, 2013), pp. 85–130.

19 Internal Review Panel, para 12.

20 Internal Review Panel, para. 61.

21 Justin Morris, "The Responsibility to Protect and the Great Powers: The Tensions of Dual Responsibility," *Global Responsibility to Protect* 7(3–4) (2015): 398–421.

22 Evan Cinq-Mars, "Too Little, Too Late: Failing to Prevent Atrocities in the Central African Republic," *Global Centre for the Responsibility to Protect Occasional Paper*, New York, 2015.

23 Office of Internal Oversight Services, *Evaluation of the Implementation and Results of Protection of Civilians Mandates in United Nations Peacekeeping Operations*, A/68/787, March 7, 2014, para. 68.

24 Office of Internal Oversight Services, "Evaluation of the Implementation and Results of protection of Cvilians Mandates in United Nations Peacekeeping Operations," A/68/787, March 7, 2014.

25 This section draws, in part, from Alex J. Bellamy and Paul D. Williams, "Protecting Civilians in Uncivil Wars," in Sara E. Davies and Luke Glanville (eds), *Protecting the Displaced: Deepening the Responsibility to Protect* (Leiden: Martinus Nijhoff, 2010), pp. 127–62.

26 Alex J. Bellamy and Paul D. Williams (eds), *Providing Peacekeepers: The Politics, Challenges and Future of United Nations Peacekeeping Contributions* (Oxford: Oxford University Press, 2013).

27 Jake Sherman, Alischa Kugel, and Andrew Sinclair, "Overcoming Helicopter Force Generation Challenges for UN Peacekeeping Operations," *International Peacekeeping* 19(1) (2012): 77–92.

28 Mary Kaldor, *New and Old Wars* (Cambridge: Polity Press, 1999), p. 125.

29 Ian Johnstone, "Dilemmas of Robust Peace Operations," in *Annual Review of Global Peace Operations 2006* (Boulder, CO: Lynne Rienner, 2006), p. 7.

30 OIOS, para. 70.

31 OIOS, para. 23.

32 OIOS, paras. 30–52.

33 SC/11274, February 14, 2014.

34 Max Kelly (with Alison Giffen), *Military Planning to Protect Civilians: Proposed Guidance for United Nations Peacekeeping Operations* (Washington, DC: The Stimson Institute, 2011), pp. 78–9.

35 Walter Dorn, "United Nations Peacekeeping Intelligence," in Loch K. Johnson (ed.), *The Oxford Handbook of National Security Intelligence* (Oxford: Oxford University Press, 2010), pp. 275–95.

36 "Unarmed Drones Aid UN Peacekeeping Efforts in Africa", *New York Times*, July 2, 2014.

37 Victoria Holt and Tobias Berkman, *The Impossible Mandate: Military Preparedness, the Responsibility to Protect and Modern Peace Operations* (Washington, DC: The Stimson Centre, 2006), pp. 166–7.

38 We are referring specifically to those elements relating to the courts and special tribunals established to prosecute individuals for grave violations of International Humanitarian Law and other international laws relating to atrocity crimes. We acknowledge that the reach of international criminal law extends beyond war and atrocity.

39 Fatou Bensouda, speech at conference on "R2P: The Next Decade," January 18, 2012, available at www.fora.tv/2012/01/18/R2P_in_2022, accessed May 12, 2016.

40 Anthony Dworkin, "International Justice and the Prevention of Atrocity," European Council on Foreign Relations, October 2014, p. 34. Available at www.ecfr.eu/page/-/ECFR115_International_Justice_Report.pdf, accessed May 18, 2016.

41 ICISS, *Responsibility to Protect*, paras. 3.30 and 6.17 respectively.

42 Ban, *Implementing the R2P*, para. 18.

43 Respectively, Michael Contarino and Melinda Negron-Gonzales, "The International Criminal Court," in Gentian Zyberi (ed.), *An Institutional Approach to the Responsibility to Protect* (Cambridge: Cambridge University Press, 2013), p. 411; and Don Wallace, "The International Criminal Court," in Daniel Silander and Don Wallace (eds), *International Organizations and the Implementation of the Responsibility to Protect: The Humanitarian Crisis in Syria* (London: Routledge, 2015).

44 Cited in Serena Sharma, *The Responsibility to Protect and the International Criminal Court: The Case of Kenya* (London: Routledge, 2016).

45 Luis Moreno Ocampo, "The Responsibility to Protect: Engaging America," November 17, 2006, www.r2pcoalition.org/content/view/61/ 86, accessed May 13, 2016.

46 Luis Moreno Ocampo, Keynote Address, Chicago, November 17, 2006, Chicago, available at www. r2pcoalition.org/content/view/61/86/, accessed May 14, 2016.

47 *Implementing the Responsibility to Protect: Report of the Secretary-General*, 2009, para. 44.

48 Jennifer M. Welsh, "The 'Narrow but Deep' Approach to Implementing the Responsibility to Protect: Reassessing the Focus on International Crimes," in Sheri P. Rosenberg, Tibi Galis, and Alex Zucker (eds), *Reconstructing Atrocity Prevention* (Cambridge: Cambridge University Press, 2016), pp. 81–94.

49 Kurt Mills, "R2P: Protecting, Prosecuting or Palliating in Mass Atrocity Situations," *Journal of Human Rights* 12 (2013): 333.

50 Carsten Stahn, "Marital Stress or Grounds for Divorce? Re-Thinking the Relationship between R2P and International Criminal Justice," *Criminal Law Forum* 26(1), 2015, pp. 13–50, p. 16.
51 Stahn, "Marital Stress," p. 32.
52 Hyeran Jo and Beth Simmons, "Can the International Criminal Court Deter Atrocity?," unpublished paper, December 18, 2014, Social Science Research Network.
53 Wes W. Widmaier and Luke Glanville, "The Benefits of Norm Ambiguity: Constructing the Responsibility to Protect Across Rwanda, Iraq and Libya," *Contemporary Politics* 21(4) (2015): 367–83.
54 *Responsibility to Protect: Timely and Decisive Response. Report of the Secretary-General.* A/66/874–S/2012/578, July 25, 2012, para. 13.
55 See Jan Egeland, *A Billion Lives: An Eyewitness Report from the Frontlines of Humanity* (New York: Simon and Schuster, 2010).
56 Heather Roff, *Global Justice, Kant, and the Responsibility to Protect: A Provisional Duty* (London: Routledge, 2014).
57 Carsten Stahn, "Responsibility to Protect: Political Rhetoric or Emerging Legal Norm?," *American Journal of International Law* 101(1) (2007): 99–120.

Chapter 7 Making a Difference: Lessons from Experience

1 United Nations, Report of the Independent Inquiry into the Actions of the United Nations During the 1994 Genocide in Rwanda, S/1999/1257, December 16, 1999, p. 31.
2 Secretary-General's Internal Review Panel on UN Action in Sri Lanka of November 2012.
3 United Nations, Report of the Secretary-General, *Early Warning, Assessment and the Responsibility to Protect*, A/64/864, July 14, 2010, p. 5, para. 10(c).
4 Ibid., p. 3, para. 7.
5 Independent Inquiry, op. cit., p. 41.
6 On the UN, see the Independent Inquiry, op. cit., pp. 31, 33, and 34.
7 *Fall of Srebrenica*, op. cit., p. 105, para. 488, and p. 107, para. 499, respectively.
8 Internal Review Panel on Sri Lanka, op. cit.
9 *Early Warning and Assessment*, op. cit., p. 5, para. 10(c).
10 Ibid., p. 8, para. 19.
11 See, for instance, Sheri P. Rosenberg, "Audacity of Hope: International Criminal Law, Atrocity Crimes, and Prevention," in Rosenberg et al., *Reconstructing Atrocity Prevention*, op. cit., pp. 151–74.
12 *Fall of Srebrenica*, op. cit., p. 104, para. 483.
13 Ibid., p. 107, para. 499.
14 Ibid., p. 107, paras. 496 and 500, respectively.
15 Ibid., p. 108, paras. 505 and 506, respectively.

Conclusion

1 Michael Ignatieff, "The New World Disorder," *The New York Review of Books*, September 25, 2014, available at http://www.nybooks.com/articles/archives/2014/sep/25/new-world-disorder/?pagination=false (accessed April 15, 2017); and

Doug Saunders, "Why Louise Arbour is Thinking Twice," *Globe and Mail*, May 28, 2015, available at http://www.theglobeandmail.com/globe-debate/why-louise-arbour-is-thinking-twice/article23667013/ (accessed April 15, 2017).

2 Jennifer Welsh, *The Return of History: Conflict, Migration and Geopolitics in the Twenty-First Century* (Toronto: House of Anansi Press, 2017).

3 Steven Pinker, *The Better Angels of Our Nature: The Decline of Violence in History and its Causes* (London: Allen Lane, 2011), p. 291.

4 UCDP/PRIO Armed Conflict Dataset version 4-2016.

5 Eric Melander, Therese Pettersson, and Lotta Themner, "Organised Violence, 1989–2015," *Journal of Peace Research* 53(5) (2016): 727–42.

6 UCDP/PRIO Armed Conflict Dataset version 4-2016.

7 Sebastian von Einseidel, "Civil War Trends and the Changing Nature of Armed Conflict," United Nations University Centre for Policy Research, Occasional Paper, No. 10, March 2017, p. 2.

8 Hugo Slim, *Killing Civilians: Method, Madness and Morality in War* (London: Hurst and Co., 2008).

9 Edward C. Luck and Dana Zaret Luck, "The Individual Responsibility to Protect," in Sheri P. Rosenberg, Tibi Galis, and Alex Zucker (eds), *Reconstructing Atrocity Prevention*),op. cit., pp. 207–48.

10 Justin Morris, "The Responsibility to Protect and the Great Powers: The Tensions of Dual Responsibility," *Global Responsibility to Protect* 7(3–4) (2015): 401–24.

11 Philippe Sands, *East West Street: On the Origins of Genocide and Crimes against Humanity* (New York: Weidenfeld and Nicolson, 2016), pp. 366–7.

12 Charlie Savage and Eric Schmitt, "Trump Eases Combat Rules in Somalia intended to Protect Civilians," *New York Times*, March 30, 2017, at https://www.nytimes.com/2017/03/30/world/africa/trump-is-said-to-ease-combat-rules-in-somalia-designed-to-protect-civilians.html .

13 UCPD/PRIO Armed Conflict Dataset version 4-2016.

14 David Cunningham, "Blocking Resolution: How External States can Prolong Civil Wars," *Journal of Peace Research* 47(2) (2010): 115–27.

15 The International, Impartial and Independent Mechanism to assist in the Investigation and Prosecution of Those Responsible for the Most Serious Crimes under International Law committed in the Syrian Arab Republic since March 2011, established by General Assembly Resolution 71/248, December 21, 2016.

16 United Nations, "Yemen Emergency Food Security and Nutrition Assessment – 2016 Preliminary Results," February 8, 2017, at http://fscluster.org/yemen/document/yemen-emergency-food-security-and-0

17 ICRC, "Crisis in Yemen: Tipping Point for International Humanitarian Action," May 20, 2015, at https://www.icrc.org/en/document/crisis-yemen-tipping-point-international-humanitarian-action

18 Hedley Bull, "The Great Irresponsibles? The United States, the Soviet Union and World Order," *International Journal* 35(3) (1980): 437–47.

19 Bull, "The Great Irresponsibles": 446.

Index